Women and Men
in the Informal Economy:
A Statistical Picture

Second Edition

Women and Men in the Informal Economy:
A Statistical Picture

Second Edition

International Labour Office, Geneva

Copyright © International Labour Organization 2013
First published 2013

Publications of the International Labour Office enjoy copyright under Protocol 2 of the Universal Copyright Convention. Nevertheless, short excerpts from them may be reproduced without authorization, on condition that the source is indicated. For rights of reproduction or translation, application should be made to ILO Publications (Rights and Permissions), International Labour Office, CH-1211 Geneva 22, Switzerland, or by email: pubdroit@ilo.org. The International Labour Office welcomes such applications.

Libraries, institutions and other users registered with reproduction rights organizations may make copies in accordance with the licences issued to them for this purpose. Visit www.ifrro.org to find the reproduction rights organization in your country.

Women and men in the informal economy: a statistical picture (second edition) / International Labour Office – Geneva: ILO, 2013

ISBN 978-92-2-128169-6 (print)
ISBN 978-92-2-128170-2 (web pdf)

International Labour Office

informal employment / women workers / men workers / temporary employment / part time employment / informal economy / urban area / data collecting / measurement / developed countries
13.01.3

ILO Cataloguing in Publication Data

The designations employed in ILO publications, which are in conformity with United Nations practice, and the presentation of material therein do not imply the expression of any opinion whatsoever on the part of the International Labour Office concerning the legal status of any country, area or territory or of its authorities, or concerning the delimitation of its frontiers.

The responsibility for opinions expressed in signed articles, studies and other contributions rests solely with their authors, and publication does not constitute an endorsement by the International Labour Office of the opinions expressed in them.

Reference to names of firms and commercial products and processes does not imply their endorsement by the International Labour Office, and any failure to mention a particular firm, commercial product or process is not a sign of disapproval.

ILO publications and electronic products can be obtained through major booksellers or ILO local offices in many countries, or direct from ILO Publications, International Labour Office, CH-1211 Geneva 22, Switzerland. Catalogues or lists of new publications are available free of charge from the above address, or by email: pubvente@ilo.org
Visit our web site: www.ilo.org/publns

Photocomposed in Switzerland JMB
Printed in Switzerland ATA

Preface

The informal economy is a major source of employment and livelihoods in many countries and interacts closely with the formal economy. Given its importance, countries are paying increasing attention to the informal economy in collecting labour force and other economic data. In 2013, the tripartite constituents of the International Labour Organization defined eight areas of critical importance for the Organization, one of which is formalization of the informal economy. More information on informality, including up-to-date statistics, is therefore crucial. The launch of the publication *Measuring Informality: A Statistical Manual on the Informal Sector and Informal Employment* in October 2013, should encourage more countries to produce and disseminate the necessary data to enlarge the knowledge base on this highly relevant topic for the world of work.

This publication, *Women and Men in the Informal Economy: A Statistical Picture* (Second Edition), is a significant step forward from the Women and Men in the Informal Economy: A Statistical Picture (2002) in that it provides, for the first time, direct measures of informal employment inside and outside informal enterprises for 47 countries. The publication also presents statistics on the composition and contribution of the informal economy as well as on specific groups of urban informal workers. Non-technical language and clear, simple statistical tables will make the information easy to understand by a large and varied audience. This publication is intended to respond to the needs of different users, including researchers, statisticians, policymakers, employers' and workers' organizations, including organizations of informal workers.

The comprehensive statistics on the informal economy were collected, compiled and analysed based on the conceptual framework for the statistical measurement of the informal sector and informal employment adopted by the International Conference of Labour Statisticians (ICLS) in 1993 and 2003, respectively. The resulting analysis confirms the feasibility and usefulness of these frameworks as a basis for the development of statistics and for data analysis for policy-making.

Chapter 1 details progress at the international level in developing definitions and methodologies for measuring the informal economy and its constituent parts. Chapter 2 presents national data on informal employment outside of agriculture, disaggregated by sex. Detailed data on specific countries are presented in the annex tables. Chapter 3 discusses non-standard employment in developed countries, and Chapter 4 focuses on specific groups of informal workers, including four groups of urban informal workers (based on national data compiled by the WIEGO network) and domestic workers (based on ILO data). Chapter 5 recommends future directions to improve the collection of data on the informal economy.

Women and Men in the Informal Economy: A Statistical Picture (Second Edition) was initiated and funded by the ILO Employment Policy Department directed by Azita Berar Awad, the ILO Department of Statistics directed by Rafael Diez de Medina and the international network, Women in Informal Employment: Globalizing and Organizing (WIEGO).

This report was prepared by Joann Vanek and Martha Chen (WIEGO), Ralf Hussmanns (ILO) and Francoise Carre. It was extensively reviewed in the ILO by many units and teams, which also provided additional inputs.

Chapter 1 was prepared by Joann Vanek (WIEGO), Martha Chen (WIEGO) and Ralf Hussmanns (ILO), with inputs by Sriani Ameratunga Kring (ILO). The ILO and WIEGO requested data from countries which were then reviewed and compiled into a database. For Latin America, Bolivar

Pino and a team at the ILO Information System for Latin America and the Caribbean (SIALC) worked with Ralf Hussmanns. The data for China were prepared by Wu Yaowu (Chinese Academy of Social Sciences) and Albert Park (Hong Kong University of Science and Technology), and for the United Republic of Tanzania by Debbie Budlender (Independent Consultant).

Jean-Michel Pasteels (ILO) prepared the first section of Chapter 2 relating to country data on employment in the informal economy, based on statistics compiled by the ILO Department of Statistics, disaggregated by sex, from 47 medium- and low-incomes countries.

Francoise Carre (University of Massachusetts/Boston and WIEGO) prepared Chapter 3 on developed countries with the assistance of Brandynn Holgate. Additional data from 2011 was collected and provided by Jean-Michel Pasteels, and the chapter was edited by Uma Amara Rani and Dorothea Schmidt-Klau (ILO).

Martha Chen (Harvard University and WIEGO) prepared Chapter 4 on categories of urban informal workers using methods developed by WIEGO and national data compiled by WIEGO. For the section relating to domestic workers, additional ILO regional and global data on domestic workers and related inputs were provided by Malte Luebker, and inputs on the Domestic Workers' Convention were provided by Martin Oelz and edited by Sriani Ameratunga Kring.

Chapter 5 was prepared by Joann Vanek, Martha Chen and Ralf Hussmanns, with additional inputs from Rafael Diez de Medina (ILO).

The annex tables and explanatory note were prepared by the ILO Department of Statistics.

Joann Vanek and Marty Chen coordinated the project on behalf of WIEGO and Azita Berar Awad and Rafael Diez de Medina provided overall guidance from the ILO.

Additional contributions were made by Jacques Charmes, formerly of the Institut de Recherche pour le développement, France; Thomas Koerner, Federal Statistical Office of Germany; Rodrigo Negrete and his colleagues, Guadalupe Luna, Tomas Ramirez, Mario Moreno and Efrain Munoz at the National Institute of Statistics, Geography and Information, Mexico (INEGI); Uma Rani of the ILO and G. Raveendran, formerly with the Central Statistical Organisation, India. Technical advice was provided by Gulab Singh, United Nations Statistics Division.

The publication also benefited from comments and reviews by the following ILO colleagues: Uma Rani Amara, Sriani Ameratunga Kring, Azita Berar Awad, Marie-Josée Da Silva Ribeiro, Rafael Diez de Medina, Ekkehard Ernst, Pablo Fleiss, Iyanatul Islam, Frédéric Lapeyre, Makiko Matsumoto, Jean-Michel Pasteels, Dorothea Schmidt-Klau, Valentina Stoevska and Dagmar Walter.

Azita Berar Awad	**Rafael Diez de Medina**	**Joann Vanek**
Director	*Director*	*Director*
ILO Employment Policy Department	ILO Statistics Department	WIEGO Statistics Programme

Table of Contents

Preface	v
Abbreviations and acronyms	ix
Main findings	xi

Chapter 1	**Measuring the informal economy: Taking up the challenge**	**1**
1.1	Introduction	1
1.2	What is new in this publication?	2
1.3	Basic statistical concepts of informality	2
1.4	New developments in statistics on the informal economy	3
1.5	Overview of this report	5

Chapter 2	**Statistics relating to the informal economy**	**7**
2.1	Country data on employment in the informal economy	7
	2.1.1 Informal employment	8
	2.1.2 Women and men in the informal economy	11
	2.1.3 Trends in employment in the informal economy	18
2.2	Economic contribution of the informal sector and informal employment	21

Chapter 3	**Statistics on Developed Countries**	**23**
3.1	Non-standard employment in developed countries	23
	3.1.1 Temporary employment	28
	3.1.2 Part-time employment	31
	3.1.3 Own-account self-employment	34

Chapter 4	**Specific Groups of Urban Informal Workers**	**39**
4.1	Domestic Workers	42
4.2	Home-Based Workers	45
4.3	Street vendors	47
4.4	Waste pickers	47
4.5	Characteristics of the four groups (based on available data)	48

Chapter 5	**Future Directions for Measuring the Informal Economy**	**55**

Annex 1 Availability of data by region 59

Annex 2 Country-Specific Tables 61

List of figures

Figure 2.1 Components of employment in the informal economy as percentage of non-agricultural employment (latest year available) 9

Figure 2.2 Informal employment as percentage of total non-agricultural employment, by sex (latest year available) 12

Figure 2.3 Informal sector employment as percentage of total non-agricultural employment, by sex (latest year available) 13

Figure 2.4 Informal employment outside the informal sector as percentage of total non-agricultural employment, by sex (latest year available) 14

Figure 4.1 Protection of domestic workers under national legislation, 2010 56

List of tables

Table 2.1 Employment in the informal economy and its components as percentage of non-agricultural employment (latest year available) 10

Table 2.2 Components of employment in the informal economy as percentage of total non-agricultural employment, by sex (latest year available) 16

Table 2.3 Employment in the informal economy and its components, selected countries, as percentage of non–agricultural employment 20

Table 2.4 Contribution of informal sector (excluding agriculture) to non-agricultural GVA in selected developing and transition economies (in percentage) 22

Table 3.1 Share of temporary employment in dependent employment (wage and salary) in selected OECD countries, 1990, 2000, 2008, 2011 29

Table 3.2 Part-time employment as share of total employment in selected OECD countries, 1990, 2000, 2008, 2011 32

Table 3.3 Own-account self-employment as a share of total employment in selected OECD Countries, 1990, 2000, 2008 (per cent) 36

Table 4.1 Global and regional estimates by the ILO of the number of domestic workers, by sex, 1995 and 2010 43

List of boxes

Box 3.1 Atypical employment and the quality of employment in Germany 26

Box 3.2 Non-standard employment in Spain 27

Box 4.1 Recent initiatives to improve estimates of domestic workers, home-based workers, street vendors and waste pickers 40

Box 4.2 Cities and countries with data on four urban informal groups, as compiled by WIEGO 41

Box 4.3 Immigrant Domestic Workers in and from Latin America 45

Box 4.4 Domestic Workers in Latin America 49

Abbreviations and acronyms

CIS	Commonwealth of Independent States
ECLAC	Economic Commission for Latin America and the Caribbean
ESCAP	Economic and Social Commission for Asia and the Pacific
EU	European Union
GDP	gross domestic product
GVA	gross value added
ICLS	International Conference of Labour Statisticians
ICSE	International Classification of Status in Employment
IILS	International Institute for Labour Studies
ILC	International Labour Conference
ILO	International Labour Organization/Office
INEGI	Instituto Nacional de Estadística y Geografía (National Institute of Statistics and Geography, Mexico)
IRD	Institut de recherche pour le développement (Institute of Research for Development, France)
ISCO	International Standard Classification of Occupations
ISE	informal sector employment
ISIC	International Standard Industrial Classification
LABORSTA	ILO database of labour statistics
MENA	Middle East and North Africa
OECD	Organization for Economic Co-operation and Development
SIALC	ILO Information System for Latin America and the Caribbean
WAP	working age population
WIEGO	Women in Informal Employment: Globalizing and Organizing

x

Main findings

Over the past decade, important advances have been made in the availability of data on informal employment, enabling this report on *Women and Men in the Informal Economy: A Statistical Picture* (Second edition) to present a more detailed and robust picture for more countries than the earlier, 2002 edition. This report presents detailed statistics on employment in the informal economy for 47 developing countries/territories and economies in transition. In the 2002 edition, data were presented for 25 countries and there were only three country-specific case studies for which detailed data were provided.

The proportion of people in informal employment in non-agricultural activities is significant in most of the reporting countries. In more than half of the countries, this share exceeds 50 per cent and in about one-third informal employment accounts for at least 67 per cent of non-agricultural employment. In all except two countries, the number of persons employed within the informal sector exceeds those in informal employment outside the informal sector, suggesting that the bulk of informal employment is concentrated in employment in the informal sector.

In **South and East Asia** (excluding China), informal employment in all the reporting countries, except Thailand, is more than 60 per cent of total non-agricultural employment. It ranges from 42 per cent in Thailand to 84 per cent in India. In all the reporting countries, the proportion of persons employed in the informal sector greatly exceeds those in informal employment outside the informal sector. The share of informal sector employment in non-agricultural activities, ranges from 44 per cent in Viet Nam to 73 per cent in Pakistan. The percentages of men and women having an informal job are relatively similar in all the countries with the exception of Sri Lanka. In the countries in South and East Asia the percentage of men in informal sector employment is higher than that of women except in Viet Nam where women's informal sector employment is slightly higher than men's. Furthermore, the bulk of informal employment of men is concentrated within the informal sector, while for women the extent of informal employment outside the informal sector (e.g. domestic workers) is also significant.

For **China**, the data, which were limited to six urban areas, indicate that informal employment is fairly significant (33 per cent), but lower than in the other reporting countries of the region. A higher proportion of women than men are in informal employment, in employment within the informal sector and in informal employment outside the informal sector.

In **sub-Saharan Africa**, informal employment in all the reporting countries accounts for a significant share of total non-agricultural employment, ranging from 33 per cent in South Africa to 82 per cent in Mali. The pattern for informal sector employment is generally similar: ranging from 9 per cent in Mauritius and 18 per cent in South Africa to 71 per cent in Mali. In all the sub-Saharan African countries for which data were available, the number of persons employed in the informal sector greatly exceeds those in informal employment outside the informal sector. In all of these countries, the percentage of women in informal employment is higher than that of men. However in contrast to the other regions, the percentage of women employed in the informal sector is generally higher than that of men in the majority of the reporting countries of the region, except in Lesotho, Mauritius, South Africa and the United Republic of Tanzania, where it is slightly lower.

In all the reporting countries in **Latin America and the Caribbean**, informal employment accounts for a significant share of non-agricultural employment, ranging from 40 per cent in Uruguay to 75 per cent in Bolivia. The proportion of employment in the informal sector as percentage of total non-agricultural employment ranges from 24 per cent in Brazil to 58 per cent in Honduras. Informal employment is generally a more important source of employment for women than for men. However in employment in the informal sector, the picture is reversed. The majority of the countries in the region (12 out of 16) registered higher percentages of men than women in informal employment. The bulk of informal employment of men is concentrated within the informal sector, while for women a large proportion also work outside the informal sector (e.g. as domestic workers).

For **North Africa and the Middle East**, informal employment in the three reporting countries/territories constitutes a significant proportion of employment: 58 per cent in the West Bank and Gaza Strip, 51 per cent in Egypt and 31 per cent in Turkey. The percentage of men in informal employment is much higher than women in two of these three countries/territories, namely Egypt and the West Bank and Gaza Strip. The higher proportion of informal employment among men partly reflects the low participation rate of women in the labour force and differences in the types of activities undertaken by men and women respectively. In Turkey, the situation is different, with similar proportions of informal employment among women and men. Women's rates of participation in the labour force are higher than in the two other reporting countries/territories, and a higher proportion of women work in the manufacturing and trade sectors.

Among the regions, the lowest percentages of informal employment are in the countries of **Eastern Europe and the Commonwealth of Independent States (CIS)**. In countries for which data were available, the share of informal employment in total non-agricultural employment ranges from 6 per cent in Serbia to 20 per cent in Armenia. The percentage of employment in the informal sector in total non-agricultural employment varies from a high of 59 per cent in Kyrgyzstan to 12 per cent in the Russian Federation and 4 per cent in Serbia. Unlike in other regions, in this region the percentages of informal employment and informal sector employment are systematically higher for men than for women in the few countries for which data were available.

This edition contains data on several specific categories of informal workers. Previously published ILO estimates show a minimum of 53 million women and men working as domestic workers globally in 2010, up from 34 million in 1995. Of these, some 16 million (or 29 per cent) are completely excluded from coverage by national labour legislation. Since domestic workers are often undercounted in labour force surveys, these figures are conservative estimates and are likely to understate the actual percentage of domestic workers. WIEGO's efforts to cross-tabulate informal employment data by occupation, branch of economic activity and place of work reveal the large proportion of informal workers in the urban labour force: **domestic workers** constitute 4 and 8 per cent of all workers in urban India and Buenos Aires, respectively, **home-based workers** represent 18 and 6 per cent of the urban workforce in India and South Africa, respectively; and **street vendors** represent 11 and 15 per cent of the urban workforce in India and South Africa, respectively. Notably, the three groups together comprise about one third of urban employment in India.

In developed countries, a large proportion of the workforce works in employment arrangements that offer limited benefits and social protection. These include certain types of own-account self-employment, temporary (or fixed-term) wage employment, and some part-time wage employment. Compilation of data on these employment arrangements provides a starting point for understanding the changes taking place in employment arrangements in developed countries.

Chapter 1

Measuring the informal economy: Taking up the challenge

1.1 Introduction

Statistics can often convey a more powerful message than other facts. Moreover, data appeal to both policy-makers and the public. And yet, until recently informal employment remained largely invisible in official statistics. Without reliable and accurate data that take into account the diversity of situations within the informal economy, it is difficult to develop effective policy solutions to address the challenges of informality.

Throughout the world, millions of people are earning a living in the informal economy. Informality exists in all labour markets, in both high- and low-income countries, although it is more prevalent in developing countries. The informal economy comprises diverse workers and entrepreneurs who are not often recognized or protected under national legal and regulatory frameworks. Viewed through the lens of what the ILO defines as Decent Work, the informal economy can be seen to encompass a broad range of vulnerabilities, such as limited access to social protection, denial of labour rights, and lack of organization and representation. On average, informal workers earn far less than formal workers. In other words, most informal workers suffer from significant decent work deficits.[1] The understanding of informality has evolved considerably over the past few decades, due largely to the joint efforts of the International Labour Office (ILO) and the Women in Informal Employment: Globalizing and Organizing (WIEGO) network. This was reflected in the discussions at the 90th session of the International Labour Conference (ILC) in 2002 which led to a Resolution concerning decent work and the informal economy.[2] This landmark resolution broadened the concept of informality, moving beyond the narrow, enterprise-based notion of the "informal sector" to a broader concept of "informal employment" which comprises all employment that lacks legal or social protection, whether in informal enterprises, formal enterprises or households.

At present, there is a renewed interest in the informal economy. This stems largely from the fact that, contrary to expectations, informal activities, enterprises and jobs have not only persisted, but have also emerged in new guises and unexpected places. The sheer size, universality and heterogeneity of the informal economy have drawn increasing attention. In addition, there is the perception that, during the recent global recession, the informal economy served as a buffer for those who lost their jobs in the formal economy; meanwhile it too was buffeted by the crisis in much the same way as the formal economy. Perhaps most crucially, the renewed interest in the informal economy stems from the recognition of the links between informality and growth, on the one hand, and informality, poverty and inequality on the other.

---

[1] ILO, *Decent work and the informal economy*, Report VI, ILC, 90th Session, Geneva, ILO, 2002.

[2] The full text of this resolution is available at: http://www.ilo.org/public/english/standards/relm/ilc/ilc90/pdf/pr-25res.pdf.

1.2 What is new in this publication?

In 2002, to support the general discussion on the informal economy at the ILC, data on informality was compiled in the first edition of *Women and Men in the Informal Economy: A Statistical Picture* in 2002.[3] That first report used an indirect, residual approach to derive the national estimates of informal employment, since the international statistical community had not yet adopted an agreed definition of informal employment. Following the 2002 ILC general discussion and the subsequent resolution[4], which proposed a new comprehensive framework for conceptualizing and measuring informal employment both inside and outside the informal sector, the 17th International Conference of Labour Statisticians (ICLS) endorsed the new and broadened concept of informal employment in 2003. This internationally accepted statistical definition of *informal employment* complements the enterprise-based definition of the *informal sector* that was adopted by the 15th ICLS in 1993.

The conceptual framework for the statistical measurement of informal employment adopted by the ICLS distinguishes between informality from the perspective of production units as observation units, on the one hand, and that of jobs as observation units on the other. Thus the two concepts which are involved form the basis of this report: employment in the informal sector, which refers to employment in informal enterprises, and informal employment, which refers to employment in informal jobs both inside and outside the informal sector. The major advances by the international statistical community in generating viable data on informal employment are described in detail in section 1.3 below.

As a result of these critical developments, this new publication differs from the earlier 2002 publication in a number of ways. Firstly, the data presented here are based on direct measures of informal employment using data from national surveys. In recent years, data on informal employment inside and outside the informal sector based on direct analyses of household and labour market surveys have become available for an increasing number of countries. The greater availability of such statistics has been made possible by the ongoing efforts to collect and analyse data that capture informal employment and distinguish it from formal employment. The improvement in data collection and analysis allows estimations of the size, breadth, composition and characteristics of the informal economy to an extent that simply was not possible a decade ago.

A second advance is that this report presents, for the first time, national data related to employment in the informal economy from 47 countries/territories. In the earlier publication, estimates were available for only 25 countries, and detailed information was presented for only three countries, while country-specific data on employment in the informal sector were disseminated in a separate publication.[5]

1.3 Basic statistical concepts of informality

In 1993, the 15th ICLS adopted a resolution concerning statistical measurement of the informal sector, including its definition. This definition is based on economic units as observation units, and refers to employment and production that take place in unincorporated small or unregistered enterprises (for example those having less than five employees).[6]

---

[3] ILO, Employment Sector, *Women and Men in the Informal Economy: A Statistical Picture*, Geneva, ILO, 2002.

[4] ILO, *Resolution and conclusions concerning decent work and the informal economy*, ILC 90th Session, Geneva, ILO, 2002.

[5] Hussmanns, R. and du Jeu, B., *Compendium of official statistics on employment in the informal sector*, STAT, Working Paper No. 1, Geneva, ILO, 2002.

[6] For the full definition, see ILO, *Report of the Fifteenth International Conference of Labour Statisticians*, Geneva, 19-28 January 2003. See also the explanatory notes to the country-specific tables in annex 2 to this publication.

Chapter 1 – Measuring the informal economy: Taking up the challenge

Ten years later in 2003, following the 2002 ILC Resolution, the 17th ICLS broadened the concept to *informal employment*.[7] Informal employment now refers to all employment arrangements that do not provide individuals with legal or social protection through their work, thereby leaving them more exposed to economic risk than the others, whether or not the economic units they work for or operate in are formal enterprises, informal enterprises or households. To further classify workers within formal or informal employment, a distinction is made according to the categories of the International Classification of Status in Employment (ICSE-93). Based on this classification, the specific groups of workers employed in the informal sector and in informal employment outside the informal sector are as follows:

Persons employed in the informal sector (including those rare persons who are formally employed in the informal sector [8]):

- Employers in informal enterprises;
- Employees in informal enterprises;
- Own-account (self-employed) workers in their own informal enterprises;
- Contributing family workers working in informal enterprises; and
- Members of informal producers' cooperatives.

Persons in informal employment outside the informal sector, specifically:

- Employees in formal enterprises not covered by social protection through their work;
- Paid domestic workers not covered by social protection through their work; and
- Contributing family workers working in formal enterprises.

A few countries also include own-account workers engaged in the production of goods exclusively for final use by their households, for instance, subsistence farming and do-it-yourself construction of own dwelling. However, most countries exclude such workers from the definition of employment.

Currently, data on agriculture is not included. Since lack of social protection characterizes much of agricultural employment, this continues to be a key goal for future work on measuring the informal economy. In this sense, it can be assumed that much of agricultural employment is informal, and it is important to note the relative size of agricultural employment in different countries when considering the prevalence of informal employment relative to total employment.

The term "informal work" is used synonymously with informal employment. (For more details see the explanatory notes in annex 2 of this report.)

1.4 New developments in statistics on the informal economy

An important consequence of the new definition of *informal employment* from the 17th ICLS was that greater priority was given to collecting data on the household-based labour force in surveys. Previously, when the *informal sector* was viewed as an enterprise-based concept, priority was often placed on collecting data through a special informal enterprise survey, either designed as an independent survey or attached to a household survey, rather than through a labour force survey. Informal sector surveys continue to be important, but they are undertaken on a less frequent basis

---

[7] For the full definition, see ILO, *Report of the Seventeenth International Conference of Labour Statisticians*, Geneva, 24 November – 3 December 2003. See also the explanatory notes to the country-specific tables in annex 2 to this publication. The conceptual change and its implications for survey design are discussed in Hussmanns, R., *Measuring the informal economy: From Employment in the Informal Sector to Informal Employment*, Geneva, ILO, 2004.

[8] In most countries, the category of formal employment in the informal sector is rather small, which is why it is not analysed in detail in this report.

than labour force surveys. Moreover, experience has shown that reliable data on employment in informal enterprises can be collected in labour force surveys. Thus the broader concept of informal employment facilitates the collection of data on both informal employment and informal sector employment as part of regular household surveys conducted by countries.

In 2003, the United Nations Statistical Commission called for an update of the *1993 System of National Accounts* to address new developments in the economy, advances in methods, and evolving users' needs. For the first time, volume 2 of the *System of National Accounts 2008* [9] contained a chapter entitled Informal Aspects of the Economy. This chapter argues that statistics on the informal sector have an important role to play in the preparation of country's national accounts. Direct survey data on the informal sector provide an improved basis for estimating relevant aspects of the household sector, and thereby a more exhaustive measure of country's gross domestic product (GDP). The chapter therefore represents an important step in the preparation of estimates of the contribution of the informal sector to GDP and also in the preparation of satellite accounts on the contribution to GDP of informal employment.

Building on the ICLS resolutions, the chapter on the informal sector in the *System of National Accounts 2008* and country experiences, the ILO coordinated the publication entitled *"Measuring Informality: A Statistical Manual on the Informal Sector and Informal Employment"*.[10] The manual was prepared in cooperation with WIEGO and other members of the International Expert Group on Informal Sector Statistics (also known as the Delhi Group). This expert group, set up by the United Nations Statistical Commission, meets regularly to address statistical issues related to the informal sector and informal employment. The manual is a guide for assisting countries in planning the collection of data on the informal sector and informal employment. It also provides guidance on the technical issues involved in each stage of the survey process – from designing and conducting a survey to tabulating and disseminating data. The final chapter concerns the use of data on the informal sector and informal employment for national accounts statistics.

By providing technical assistance and training for countries, the ILO Department of Statistics, in cooperation with ILO field offices, has contributed to increasing the number of countries that regularly collect and disseminate data on employment in the informal sector and on informal employment. In addition, two projects – Interregional Cooperation on the Measurement of the Informal Sector and Informal Employment, coordinated by the United Nations Economic and Social Commission for Asia and the Pacific (ESCAP), and a project of the Asian Development Bank (ADB) – were undertaken to improve the available data, especially in Asia.[11] Furthermore, a project on Informal Employment, Poverty and Growth in India and China, which the global network WIEGO helped initiate, contributed to the collection of data on informal employment and employment in the informal sector through the China Urban Labour Survey that was carried out in six cities in China. The survey was conducted by the Chinese Academy of Social Sciences working closely with the city offices of the National Bureau of Statistics in China. An international advisory committee with members from both the ILO and WIEGO ensured that the definitions used were consistent with the ICLS recommendations. The resulting data in chapter 2 and in the country-specific tables in annex 2 are the first estimates of informal employment in China.

The ILO Department of Statistics, working with the ILO's Information System for Latin America and the Caribbean (SIALC) and WIEGO, has compiled data from nearly 50 countries on informal employment both outside and inside the informal sector in the region. These include virtu-

---

[9] Commission of the European Communities, International Monetary Fund, Organisation for Economic Co-operation and Development, United Nations and World Bank, *System of National Accounts, 2008*, New York, United Nations publication, Sales No, E.08.XVII.29.

[10] Available at: http://www.ilo.org/global/publications/ilo-bookstore/order-online/books/WCMS_222979/lang--en/index.htm.

[11] The countries/territories where surveys were undertaken through the ESCAP-coordinated project are: Mongolia, the Philippines, Sri Lanka, St. Lucia and West Bank and Gaza; the countries/areas covered by the ADB project are: Armenia, Bangladesh and two provinces of Indonesia. As a result of the project in Indonesia, a national level survey is now being carried out.

ally all Latin American countries which collect data on informal employment and employment in the informal sector through their labour force surveys on a regular basis. An increasing number of Sub-Saharan African countries and transition countries also collect such data. These data are presented in the country-specific tables in annex 2. However, data gaps still exist for many Asian countries, as well as for countries in the Middle East and North Africa.

The ILO and WIEGO have also initiated several activities to improve the availability of statistics on informal employment and on specific categories of workers, as well as to promote the use of those statistics. These activities reflect the joint collaboration of activists, researchers and statisticians to improve statistics on the informal economy. In 2008, the ILO and WIEGO organized a meeting of experts to explore the steps required for ensuring the collection of comprehensive data on all forms of informal employment in developed countries.[12] There is a considerable and increasing amount of non-standard employment in developed countries that offers limited or no benefits and social protection.[13] Many relevant data for obtaining a detailed picture of the different forms of informal arrangements in developed countries have been collected and analysed. The section on developed countries in chapter 3 presents an analysis of such data from countries of the Organisation of Economic Co-operation and Development (OECD).

Moreover, the ILO and WIEGO have focused on making currently available statistics on informal employment and specific categories of informal workers more accessible to researchers, policy-makers and advocates. As part of the global project entitled Inclusive Cities for the Working Poor, WIEGO has commissioned data analysts to generate estimates of urban informal employment, including estimates of paid domestic workers, home-based workers, street vendors and waste pickers, in a number of cities and countries. Among others, DIAL, a research unit of the French Institut de Recherche pour le Développement (IRD), analysed data for 11 cities in 10 countries from its database. Regional and global estimates of domestic work, published by the ILO in 2013 using data from 117 countries and territories, show the magnitude of that sector around the world. These analyses provide the main source of data for the section on specific categories of urban informal workers discussed in chapter 4 of this report.

1.5 Overview of this report

Chapter 1 of this report reviews developments at the international level with regard to measuring the informal economy. Chapter 2 presents, for the first time, national data from 47 countries and territories, most of them concerning informal employment inside and outside the informal sector. Also national data on employment in the informal economy for 13 countries covering more than one year are presented. This chapter includes a section on the economic contribution of the informal sector and informal employment. Chapter 3 focuses on statistics concerning non-standard employment in developed countries. Chapter 4 presents statistics prepared by WIEGO on specific groups of urban informal workers, and explains the methods used for identifying these groups. This chapter includes recent ILO regional and global estimates of domestic work. Chapter 5

---

[12] The report of this meeting is available at: http://wiego.org/sites/wiego.org/files/reports/files/Measuring-Inf-Employment-Developed-Countries-2008.pdf.

[13] The statistical concept of informal employment has been applied by official statisticians mainly to developing countries. However, some forms of employment in developed countries demonstrate tenuous links between workers and formal structures. Workers in those kinds of employment have little, if any, access to fundamental labour rights and protection and employment-based social protection. The term most often used to describe such work arrangements is "non-standard employment". Part-time employment, temporary employment, own-account self-employment, subcontracted work and day labour are all categories of such non-standard employment. These concepts are related, but not identical, to the concept of informal employment; for instance, not all non-standard employment in developed countries is informal, and not all informal employment is non-standard. Therefore non-standard work should not be considered as proxy for informal employment.

revisits and updates a plan of action for improving statistics on the informal economy and their dissemination. Annex 1 describes data coverage on informal employment and employment, both within and outside the informal sector, for all the regions, while annex 2 contains country-specific tables and explanatory notes, with information on the methodology used for compiling the data shown in the tables.

Chapter 2

Statistics relating to the informal economy

National data on the informal economy have improved significantly as countries increasingly adopt the ICLS recommendations for defining informal employment and the informal sector (see chapter 1). Increasing availability of such statistics has been made possible by ongoing the efforts to collect and analyse data that capture informal employment and distinguish it from formal employment. The improvement in data collection and analysis allows estimations of the size, breadth, composition and characteristics of the informal economy to an extent that was not possible a decade ago.

However, some challenges to comparability remain: survey questions and the variables used to define informal employment vary to some extent, despite a common overarching framework. In most cases, these differences stem from legal and institutional variations across countries, which are necessarily reflected in the survey design. Survey responses are also typically context specific – a common difficulty for comparing labour market statistics across countries.

Statistics on employment in the informal economy are now available for many developing countries/territories and economies in transition including a large number of the most populated countries, such as Brazil, China, India and Indonesia. However, many other countries still lack reliable estimates. In some countries, there have not been any surveys; in others, the surveys do not collect enough information to allow an analysis of informal employment and the informal sector. In other countries, even though data exist, they are not able to analyse them due to the lack of the appropriate human resources and technical skills. The availability of data also differs in different regions. For example, in Latin America, the efforts to collect data on informal employment over time resulted in the availability of data for 16 countries covering 89 per cent of the working age population in the region. However, the paucity of basic statistics on the informal economy for many countries remains a challenge for developing a comprehensive set of regional estimates on the size and composition of informal employment.

This chapter presents country/territory data on different measures of employment in the informal economy. The first section presents statistics collected by the ILO Department of Statistics for 47 countries and territories. More detailed data for these countries/territories are presented in annex 2 to this report. This section also presents country-specific data on informal employment inside and outside the informal sector which were available for 13 countries covering a period of more than one year. Section 2 of this chapter presents estimates of gross value added (GVA) of the informal sector, excluding agriculture, for 28 countries.

2.1 Country data on employment in the informal economy

In 2011, the ILO compiled statistics on employment in the informal economy, disaggregated by sex from 47 medium- and low-income countries/territories. The statistics relate to the number of persons whose main (or only) jobs were in non-agricultural informal employment, including both inside and outside the informal sector.

2.1.1 Informal employment

In 15 countries out of 41 for which data were available, informal employment represents at least two thirds of total (formal plus informal) non-agricultural employment, and in 24 countries it exceeds 50 per cent (see table 2.1 and figure 2.1). In all except two countries, employment in the informal sector exceeds informal employment outside the informal sector.

In Latin America and the Caribbean, informal employment in all reporting countries constitutes a significant proportion of non-agricultural employment, ranging from 39.8 per cent in Uruguay to 75.1 per cent in the Plurinational State of Bolivia. Informal sector employment ranges from 24.3 per cent in Brazil to 58.3 per cent in Honduras, where informal employment is concentrated in the informal sector. The countries with the highest percentage of informal employment outside the informal sector are Paraguay, Ecuador and the Plurinational State of Bolivia.

Among the regions, Eastern European countries and member states of the Commonwealth of Independent States (CIS) have the lowest percentage of informal employment. In four countries for which data were available on informal employment, the proportion of workers in informal non-agricultural employment ranges from 6.1 per cent in Serbia to 19.8 per cent in Armenia. Data on informal sector employment, which were available for seven countries, show that the percentage of informal sector employment in total non-agricultural employment varies from a high of 59.2 per cent in Kyrgyzstan to 12.1 per cent in the Russian Federation and 3.5 per cent in Serbia.

In Sub-Saharan Africa, informal employment in all reporting countries accounts for a significant percentage of total non-agricultural employment. However, the pattern differs between Southern Africa and the other sub-regions. In Southern Africa, informal employment is much lower, ranging from 32.7 per cent in South Africa to 43.9 per cent in Namibia. In the other seven countries for which data were available, the percentage exceeds 50 per cent and reaches as high as 76.2 per cent in the United Republic of Tanzania and 81.8 per cent in Mali. The pattern for informal sector employment is generally the same. The richer countries show the lowest percentages of informal sector employment: 9.3 per cent in Mauritius and 17.8 per cent in South Africa.

In all Sub-Saharan African countries for which data were available, the number of persons employed in the informal sector greatly exceeds those in informal employment outside the informal sector. For example in 2004, in Mali, the percentage of informal sector employment was estimated to be 71.4 per cent comparing with 11.3 per cent of informal employment outside the informal sector.

In South and East Asia, excluding China, informal employment in all reporting countries constitutes a significant proportion of total employment, ranging from 42.3 per cent in Thailand to 83.6 per cent in India, and for all countries except Thailand it is more than 60 per cent.

In all reporting countries the proportion of persons employed in the informal sector greatly exceeds those in informal employment outside the informal sector. For informal sector employment, the percentage ranges from 43.5 per cent in Viet Nam to 73 per cent in Pakistan. In Pakistan, the percentage of informal employment outside the informal sector is estimated to be only 8.3 per cent. The countries with the highest percentage of informal employment outside the informal sector are India (16.8 per cent) and Viet Nam (25 per cent).

For China, data were limited to six urban areas, including Fuzhou, Guangzhou, Shanghai, Shenyang, Wuhan and Xi-an. The percentage of informal employment is significant (32.6 per cent), but it is lower than in the other reporting countries of the region.

For North Africa and the Middle East, informal employment in the three reporting countries/territories accounts for a substantial proportion of employment; 58.5 per cent in the West Bank and Gaza Strip, 51.2 per cent in Egypt and 30.6 per cent in Turkey.

Chapter 2 – Statistics relating to the informal economy

Figure 2.1: Components of employment in the informal economy as percentage of non-agricultural employment (latest year available)

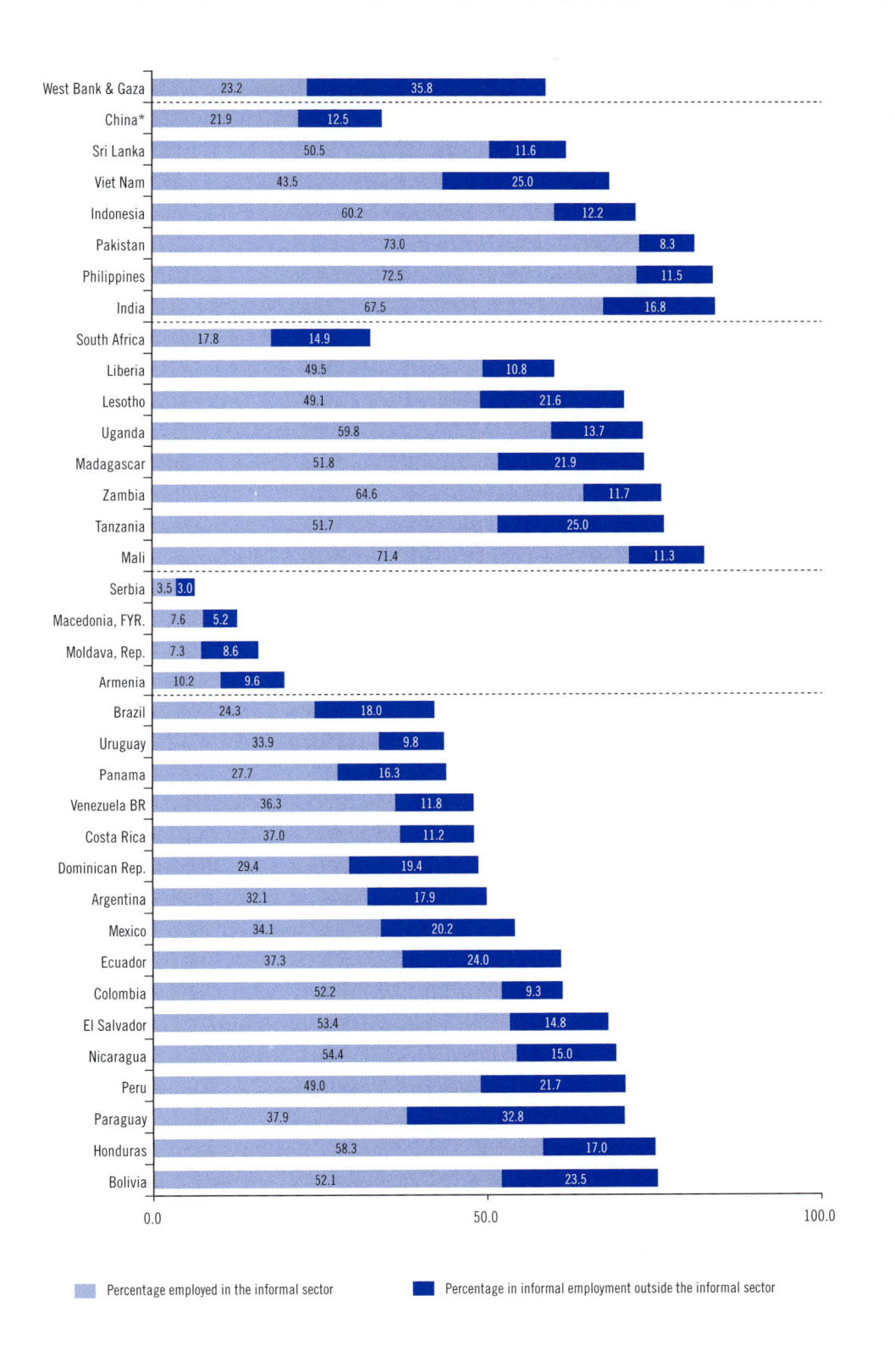

Country	Percentage employed in the informal sector	Percentage in informal employment outside the informal sector
West Bank & Gaza	23.2	35.8
China*	21.9	12.5
Sri Lanka	50.5	11.6
Viet Nam	43.5	25.0
Indonesia	60.2	12.2
Pakistan	73.0	8.3
Philippines	72.5	11.5
India	67.5	16.8
South Africa	17.8	14.9
Liberia	49.5	10.8
Lesotho	49.1	21.6
Uganda	59.8	13.7
Madagascar	51.8	21.9
Zambia	64.6	11.7
Tanzania	51.7	25.0
Mali	71.4	11.3
Serbia	3.5	3.0
Macedonia, FYR.	7.6	5.2
Moldava, Rep.	7.3	8.6
Armenia	10.2	9.6
Brazil	24.3	18.0
Uruguay	33.9	9.8
Panama	27.7	16.3
Venezuela BR	36.3	11.8
Costa Rica	37.0	11.2
Dominican Rep.	29.4	19.4
Argentina	32.1	17.9
Mexico	34.1	20.2
Ecuador	37.3	24.0
Colombia	52.2	9.3
El Salvador	53.4	14.8
Nicaragua	54.4	15.0
Peru	49.0	21.7
Paraguay	37.9	32.8
Honduras	58.3	17.0
Bolivia	52.1	23.5

Notes: Horizontal lines separate geographical regions. The countries are presented in ascending order of employment in the informal economy within each geographical region. * Data for China cover six cities, including Fuzhou, Guangzhou, Shanghai, Shenyang, Wuhan and Xi-an.

Women and men in the informal economy: A statistical picture

Table 2.1: Employment in the informal economy and its components as percentage of non-agricultural employment (latest year available)

Year/Period	Country or Region	Informal employment (Thousands)	Informal employment (% of non-agricultural emplyment)	Employment in the informal sector (Thousands)	Employment in the informal sector (% of non-agricultural emplyment)	Informal employment outside the informal sector (Thousands)	Informal employment outside the informal sector (% of non-agricultural emplyment)
Latin Amercica and the Carribbean							
2009 IV Qtr.	Argentina	5,138	49.7	3,317	32.1	1,850	17.9
2006	Bolivia	2,069	75.1	1,436	52.1	647	23.5
2009	Brazil	32,493	42.2	18,688	24.3	13,862	18.0
2010 II Qtr.	Colombia	9,307	59.6	8,144	52.2	1,444	9.3
2009 July	Costa Rica	754	43.8	638	37.0	193	11.2
2009	Dominican Rep.	1,484	48.5	898	29.4	593	19.4
2009 IV Qtr.	Ecuador	2,691	60.9	1,646	37.3	1,062	24.0
2009	El Salvador	1,242	66.4	998	53.4	277	14.8
2009	Honduras	1,454	73.9	1,146	58.3	334	17.0
2009 II Qtr.	Mexico	20,258	53.7	12,861	34.1	7,620	20.2
2009	Nicaragua	1,024	65.7	847	54.4	234	15.0
2009 Aug.	Panama	517	43.8	327	27.7	192	16.3
2009	Paraguay	1,473	70.7	790	37.9	683	32.8
2009	Peru	7,458	69.9	5,223	49.0	2,313	21.7
2009	Uruguay	572	39.8	487	33.9	141	9.8
2009 I Qtr.	Venezuela BR	5,131	47.5	3,920	36.3	1,275	11.8
Eastern Europe and CIS countries							
2009	Armenia	138	19.8	71	10.2	67	9.6
2009	Kyrgyztan	n.a.	n.a.	887	59.2	n.a.	n.a.
2010	Macedonia, FYR.	65	12.6	39	7.6	27	5.2
2009	Moldova, Rep.	136	15.9	62	7.3	73	8.6
2010	Russian Fed.	n.a.	n.a.	7,785	12.1	n.a.	n.a.
2010	Serbia	113	6.1	66	3.5	57	3.0
2009	Ukraine	n.a.	n.a.	1,525	9.4	n.a.	n.a.
Sub-Saharan Africa							
2008	Cote d'Ivoire	n.a.	n.a.	2,434	69.7	n.a.	n.a.
2004	Ethiopia**	n.a.	n.a.	1,089	41.4	n.a.	n.a.
2008	Lesotho	160	34.9	255	49.1	99	21.6
2010	Liberia	343	60.0	284	49.5	62	10.8
2005	Madagascar	1,271	73.6	893	51.8	378	21.9
2004	Mali	1,180	81.8	1,029	71.4	163	11.3
2009	Mauritius	n.a.	n.a.	57	9.3	n.a.	n.a.
2008	Namibia	121	43.9	n.a.	n.a.	n.a.	n.a.
2010	South Africa	4,089	32.7	2,225	17.8	1,864	14.9
2005/2006	Tanzania	3,467	76.2	2,353	51.7	1,137	25.0
2010	Uganda	2,720	69.4	2,344	59.8	537	13.7
2008	Zambia	920	69.5	854	64.6	155	11.7
2004	Zimbabwe	909	51.6	698	39.6	n.a.	n.a.

Chapter 2 – Statistics relating to the informal economy

Year/ Period	Country or Region	Informal employment (Thousands)	Informal employment (% of non-agricultural employment)	Employment in the informal sector (Thousands)	Employment in the informal sector (% of non-agricultural employment)	Informal employment outside the informal sector (Thousands)	Informal employment outside the informal sector (% of non-agricultural employment)
South and East Asia							
2010	China*	36,030	32.6	24,220	21.9	13,850	12.5
2009/2010	India	185,876	83.6	150,113	67.5	37,409	16.8
2009	Indonesia	3,157	72.5	2,621	60.2	532	12.2
2009/2010	Pakistan	21,913	78.4	20,416	73.0	2,319	8.3
2008	Philippines	15,150	70.1	15,680	72.5	2,490	11.5
2009	Sri Lanka	3,184	62.1	2,588	50.5	597	11.6
2010	Thailand	9,642	42.3	n.a.	n.a.	n.a.	n.a.
2009	Viet Nam	17,172	68.2	10,948	43.5	6,303	25.0
Middle East and North Africa							
2009	Egypt	8,247	51.2	n.a.	n.a.	n.a.	n.a.
2009	Turkey	4,903	30.6	n.a.	n.a.	n.a.	n.a.
2010	West Bank & Gaza	375	58.5	140	23.2	235	35.8

Sources: ILO, Department of Statistics; country responses to ILO request for data; special tabulations of data from national labour force survey, extracts from national survey reports. For Latin American countries, ILO/SIALC household survey micro-data database.

Notes: Due to the possible existence of some formal wage employment in the informal sector, estimates of total informal employment may be slightly lower than the sum of informal sector employment and informal employment outside the informal sector. *For China, data cover six cities (Fuzhou, Guangzhou, Shanghai, Shenyang, Wuhan and Xi-an); ** Urban Areas; n.a. =Not available.

For detailed definitions of the concepts, see the conceptual framework in annex 2.

2.1.2 Women and men in the informal economy

In 30 of the 41 countries for which data were available by sex, the percentage of women in informal non-agricultural employment is higher than that of men (table 2.2 and figure 2.2). By contrast, the majority of countries have a higher percentage of men than women in informal sector employment (table 2.2 and figure 2.3).

In Latin America and the Caribbean, informal employment is generally a more important source of employment for women than for men. The two exceptions of the 16 countries for which data were available are Argentina and the Bolivarian Republic of Venezuela, where there is a slightly higher percentage of men than women in informal employment. However, for informal sector employment, the picture is reversed: the majority of the countries in the region (12 out of 16) registered higher percentages of men in informal sector employment as compared with women. For men, the bulk of informal employment is concentrated within the informal sector, while for women there is a large proportion of informal employment outside the informal sector, such as domestic work, shown in table 2.2 and figure 2.4. In three countries, including Brazil, the Dominican Republic and Paraguay, the proportion of women in informal employment outside the informal sector exceeds the percentage of women in informal sector employment. For example, in Brazil, out of an estimated 15.9 million women in informal employment, nearly 5 million of them were reported to work informally in households.

The Eastern Europe and CIS region shows a different pattern than the other regions. The percentages of informal employment and informal sector employment are consistently higher for men than for women in the few countries for which data were available. In Kyrgyzstan, 65.4 per cent of men are in informal sector employment comparing with 50.7 per cent of women. In the Russian Federation, the percentages of both men and women employed in the informal sector are low, and the difference between the rates for men and women is smaller: 13.3 per cent for men and 10.9 per cent for women.

Women and men in the informal economy: A statistical picture

Figure 2.2 Informal employment as percentage of total non-agricultural employment, by sex (latest year available)

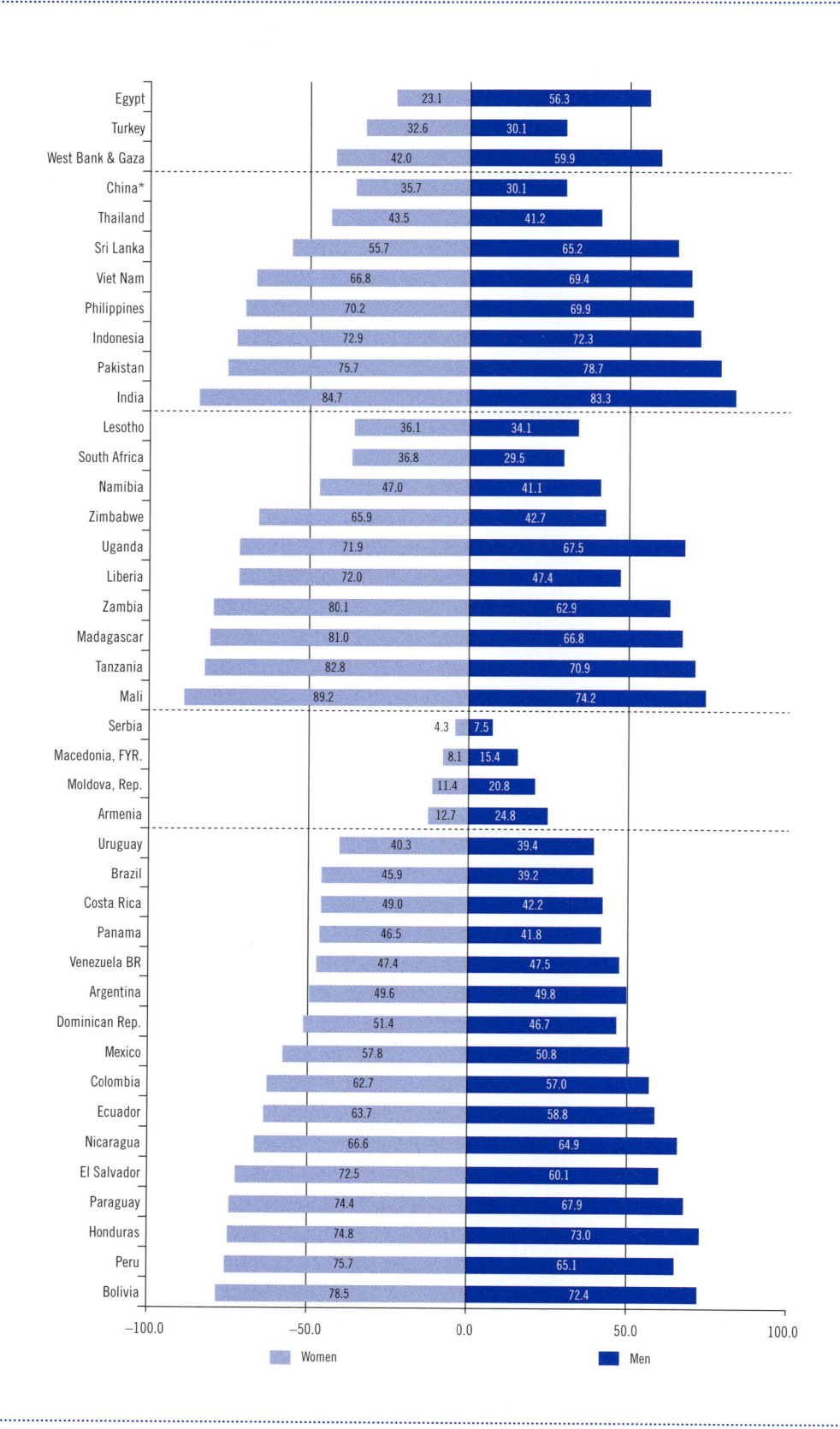

Country	Women	Men
Egypt	23.1	56.3
Turkey	32.6	30.1
West Bank & Gaza	42.0	59.9
China*	35.7	30.1
Thailand	43.5	41.2
Sri Lanka	55.7	65.2
Viet Nam	66.8	69.4
Philippines	70.2	69.9
Indonesia	72.9	72.3
Pakistan	75.7	78.7
India	84.7	83.3
Lesotho	36.1	34.1
South Africa	36.8	29.5
Namibia	47.0	41.1
Zimbabwe	65.9	42.7
Uganda	71.9	67.5
Liberia	72.0	47.4
Zambia	80.1	62.9
Madagascar	81.0	66.8
Tanzania	82.8	70.9
Mali	89.2	74.2
Serbia	4.3	7.5
Macedonia, FYR.	8.1	15.4
Moldova, Rep.	11.4	20.8
Armenia	12.7	24.8
Uruguay	40.3	39.4
Brazil	45.9	39.2
Costa Rica	49.0	42.2
Panama	46.5	41.8
Venezuela BR	47.4	47.5
Argentina	49.6	49.8
Dominican Rep.	51.4	46.7
Mexico	57.8	50.8
Colombia	62.7	57.0
Ecuador	63.7	58.8
Nicaragua	66.6	64.9
El Salvador	72.5	60.1
Paraguay	74.4	67.9
Honduras	74.8	73.0
Peru	75.7	65.1
Bolivia	78.5	72.4

Notes: Horizontal lines separate geographical regions. The countries are listed by ascending order of the indicator for women within each geographical region. *Six cities (see note to table 2.1).

Chapter 2 – Statistics relating to the informal economy

Figure 2.3 Informal sector employment as percentage of total non-agricultural employment, by sex (latest year available)

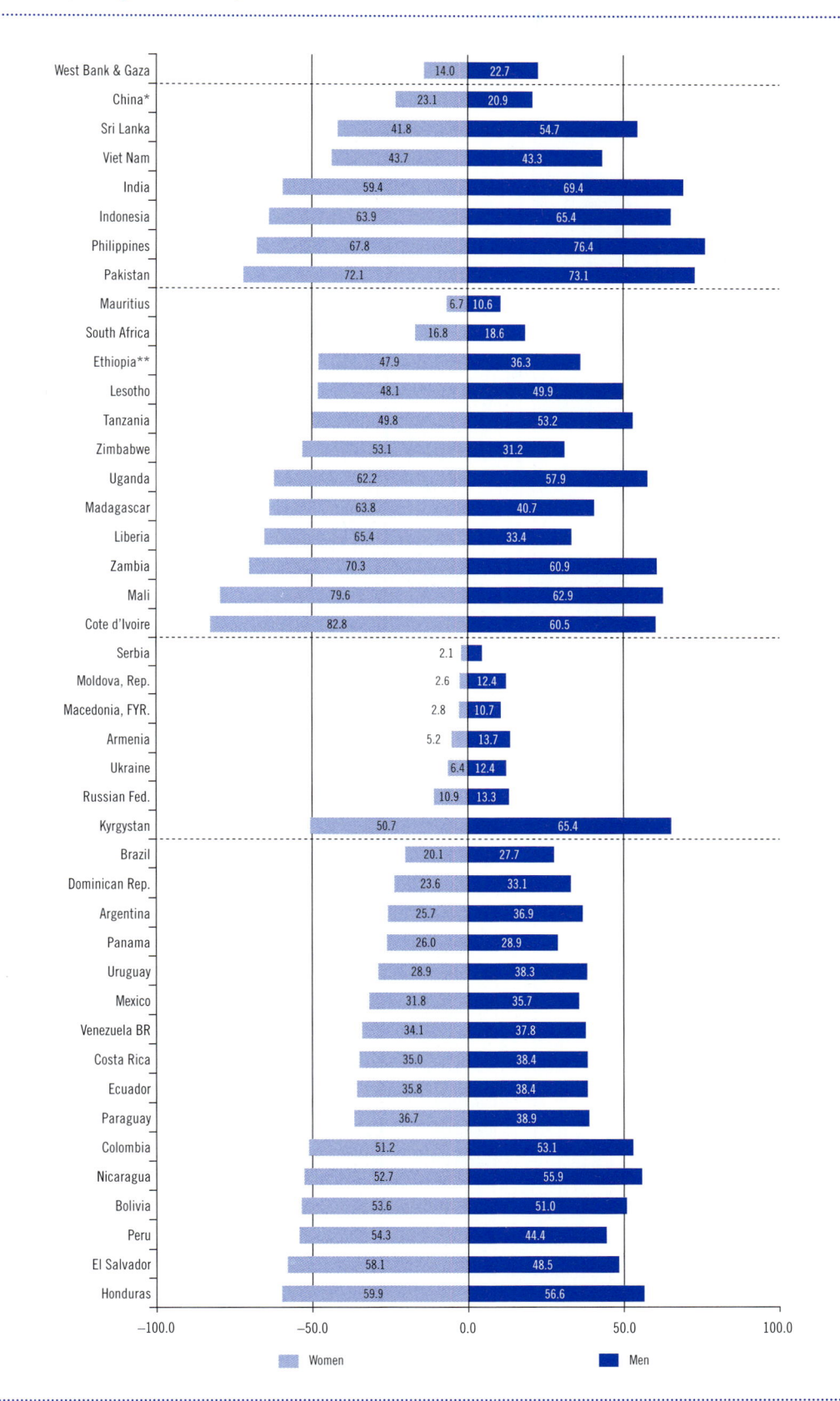

Country	Women	Men
West Bank & Gaza	14.0	22.7
China*	23.1	20.9
Sri Lanka	41.8	54.7
Viet Nam	43.7	43.3
India	59.4	69.4
Indonesia	63.9	65.4
Philippines	67.8	76.4
Pakistan	72.1	73.1
Mauritius	6.7	10.6
South Africa	16.8	18.6
Ethiopia**	47.9	36.3
Lesotho	48.1	49.9
Tanzania	49.8	53.2
Zimbabwe	53.1	31.2
Uganda	62.2	57.9
Madagascar	63.8	40.7
Liberia	65.4	33.4
Zambia	70.3	60.9
Mali	79.6	62.9
Cote d'Ivoire	82.8	60.5
Serbia	2.1	
Moldova, Rep.	2.6	12.4
Macedonia, FYR.	2.8	10.7
Armenia	5.2	13.7
Ukraine	6.4	12.4
Russian Fed.	10.9	13.3
Kyrgystan	50.7	65.4
Brazil	20.1	27.7
Dominican Rep.	23.6	33.1
Argentina	25.7	36.9
Panama	26.0	28.9
Uruguay	28.9	38.3
Mexico	31.8	35.7
Venezuela BR	34.1	37.8
Costa Rica	35.0	38.4
Ecuador	35.8	38.4
Paraguay	36.7	38.9
Colombia	51.2	53.1
Nicaragua	52.7	55.9
Bolivia	53.6	51.0
Peru	54.3	44.4
El Salvador	58.1	48.5
Honduras	59.9	56.6

Notes: Horizontal lines separate geographical regions. The countries are listed by ascending order of the indicator for women within each geographical region. *Six cities (see note in table 2.1).

Women and men in the informal economy: A statistical picture

Figure 2.4 Informal employment outside the informal sector as percentage of total non-agricultural employment, by sex (latest year available)

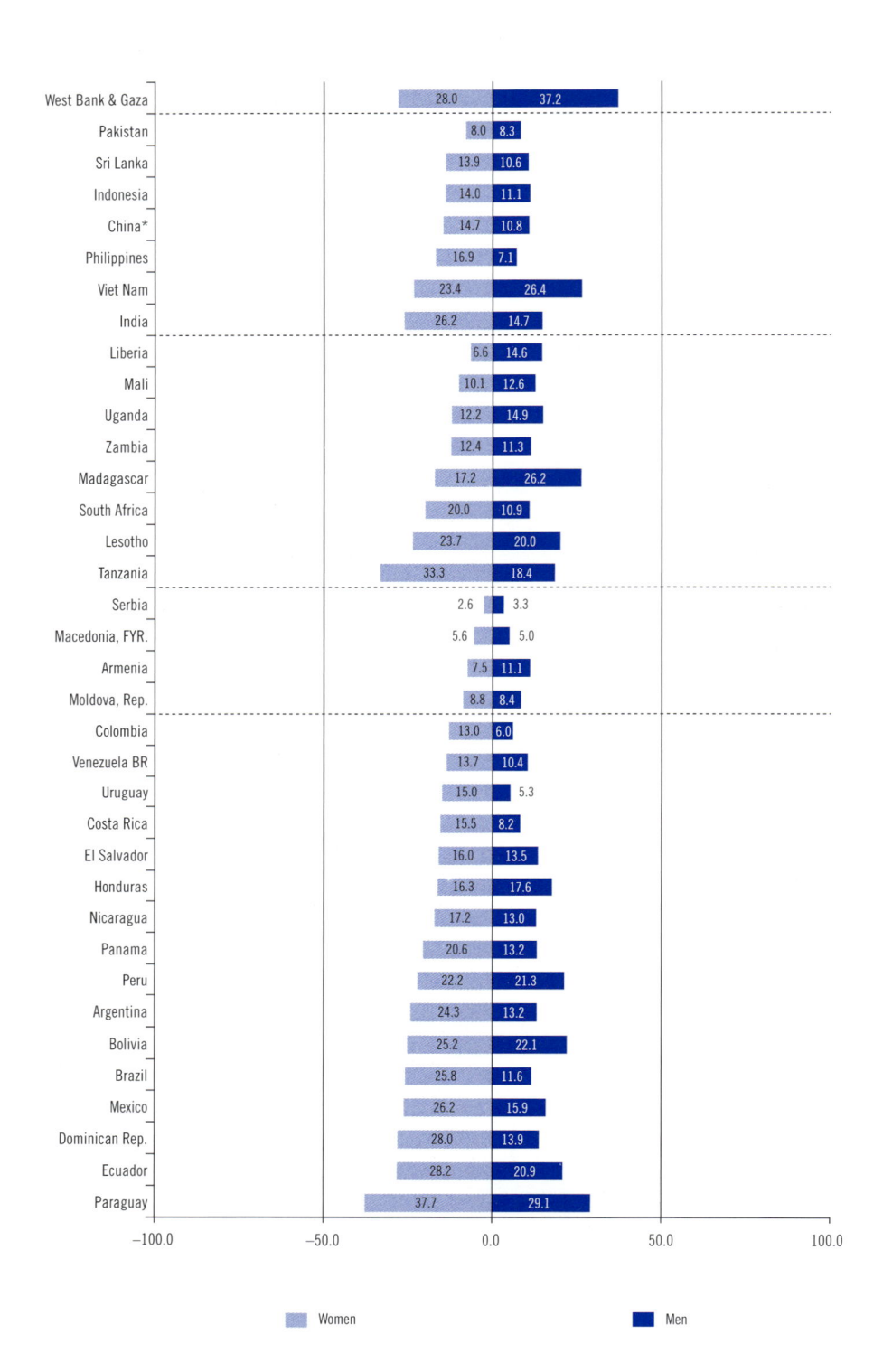

Country	Women	Men
West Bank & Gaza	28.0	37.2
Pakistan	8.0	8.3
Sri Lanka	13.9	10.6
Indonesia	14.0	11.1
China*	14.7	10.8
Philippines	16.9	7.1
Viet Nam	23.4	26.4
India	26.2	14.7
Liberia	6.6	14.6
Mali	10.1	12.6
Uganda	12.2	14.9
Zambia	12.4	11.3
Madagascar	17.2	26.2
South Africa	20.0	10.9
Lesotho	23.7	20.0
Tanzania	33.3	18.4
Serbia	2.6	3.3
Macedonia, FYR.	5.6	5.0
Armenia	7.5	11.1
Moldova, Rep.	8.8	8.4
Colombia	13.0	6.0
Venezuela BR	13.7	10.4
Uruguay	15.0	5.3
Costa Rica	15.5	8.2
El Salvador	16.0	13.5
Honduras	16.3	17.6
Nicaragua	17.2	13.0
Panama	20.6	13.2
Peru	22.2	21.3
Argentina	24.3	13.2
Bolivia	25.2	22.1
Brazil	25.8	11.6
Mexico	26.2	15.9
Dominican Rep.	28.0	13.9
Ecuador	28.2	20.9
Paraguay	37.7	29.1

Notes: Horizontal lines separate geographical regions. The countries are listed by ascending order of the indicator for women within each geographical region. *Six cities (as in note to table 2.1).

In all Sub-Saharan African countries, for which data were available, the percentage of women in informal employment is higher than that of men, particularly in Liberia, where it is 72 per cent for women comparing with 47.4 per cent for men.

However, in contrast to other regions, more women than men are employed in the informal sector in the majority of countries in the region for which data were available. In Liberia, the percentage of women employed in the informal sector is significantly higher than that of men (65.4 per cent compared with 33.4 per cent respectively), but it is lower in Lesotho, Mauritius, South Africa and the United Republic of Tanzania. Concerning informal employment outside the informal sector, there is no significant difference between women and men. In four out of the eight countries for which data were available, the percentage of women in informal employment outside the informal sector exceeded that of men, while it was the opposite in the other four countries. In the United Republic of Tanzania, a significant higher percentage of women were in informal employment outside the informal sector, and in Madagascar, there was a higher proportion of man holding informal employment outside the informal sector.

In South and East Asia, there are fairly similar percentages of men and women having an informal job in all the countries with the exception of Sri Lanka. In Sri Lanka, there is a significantly higher proportion of men in informal employment (65.2 per cent) than women (55.7 per cent).

In five out of seven countries in South and East Asia, the percentage of men in informal sector employment is higher than that of women. Furthermore, the bulk of informal employment of men is concentrated in employment in the informal sector while that of women is outside the informal sector, for instance, domestic work. For example, in India, 26.2 per cent of employed women are in informal employment outside the informal sector in contrast to 14.7 per cent of men. Viet Nam shows a different pattern than other countries of the region, with a higher proportion of men in informal employment outside the informal sector (26.4 per cent compared with 23.4 per cent for women).

For the six cities in China for which data were available, there are higher participation rates for women than for men across all three indicators: informal employment, employment in the informal sector and informal employment outside the informal sector.

In North Africa and the Middle East, the percentages of men in informal employment are much higher than those of women in two of the three countries/territories for which data were available; Egypt, and the West Bank and Gaza Strip. The higher proportion of informal employment for men reflects, at least partly, the low participation rate of women in the labour force and the difference in the types of activities undertaken by men and women. For example, in Egypt,[14] women's employment, both formal and informal, is concentrated in "services other than trade or transportation" activities, which accounts for 78.1 per cent of total women's employment, and this activity has a lower level of informality than the other sectors of the economy, approximately 20 per cent for both men and women. In contrast, the construction sector has the highest rate of informal employment, accounting for 92.1 per cent of total employment, and is a significant source of employment for men, approximately 18 per cent of total non-agricultural employment; on the other hand, it accounts for only 0.6 per cent of total non-agricultural employment for women.

In Turkey, the situation is different, with similar proportions of informal employment for women and men. Moreover, the participation rate of women in the labour force is higher in Turkey than in the two other reporting countries/territories, and a greater proportion of women work in the manufacturing and trade sectors.

---

[14] See detailed data in annex 2.

Women and men in the informal economy: A statistical picture

Table 2.2 Components of employment in the informal economy as percentage of total non-agricultural employment, by sex (latest year available)

Country (Year)	Sex	Informal employment (Thousands)	Informal employment (% of non-agricultural emplyment)	Employment in the informal sector (Thousands)	Employment in the informal sector (% of non-agricultural emplyment)	Informal employment outside the informal sector (Thousands)	Informal employment outside the informal sector (% of non-agricultural emplyment)
Latin Amercica and the Carribbean							
Argentina (2009 IV Qtr.)	Women	2,189	49.6	1,131	25.7	1,071	24.3
	Men	2,949	49.8	2,186	36.9	779	13.2
Bolivia (2006)	Women	972	78.5	664	53.6	311	25.2
	Men	1,097	72.4	772	51.0	336	22.1
Brazil (2009)	Women	15,909	45.9	6,982	20.1	8,944	25.8
	Men	16,585	39.2	11,706	27.7	4,918	11.6
Colombia (2010 II Qtr.)	Women	4,532	62.7	3,702	51.2	943	13.0
	Men	4,775	57.0	4,442	53.1	502	6.0
Costa Rica (2009 July)	Women	323	46.0	246	35.0	109	15.5
	Men	432	42.2	392	38.4	84	8.2
Dominican Rep. (2009)	Women	615	51.4	283	23.6	335	28.0
	Men	869	46.7	616	33.1	258	13.9
Ecuador (2009 IV Qtr.)	Women	1,214	63.7	682	35.8	537	28.2
	Men	1,477	58.8	964	38.4	525	20.9
El Salvador (2009)	Women	693	72.5	555	58.1	153	16.0
	Men	549	60.1	443	48.5	123	13.5
Honduras (2009)	Women	724	74.8	580	59.9	158	16.3
	Men	729	73.0	566	56.6	176	17.6
Mexico (2009 II Qtr.)	Women	9,066	57.8	4,993	31.8	4,115	26.2
	Men	11,192	50.8	7,868	35.7	3,504	15.9
Nicaragua (2009)	Women	505	66.6	400	52.7	130	17.2
	Men	519	64.9	447	55.9	104	13.0
Panama (2009 Aug.)	Women	232	46.5	130	26.0	103	20.6
	Men	285	41.8	197	28.9	90	13.2
Paraguay (2009)	Women	666	74.4	328	36.7	338	37.7
	Men	806	67.9	462	38.9	345	29.1
Peru (2009)	Women	3,691	75.7	2,650	54.3	1,081	22.2
	Men	3,767	65.1	2,572	44.4	1,232	21.3
Uruguay (2009)	Women	270	40.3	194	28.9	101	15.0
	Men	302	39.4	294	38.3	41	5.3
Venezuela BR (2009 I Qtr.)	Women	2,159	47.4	1,552	34.1	623	13.7
	Men	2,972	47.5	2,367	37.8	652	10.4
Eastern Europe and CIS countries							
Armenia (2009)	Women	37	12.7	15	5.2	22	7.5
	Men	101	24.8	56	13.7	45	11.1
Kyrgyztan (2009)	Women	n.a.	n.a.	321	50.7	n.a.	n.a.
	Men	n.a.	n.a.	566	65.4	n.a.	n.a.
Macedonia, FYR. (2010)	Women	16	8.1	5	2.8	11	5.6
	Men	49	15.4	33	10.7	16	5.0
Moldova, Rep. (2009)	Women	50	11.4	11	2.6	39	8.8
	Men	85	20.8	51	12.4	35	8.4

Chapter 2 – Statistics relating to the informal economy

Country (Year)	Sex	Informal employment (Thousands)	% of non-agricultural employment	Employment in the informal sector (Thousands)	% of non-agricultural employment	Informal employment outside the informal sector (Thousands)	% of non-agricultural employment
Russian Fed. (2010)	Women	n.a.	n.a.	3,536	10.9	n.a.	n.a.
	Men	n.a.	n.a.	4,249	13.3	n.a.	n.a.
Serbia (2010)	Women	35	4.3	17	2.1	21	2.6
	Men	79	7.5	48	4.6	35	3.3
Ukraine (2009)	Women	n.a.	n.a.	518	6.4	n.a.	n.a.
	Men	n.a.	n.a.	1,006	12.4	n.a.	n.a.

Sub-Saharan Africa

Country (Year)	Sex	Informal employment (Thousands)	%	Employment in the informal sector (Thousands)	%	Informal employment outside the informal sector (Thousands)	%
Cote d'Ivoire (2008)	Women	n.a.	n.a.	1,194	82.8	n.a.	n.a.
	Men	n.a.	n.a.	1,240	60.5	n.a.	n.a.
Ethiopia** (2004)	Women	n.a.	n.a.	561	47.9	n.a.	n.a.
	Men	n.a.	n.a.	528	36.3	n.a.	n.a.
Lesotho (2008)	Women	70	36.1	94	48.1	46	23.7
	Men	90	34.1	131	49.9	53	20.0
Liberia (2010)	Women	206	72.0	188	65.4	19	6.6
	Men	136	47.4	96	33.4	42	14.6
Madagascar (2005)	Women	671	81.0	528	63.8	143	17.2
	Men	600	66.8	365	40.7	235	26.2
Mali (2004)	Women	652	89.2	582	79.6	74	10.1
	Men	528	74.2	447	62.9	89	12.6
Mauritius (2009)	Women	n.a.	n.a.	14	6.7	n.a.	n.a.
	Men	n.a.	n.a.	43	10.6	n.a.	n.a.
Namibia (2008)	Women	62	47.0	n.a.	n.a.	n.a.	n.a.
	Men	59	41.1	n.a.	n.a.	n.a.	n.a.
South Africa (2010)	Women	2,018	36.8	922	16.8	1,096	20.0
	Men	2,071	29.5	1,303	18.6	768	10.9
Tanzania (2005/2006)	Women	1,672	82.8	1,006	49.8	672	33.3
	Men	1,795	70.9	1,347	53.2	465	18.4
Uganda (2010)	Women	1,232	71.9	1,066	62.2	209	12.2
	Men	1,488	67.5	1,277	57.9	328	14.9
Zambia (2008)	Women	407	80.1	357	70.3	63	12.4
	Men	513	62.9	497	60.9	92	11.3
Zimbabwe (2004)	Women	447	65.9	360	53.1	n.a.	n.a.
	Men	462	42.7	338	31.2	n.a.	n.a.

South and East Asia

Country (Year)	Sex	Informal employment (Thousands)	%	Employment in the informal sector (Thousands)	%	Informal employment outside the informal sector (Thousands)	%
China* (2010)	Women	17,230	35.7	11,150	23.1	7,100	14.7
	Men	18,794	30.1	13,062	20.9	6,761	10.8
India (2009/2010)	Women	34,921	84.7	24,475	59.4	10,793	26.2
	Men	150,955	83.3	125,639	69.4	26,615	14.7
Indonesia (2009)	Women	1,180	72.9	1,034	63.9	227	14.0
	Men	1,977	72.3	1,788	65.4	305	11.1
Pakistan (2009/2010)	Women	2,079	75.7	1,979	72.1	219	8.0
	Men	19,834	78.7	18,437	73.1	2,100	8.3
Philippines (2008)	Women	6,854	70.2	6,618	67.8	1,646	16.9
	Men	8,296	69.9	9,062	76.4	843	7.1

17

Women and men in the informal economy: A statistical picture

Country (Year)	Sex	Informal employment Thousands	Informal employment % of non-agricultural emplyment	Employment in the informal sector Thousands	Employment in the informal sector % of non-agricultural emplyment	Informal employment outside the informal sector Thousands	Informal employment outside the informal sector % of non-agricultural emplyment
Sri Lanka (2009)	Women	933	55.7	700	41.8	232	13.9
	Men	2,252	65.2	1,888	54.7	364	10.6
Thailand (2010)	Women	4,730	43.5	n.a.	n.a.	n.a.	n.a.
	Men	4,912	41.2	n.a.	n.a.	n.a.	n.a.
Viet Nam (2009)	Women	7,800	66.8	5,106	43.7	2,738	23.4
	Men	9,372	69.4	5,842	43.3	3,565	26.4
Middle East and North Africa							
Egypt (2009)	Women	572	23.1	n.a.	n.a.	n.a.	n.a.
	Men	7,675	56.3	n.a.	n.a.	n.a.	n.a.
Turkey (2009)	Women	1,116	32.6	n.a.	n.a.	n.a.	n.a.
	Men	3,788	30.1	n.a.	n.a.	n.a.	n.a.
West Bank & Gaza (2010)	Women	42	42.0	14	14.0	28	28.0
	Men	333	59.9	126	22.7	207	37.2

Sources: ILO, Department of Statistics; country responses to ILO request for data; special tabulations of national labour force survey data and extracts from survey reports. For Latin American countries, ILO/SIALC household survey micro-data database.

Notes: * Six cities (as in note to table 2.1); ** Urban areas only; n.a. = Not available.

2.1.3 Trends in employment in the informal economy

The cross-country estimates provide a comparative picture across the world of the significance of informal employment and its components. But what about the picture across time? The collection of data on informal employment and employment in the informal sector on a regular basis as part of official statistics of countries allows the observation of changes over time in total informal employment and in its components. Many countries now regularly collect data on employment in the informal sector and, increasingly, on informal employment outside the informal sector. While these countries generally follow the ICLS guidelines for measuring informal employment both within and outside the informal sector, differences in observing the definitions of the concepts in the design of surveys among countries make comparisons somewhat difficult across time and space. Nonetheless, an initial examination of the available data is useful for understanding the trends in informal employment.

While many countries have started to collect these data, only a few of them have been able to provide the ILO with data for more than one year over a period of time. The ILO Department of Statistics has gathered time series data for 13 countries. Table 2.3 shows data on total informal employment, employment in the informal sector and informal employment outside the informal sector as share of total non-agricultural employment for only two or three years over a period of time: in or around 2000, 2005 and 2010. The available data suggest that total informal employment declined in most of the reporting countries, though it increased in India and Zambia. In the three transition economies with time series data, including the Republic of Moldova, the Russian Federation and Ukraine, employment in the informal sector increased.

In Latin America, informal sector employment and informal employment outside the informal sector as share of total non-agricultural employment declined steadily and consistently in five of the six countries with time series data: Argentina, Ecuador, Panama, Peru and Uruguay. In 2009, in those five countries, total informal employment accounted for about 50 per cent, 61 per cent, 44 per cent, 70 per cent and 40 per cent, respectively, of non-agricultural employment; employment in the informal sector accounted for about 32 per cent, 37 per cent, 28 per cent, 49 per cent and

34 per cent respectively; and informal employment outside the informal sector was about 18 per cent, 24 per cent, 16 per cent, 22 per cent and 10 per cent respectively. Among those five countries, the decrease in informal employment was the most significant in Argentina, from 60.8 per cent in 2003 to 57 per cent in 2005 and 49.7 per cent in 2009, albeit remaining at relatively high levels.

In Mexico, the overall rate of informal employment changed little over time, with only a slight increase outside the informal sector and a slight decrease within that sector. In 2009, the share of informal employment in total non-agricultural employment was 53.7 per cent, that of employment in the informal sector was 34.1 per cent, and that of informal employment outside the informal sector was 20.2 per cent.

Only two countries in Sub-Saharan Africa reported time series data: South Africa and Zambia. In Zambia, the share of total informal employment in non-agricultural employment increased from 59.4 to 69.5 per cent between 2005 and 2009. However, no data on employment in the informal sector and informal employment outside the informal sector were reported for 2005. In South Africa, total informal employment and its two components decreased significantly between 2005 and 2010. In 2010, total informal employment represented approximately 33 per cent of non-agricultural employment, and employment in the informal sector and informal employment outside the informal sector represented approximately 18 per cent and 15 per cent respectively. South Africa has a higher rate of unemployment and a lower rate of informal employment than other developing countries in Sub-Saharan Africa and other regions.

Time series data were available for only two countries in Asia – India and Thailand. In India, between 2004/05 and 2011/12, the total informal employment and informal employment outside the informal sector as share of non-agricultural employment increased, while employment within the informal sector decreased. This reflects wider changes in the Indian labour market between these years over time: notably, a marked slowdown in employment growth, and a decline in both self-employment and in the participation rate of women in the labour force.[15] By contrast, in the five years between 1999/00 and 2004/05 in India, employment grew at a steady rate, and both employment in the informal sector and self-employment increased.[16] In 2011/12, informal employment accounted for nearly 85 per cent of total non-agricultural employment; the shares of employment in the informal sector and informal employment outside the informal sector were 66.8 per cent and 17.9 per cent respectively.

In Thailand, the total informal employment decreased slightly between 2006 and 2010, from 42.6 per cent to 42.3 per cent of total non-agricultural employment. Data on employment in the informal sector and informal employment outside the informal sector were not available.

Three transition economies – the Republic of Moldova, the Russian Federation and Ukraine – are included in the data set. Only the Republic of Moldova had time series data on total informal employment and its two components, which indicate mixed trends: the total informal employment decreased, the employment in the informal sector increased slightly, and the informal employment outside the informal sector fell significantly between 2005 and 2009. The Russian Federation and Ukraine had time series data only for employment in the informal sector: in the Russian Federation, its share in total non-agricultural employment increased significantly between 2000 and 2005 but then fell slightly to 12.1 per cent in 2009; in the Ukraine it increased steadily, from 7 per cent in 2000 to 9.4 per cent in 2009.

---

[15] Chen, M.; Raveendran, G., "Urban employment in India: Recent trends and future prospects", Special issue on Informality, New Delhi, National Council for Applied Economics Research, 2012.

[16] Ibid.

Women and men in the informal economy: A statistical picture

Table 2.3: Employment in the informal economy and its components, selected countries, as percentage of non–agricultural employment

Region/country	Year (Quarter)	Informal employment	Employment in the informal sector	Informal employment outside the informal sector
		Share in total non-agricultural employment (%)		
Latin Amercica and the Carribbean				
Argentina	2003 (IV)	60.8	35.5	25.5
	2005 (IV)	57.0	33.4	23.7
	2009 (IV)	49.7	32.1	17.9
Ecuador	2005 (IV)	65.7	40.2	26.0
	2009 (IV)	60.9	37.3	24.0
Mexico	2005 (II)	53.2	34.9	19.1
	2009 (IV)	53.7	34.1	20.2
Panama	2005 (Aug.)	48.2	30.6	17.7
	2009 (Aug.)	43.8	27.7	16.3
Peru	2005	76.3	52.7	24.0
	2009	69.9	49.0	21.7
Uruguay	2006	43.4	37.4	10.8
	2009	39.8	33.9	9.8
Sub-Saharan Africa				
South Africa	2001	46.2	24.6	21.6
	2005	39.1	20.3	18.8
	2010 (IV)	32.7	17.8	14.9
Zambia	2005	59.4		
	2008	69.5	64.6	11.7
Central and Eastern Europe and CIS Countries				
Moldova, Rep.	2005	19.4	6.3	13.1
	2009	15.9	7.3	8.6
Russian Fed.	2000		8.2	
	2005		13.0	
	2010		12.1	
Ukraine	2000		7.0	
	2005		7.8	
	2009		9.4	
Asia				
India	1999–2000	80.4	67.7	13.5
	2004–2005	83.5	68.8	15.4
	2009–2010	83.6	84.7	67.5
	2011–2012*	84.7	66.8	17.9
Thailand	2006	42.6		
	2010	42.3		

Source: ILO Department of Statistics.

Note: *Due to the existence of some formal wage employment in the informal sector and the possibility of double counting, for some countries, total informal employment is slightly different than the sum of informal sector employment and informal employment outside the informal sector.* * based on the *2011–12 Survey of Employment and Unemployment in India.*

2.2 Economic contribution of the informal sector and informal employment

Data on employment in the informal sector are important as they enable a quantification of the contribution of the sector to the national economy. The contribution of economic activities undertaken in the informal sector to total (GDP) or GVA provides a key indicator for measuring the performance of the informal economy, and indeed the economy as a whole.

A new chapter, "Informal aspects of the economy" (chapter 25), in the System of National Accounts 2008 represents an important step in encouraging countries to prepare estimates of the contribution of the informal sector in their national accounts.[17] This chapter recognizes that measuring the informal sector would help to improve the quality of the national accounts by providing more exhaustive coverage of the contribution of all economic activities to the estimates of GDP. It lays the foundation for such estimates by developing links between the ICLS resolutions and the framework and concepts of the system of national accounts.

Estimates shown in table 2.4 indicate that the share of the informal sector, excluding agriculture, in non-agricultural GVA is significant. The contribution is the highest in the countries of West Africa. For example, in Benin, Niger and Togo, the informal sector, excluding agriculture, accounts for more than 50 per cent of non-agricultural GVA. In India, the contribution of the informal sector to the economy, excluding agriculture, is also very high, at 46 per cent of non-agricultural GVA in 2008.

Another key indicator of the contribution of the informal economy to GDP/GVA is that of total informal employment, both inside and outside the informal sector. While this is more difficult to estimate, it is an important indicator from the policy perspective. The fact that informal workers in the formal sector are scattered across all industrial sectors of the economy and it is difficult to measure their contribution by using data from available sources. Although the national accounts methodology takes account of the contribution of these workers implicitly, it does not provide specific guidelines on how to prepare explicit estimates of their contribution to GDP. Measurement of their contribution can only be based on data provided outside the national accounts, from satellite accounts based on estimates of informal employment outside the informal sector and an imputation of value added for these workers.

In recent years, Mexico has conducted studies that aimed at estimating the contribution of total informal employment to the economy, including estimates of the contribution of both the informal sector as well as the informal employment outside the informal sector. The research unit of Mexico's National Statistical Institute, INEGI, first prepared estimates of the informal sector's contribution to GDP in the late 1990s to explore its potential for tax income. While the need for information to inform tax policies continues, additional and broader concerns have also emerged. These include the need for statistics on labour productivity which encompass both employment in the informal sector and informal employment outside the informal sector.

The improvements made by INEGI in recent years in its surveys and censuses provide the needed data to prepare estimates of the contribution not only of the informal sector but also of informal employment outside the informal sector. The estimates reported here are based on the year 2008, which is the time reference of the last economic census, the biannual income–expenditure survey and the labour force survey's module on micro-businesses.

The two main steps used by INEGI in assessing the contribution of informal employment to GDP were: first, using the above sources plus the Mexican labour force survey, the construction of a labour matrix and an associated productivity coefficient; second, as required by national accounts methodology, an estimation of GVA by adjusting data on the consumption of goods and services, taking into account its allocation by institutional sectors, in other words data from the production

---

[17] European Commission, International Monetary Fund, OECD, United Nations and World Bank, *System of National Accounts 2008* (ST/ESA/STAT/SER.F/2/Rev.5). United Nations Publication, Sales No. E.08XVII.29; available at: http://unstats.un.org/unsd/nationalaccount/docs/SNA2008.pdf.

Women and men in the informal economy: A statistical picture

Table 2.4 Contribution of informal sector (excluding agriculture) to non-agricultural GVA in selected developing and transition economies (in percentage)

Sub-Saharan Africa		Latin America	
Benin (2000)	61.8	Colombia (2006)	32.2
Burkina Faso (2000)	36.2	Guatemala (2006)	34.0
Cameroon (2003)	46.3	Honduras (2006)	18.1
Niger (2009)	51.5	Venezuela, Bolivarian Rep. of (2006)	16.3
Senegal (2000)	48.8	**Transition economies**	
Togo (2000)	56.4	Armenia (2008)	19.5
MENA		Azerbaijan (2008)	13.1
Algeria (2003)	30.4	Belarus (2008)	3.7
Egypt (2008)	16.9	Bulgaria (2006)	16.5
Islamic Rep. of Iran (2007)	31.1	Estonia (2008)	10.1
Tunisia (2004)	34.1	Kazakhstan (2009)	20.0
Palestine (2007)	33.4	Kyrgyzstan (2008)	27.5
Asia		Latvia (2007)	10.2
India (2008)	46.3	Lithuania (2008)	11.8
		The former Yugoslav Rep of Macedonia (2008)	14.9
		Russian Federation (2009)	8.6
		Ukraine (2008)	12.9

Sources: United Nations Department of Economic and Social Affairs, Statistics Division, *National Accounts Statistics*, vol. 2, 2004, Main aggregates and detailed tables: 2002–2003, p. 1332 and p. 1302 for data on the household institutional sector. For the countries of the West African Economic and Monetary Union, data were drawn from national accounts.

Note: Estimates of GVA instead of GDP have been used, as the information on taxes on products by economic activities was not available in many countries.

or supply side were adjusted by data on the demand side. The resulting calculation shows that the informal economy contributes 30.4 per cent of total GVA in Mexico – a substantial amount, especially considering that the Mexican economy is the fourteenth largest in the world.[18] Furthermore, the contribution of informal employment outside the informal sector is greater than that of the informal sector (17.1 per cent compared with 13.3 per cent).

Considering the contribution of the informal economy by field of economy activity, the greatest contribution to GVA is from trade (31.4 per cent) followed by manufacturing (15.2 per cent) and construction (13.4 per cent), repair and personal services (11.2 per cent), and food and beverage preparation, and trade services (8.9 per cent). The contributions of informal employment in transport and agriculture to GVA are each less than four per cent.

Women account for 28.7 per cent of the informal economy's contribution to GVA, while men's share is 71.3 per cent. By component of the informal economy, women's share is higher in informal employment outside the informal sector than within the informal sector (30.6 per cent compared with 26.5 per cent).

---

[18] Both the data and the text on Mexico were prepared by Rodrigo Negrete and Guadalupe with the support of Tomas Ramirez, Mario Moreno and Efrain Munoz from the Instituto Nacional de Estadistica, Geografia e Informatica (INEGI), Mexico.

Chapter 3

Statistics on Developed Countries

Informality, as defined in developing countries, does not affect the majority of the workforce in developed countries. However, a large proportion of the workforce in developed countries works under employment arrangements which offer limited benefits and social protection. These include certain types of own-account self-employment, temporary (or fixed-term) wage employment, and part-time wage employment. The number of such non-standard employment arrangements in these countries is considerable and is increasing in many of them. Relevant indicators for obtaining a detailed picture of the different forms of informal arrangements in developed countries have been collected and are analysed in this chapter.

The concepts used in the developed-country context are related to the concept of informal employment but are not identical to it. Not all non-standard employment in developed countries is informal, and not all informal employment is non-standard. The same applies to undeclared work.[19] Neither non-standard nor undeclared work can therefore be considered as proxy for informal employment.

This chapter presents recent data on three categories of non-standard work in selected OECD countries. The use of these long-standing statistical categories is part of a WIEGO initiative to develop measures of informality in developed countries, as described in the following section. Comprehensive and internationally comparable data on undeclared work were not available.

3.1 Non-standard employment in developed countries

An increasing proportion of the labour force in developed countries works under arrangements which offer limited benefits and social protection. The arrangements in question generally refer to non-standard employment because they tend to deprive workers of the protection of regular, full-time, year-round wage employment. Non-standard arrangements include: own-account self-employed workers without employees, temporary (or fixed-term) employment (including through temporary help agencies) and on-call workers,[20] as well as some part-time workers.

The significance of non-standard employment arrangements in developed countries is illustrated for selected OECD countries in tables 3.1, 3.2 and 3.3. The following patterns may be observed:

- Temporary work ranges from a high of 27 per cent of *wage and salary employment* in Poland to a low of about 6 per cent in the United Kingdom; in 2011, of the 27 countries for which data

---

[19] Undeclared work is generally understood as a legal and remunerated activity that is hidden from the State for tax and social security reasons, although legal definitions, if they exist, vary from one country to the other. It is encompassed in the broader parameters of the ILO's analysis of the informal economy, which is not limited to undeclared work but includes work that falls outside the scope of the law, i.e. "all economic activities by workers and economic units that are – in law or in practice – not covered or sufficiently covered by formal arrangements" in the ILC Resolution concerning decent work and the informal economy, 2002, at: http://www.ilo.org/public/english/standards/relm/ilc/ilc90/pdf/pr-25res.pdf. See also Brief 4.b5, "Strategies for transforming undeclared work into regulated work", in: ILO, *The informal economy and decent work: A policy resource guide, supporting transitions to formality*, Geneva, 2013.

[20] The United States also includes contract company workers.

were available, temporary employment was higher than 20 per cent of wage and salary work in four countries, from 10 to 18 per cent in 14 countries and from six to 9.6 per cent in 9 countries.

- Part-time employment as percentage of *total employment* was 20 per cent and higher in nine of the 32 countries for which data were available for 2011, reaching a high of 37 per cent in the Netherlands. It was between 11 and 20 per cent in 16 countries and less than 10 per cent in seven countries.

- Own account self-employment as a share of *total employment* in 2008 was as high as 20 per cent in Greece and Turkey; for 11 of the 28 countries for which data were available, it ranged from 10 to 19 per cent; and for the remaining 15 countries, it was between four per cent and nine per cent.

Since these estimates are based on a variety of published data sources, it is not possible to add the three categories to obtain an overall measure of total non-standard employment. A summary statistic would require eliminating the double counting of part-time workers among these categories – an important distinction, because temporary workers often are more likely to work part-time than standard workers.[21] Furthermore, all percentages would need to be based on total employment. In the data above, the percentages of temporary workers are based on wage and salary employment only, because more countries reported data on this indicator. Moreover, in developed countries, an estimate of total non-standard employment would not be an exhaustive or accurate indicator of informal employment in a country because there may be forms of non-standard employment not reflected in the statistics; that is, employment with aspects of informality might be counted as part of regular employment. Also, not all workers in non-standard employment arrangements should be classified as being in informal employment. Some temporary and part-time workers are covered by social protection and labour legislation while others are not; this varies by country. Some self-employed are entitled to or can afford to pay for their own social protection (see discussion of benefits under each category below). On the other hand, there may be persons in standard employment who hold informal jobs. An example would be regular, full-time, year-round employees whose employers do not pay all or part of their social security contributions in order to reduce labour costs and increase the employee's take-home pay.

In 2008, the WIEGO Statistics Programme organized a meeting of experts to explore the steps required for collecting comprehensive data on all forms of informal and non-standard employment in OECD countries. The long-term goal of these efforts is to enable classification and analysis of the full set of employment situations in both developed and developing countries. The WIEGO meeting recommended developing markers of informality which would bridge ICLS definitions of informal employment with developed country statistics on employment, particularly non-standard employment categories.[22] These markers would override differences in institutional settings across countries, for example, the difference between countries with universal health insurance and those where it is tied to standard employment only. They would enable a comparison of the size of informal employment in different national institutional contexts. Criteria would include whether or not workers receive social protection and labour standard protection coverage, and whether they experience significant economic uncertainty due to their employment arrangement, such as casual or day labour.

It is also important to recognize that most official employment data are based on de jure distinctions between employment arrangements. De facto informality, such as that resulting from evasion of employment regulations or outright violation of labour standards, is not readily apparent,

---

[21] For example, in Canada in 2008, the average working hours per week were 33 hours for men in temporary work (compared with 38 hours for men in standard jobs) and 27 hours for women in temporary work (compared with 34 hours for women in standard jobs).

[22] This section, summarizing discussions from an expert workshop held at Harvard University by WIEGO in November 2008, draws extensively on Carré, F. and Heintz, J, Issues in developing a common framework on informal employment, (Cambridge, MA, WIEGO), 2009 (revised in May); available at: http://previous.wiego.org/reports/statistics/nov-2008/Carre_and_Heintz_Common_Framework.pdf.

and is therefore only partially measured. In a number of OECD countries, primarily middle- and low-income countries, so-called "undeclared" (or under-declared) employment has been highlighted as a form of informal employment. "Undeclared" work refers to the work that has not been declared to one or more administrative authorities as mandated, most notably to tax authorities, but it is not an illegal activity and is considered as employment in statistical definitions.[23] Fiscal and GDP measurement impacts are of primary concern in using the concept of undeclared work, but there is also a recognition that people in undeclared work are deprived of access to social protection that would otherwise be mandated and they may receive lower wages when they are paid in cash.[24] Also, employment arrangements that are somewhere between wage employment and self-employment, or which are too novel to have prompted a categorical definition, are not measured separately.

Many countries are collecting and publishing data on changing employment arrangements and on the exposure of workers to greater risk and vulnerability. The work of the Federal Statistical Office of Germany is noteworthy in this respect. It not only publishes statistics on atypical employment (i.e. non-standard wage and salaried employment) and on the quality of employment, but it has also developed certain "markers of economic risk" among workers in the country (box 3.1).

Given cross-national differences in employment regulations and contexts, some research has sought to develop a single criterion and shared measure of informal employment for countries that have broadly similar norms for employment. In European countries, for example, informal wage employment has been defined by some research as employees without a contract or uncertain about having a contract. Informal self-employment has been defined as non-professional, own-account workers and self-employed employers with fewer than five workers.[25] The criteria to be used are still under examination; for example, should employees with a short-term or fixed-term (non-standard) contract be considered formal because they, at least, have a written contract? And does having a contract necessarily ensure registration with social insurance schemes?

Many of the transition economies in Eastern Europe as well as Turkey already applied the ICLS concept of informal employment in their labour force surveys, specifically the Former Yugoslav Republic of Macedonia, the Republic of Moldova, the Russian Federation, Serbia and the Ukraine. To continue moving forward on the topic of informality, it will be important to compare data on informal employment and non-standard employment. In two cases where data are now available, the proportion of workers in informal wage employment is quite similar to those in non-standard employment. In 2007 in the Former Yugoslav Republic of Macedonia, temporary employment accounted for 77 per cent of all informal wage employment, and non-standard employment accounted for 78 per cent. In 2008 in Serbia, about one third of workers in non-standard wage employment were informal. However, considering informal employees only, most were in non-standard employment. For example, 81 per cent of informal employees had temporary contracts and 82 per cent were in non-standard jobs.[26]

---

[23] OECD, *Employment Outlook 2004* (Paris), p. 232.

[24] Estimates of the share of workers who are not registered and thus do not necessarily benefit from mandatory social security or who work without an employment contract are provided as partial measures of undeclared work. For example, 26 per cent of workers in the Republic of Korea (2005) are not registered for mandatory social security and 1.8 per cent of workers in the Czech Republic (2006/07) do not have an employment contract (OECD, *Employment Outlook 2008*, Paris, p. 86).

[25] Hazans, M., *Informal workers across Europe: Evidence from 30 countries*, Discussion Paper No. 5871, July (Bonn, Institute for the Study of Labor), 2011, p. 32. The premise is that employees with a verbal contract in countries where this is the norm would answer "yes" to the European Social Survey question about whether they have a contract.

[26] Heintz, J., *Estimating informal employment in Serbia, Kazakhstan, and the Former Yugoslav Republic of Macedonia: Definitions, recommendations and applications*. Report prepared for a joint project of the United Nations Economic Commission for Europe and the ILO (Geneva), April 2009.

> **Box 3.1 Atypical employment and the quality of employment in Germany**
>
> Employment in Germany is highly formalized. Most workers are registered and are therefore covered by labour laws as well as by social protection. However employment arrangements in Germany are changing and workers are being exposed to greater economic risk and vulnerability. To monitor these changes, the Federal Statistical Office of Germany prepares statistics on atypical employment[27] and on quality of employment.[28] A starting point for these analyses are the categories of non-standard employment explored in this chapter, i.e. part-time work of no more than 20 hours per week, temporary employment and own-account self-employment. In 2010, 7.8 million persons were in non-standard wage employment (or atypical employment), accounting for a quarter of wage employment. If own-account self-employment is included, the number of people in non-standard employment increases to 10 million, or 27 per cent of total employment. In contrast to standard employment, which generally should be able to fully finance a person's living requirements and possibly those of dependants, many atypical employment forms can only partially meet those requirements. However, given the legal and institutional framework in Germany, not all workers in these employment categories can be identified as being in informal employment. To identify persons within these categories who are working under informal employment arrangements, the Statistical Office of Germany uses the following "markers" of economic risk and exposure:
>
> - **Marginal workers**, defined in German social law as employees earning no more than 400 euros a month, irrespective of the hours worked. Marginal employees are entitled to significant social benefits and employers pay social insurance contributions for these workers at a reduced rate. Marginal employees account for nearly half of all part-time employees and usually work no more than 20 hours per week. In 2010, such workers constituted eight per cent of wage employment and 13 per cent of women's wage employment. Since 1999 marginal employment is required to be registered.
>
> - **Involuntary part-time employment** concerns persons in part-time work who would prefer to work full time. In 2010, about one fifth of persons (22 per cent) were in part-time work because they could not find a full-time job.[29] This is a fourfold increase from 1992 when only six per cent of workers were in involuntary part-time work. About 38 per cent of men but only 19 per cent of women in part-time work would have preferred a full-time job, but could not find one. At the same time, 50 per cent of the women cited family-related obligations as the main reason for working part-time; in a context where child-care facilities are limited, some of these workers might be deemed "involuntary" part-time workers.
>
> - **Involuntary fixed-term employment** concerns persons who sought a permanent job but did not find one. For these persons, both long-term occupational and personal life planning are difficult. Of the 57 per cent of persons who cited reasons for having a fixed-term contract, 48 per cent mentioned this was because they could not find a permanent job – an increase from 42 per cent in 1999.[30]

As a starting point for an understanding of informal employment in developed countries – and relying on the data based on shared definitions – this section reviews data for developed countries on the three components of non-standard employment. It covers the period 1990–2011 for temporary employment and part-time employment, and the period 1990–2008 for own-account self-employment. Additional data which contribute to developing markers of informality (i.e. access to benefits and earnings) are also analysed.

---

[27] Federal Statistical Office of German, Atypical employment decreasing in crisis year 2009 http://www.destatis.de/jetspeed/portal/cms/Sites/destatis/Internet/EN/Content/Statistics/AR and calculations provided by Thomas Koerner of the Federal Statistical Office.

[28] Federal Statistical Office of Germany, *Quality of employment: Earning money and what else counts* (Wiesbaden), 2011.

[29] Ibid, p. 32-33.

[30] Ibid, pp. 40-41.

Chapter 3 – Statistics on developed countries

> **Box 3.2   Non-standard employment in Spain**[31]
>
> A unique feature of the Spanish labour market is the dual nature of its employment protection legislation, which distinguishes between workers with regular contracts of an indefinite duration and those with temporary employment contracts. It has been observed that, despite reforms over the past 15 years, the costs entailed in dismissing workers on regular contracts continue to remain high and have encouraged the massive use of temporary workers.[32] The recession has accentuated the duality in Spain's labour market: since the beginning of the recession, nearly 80 per cent of the job losses in Spain have been in non-standard employment arrangements. Temporary workers have been the worst affected.
>
> In 2010, 5.7 million workers – or 31 per cent of total wage employment – were in the following non-standard wage employment arrangements: irregular work,[33] temporary employment and part-time work (i.e. less than 20 hours of work per week). In 2007, before the onset of the financial crisis, non-standard wage employment was much higher, involving 7.4 million workers (37 per cent of wage employment). About 1.7 million temporary wage workers have been laid off since the beginning of the crisis. If own-account self-employment were included, the number of workers in non-standard employment would increase to 7.6 million in 2010. Non-standard employment comprised 47 per cent of total employment in 2007 and only about 41 per cent in 2010.
>
> Temporary employment affects entry into the labour force for many young people in Spain. A large proportion of young workers are in temporary employment: 57 per cent in the age group 15 to 24 years in 2010 compared with 23 per cent of workers aged 25 to 60 years. However this represents a sharp drop since 2007, when 62 per cent of young workers were in temporary employment.
>
> In 2010, 18 per cent of the workforce was in part-time employment, a slight decline from 2007 when it was 19 per cent. Part-time work was quite high in public sector wage employment (20 per cent). Only 11 per cent of part-time workers chose this form of employment. Another 9 per cent were in part-time work because they were engaged in "further education or training." Perhaps most significant were the many persons in involuntary part-time work. About 43 per cent could not find a full-time job, with similar proportions for women and men. Women part-time workers are particularly affected by care-giving constraints: about 27 per cent work part-time because of their responsibilities for child care, care for the elderly and family-related obligations.
>
> Wage employees, both in the public and private sectors, were less likely to choose part-time employment than workers overall. Furthermore, among wage workers, temporary workers were less likely to report that they chose to work part-time than workers overall.

The data do not show a clear trend over the last two decades, either within or across countries. One reason is that countries include different non-standard arrangements under these three general categories. Countries capture the non-standard arrangements which are of the greatest concern to them in that they are seen to expose workers to economic risk, but this is not consistent across countries. For example, the United States lists contract company workers under temporary employment, whereas this is not the tendency in countries of the European Union (EU). In some countries there are contracts for "intermittent" employment and these workers are counted separately from other workers; other countries do not have a specific statistical category for intermittent workers, and therefore do not count them separately from other workers.

---

[31] This box was prepared by Uma Rani of the ILO. The analysis was based on surveys of the economically active population (Encuesta de poblacion Activa) in 2007 and 2010 by the Instituto Nacional de Estadisticas, Madrid, Spain.

[32] OECD, *Employment Outlook 2010* (Paris).

[33] Irregular work falls in the category of "discontinuous permanent employment."

Secondly, since the economic situation varies considerably across these countries, it is difficult to track any consistent changes among the three employment arrangements across countries. For example, recessions tend to trigger increase in the incidence of temporary employment as a proportion of total wage employment. Either temporary employment grows faster than total employment, or it declines more slowly than total employment. For instance, in Canada, temporary employment as a proportion of wage employment increased between 2008 and 2009 because permanent employment declined faster than temporary employment during the global crisis.[34] However data from Spain show that, with the recent global crisis, both non-standard employment and non-standard wage employment dropped significantly between 2007 and 2010 (box 3.2).

3.1.1 Temporary employment

Temporary employment tends to be associated with not only a shorter job duration than standard employment, and possibly greater exposure to spells of unemployment, but also less coverage of employer-sponsored benefits and greater fluctuations of earnings (because work duration is less predictable). In addition, it tends to be associated with lower pay, despite regulations to prevent pay disparity. Many countries, the members states of the EU in particular, honour directives for pay parity between temporary and regular jobs. However, even in these countries temporary jobs may be concentrated in certain job categories. As a result, such directives may have limited effects. There is also a relationship between labour legislation and temporary employment. Countries with strong legal protection against dismissal of employees tend to have higher rates of temporary employment than those with less regulated labour markets.

Temporary employment encompasses all short-term employment arrangements, whether through an intermediary, for instance, a temporary job agency or labour broker[35], or through direct hire for a fixed term. Countries define temporary employment somewhat differently. All countries, however, report a mix of short-term direct employment and employment through a temporary job agency.[36]

The data on temporary employment reported here are based on the share of wage and salary employment, excluding self-employment, rather than on total employment, since temporary employment is considered as form of wage employment in virtually all OECD countries[37] (table 3.1). During the global financial and economic crisis, some countries continued to record high rates of temporary employment among wage and salary workers: Poland (27 per cent), Spain (25 per cent), the Republic of Korea (24 per cent) and Portugal (22 per cent) in 2011. Spain witnessed a decline in temporary employment during the crisis, while the unemployment rate increased significantly. As highlighted in box 3.2, in Spain, job losses were higher among temporary workers than among permanent ones.

Countries with the greatest increase in temporary employment between 1990 and 2011 were Italy (8.2 percentage points) and the Netherlands (10.8 percentage points). In Poland, temporary employment increased from 12 per cent to 27 per cent of wage and salary employment between

---

[34] Galarneau D, "Temporary employment in the downturn", in *Perspectives* No. 75-001-X, Nov. 2010 (Ottawa, Statistics Canada), p. 6, table 1.

[35] For example, an industry association estimated that 12 million workers used temporary job agencies in Europe in 2010 (Eurociett, 2011).

[36] Sources: OECD online database, "Employment by Permanency of the Job", available at: http://stats.oecd.org/Index.aspx?DataSetCode=TEMP_D (accessed 2010); for European countries, the OECD used the Eurostat Labour Force Survey Temporary employment is defined as fixed-term, or limited duration employment, temporary agency work and, depending on the country, seasonal employment, training contracts and apprenticeships. (Country definitions are available through the OECD.) For other countries, national labour force surveys (monthly, or quarterly) were used.

[37] These arrangements are forms of wage employment and do not apply to self-employment, with the exception of the United States, which uses expectation of employment duration regardless of status in employment. In the United States, temporary workers are those who do not expect their jobs to last, and include temporary help workers and contract company workers are included. Source used by the OECD is the Current Population Survey Supplement on Contingent and Alternative Work Arrangements.

Chapter 3 – Statistics on developed countries

Table 3.1: Share of temporary employment in dependent employment (wage and salary) in selected OECD countries, 1990, 2000, 2008 and 2011

	All persons				Women			
	1990	2000	2008	2011	1990	2000	2008	2011
Australia [c]		4.8				5.4		
Austria		7.9	9.0	9.6		8.4	9.1	9.5
Belgium	5.3	9.0	8.3	9.0	8.6	12.1	10.2	10.3
Canada		12.5	12.3	13.7		13.2	12.7	14.0
Czech Republic [b]	5.5	9.3	8.0	8.5	4.9	9.4	9.8	10.1
Denmark	10.8	10.2	8.5	8.8	11.0	11.7	9.4	9.4
Finland		16.5	15.1	15.7		19.8	18.8	18.5
France	10.5	15.5	14.9	15.3	12.0	16.5	16.1	15.8
Germany	10.5	12.7	14.7	14.7	11.6	13.1	14.8	14.8
Greece	16.6	13.1	11.5	11.6	15.9	15.7	13.7	13.0
Hungary		7.1	7.9	8.9		6.5	7.0	8.4
Iceland [a]	14.4	12.2	9.5	12.2	15.2	12.9	9.9	12.2
Ireland	8.5	4.7	8.5	10.0	11.4	6.0	9.8	10.4
Italy	5.2	10.1	13.3	13.4	7.6	12.2	15.6	14.7
Japan	10.6	12.5	13.6	13.7	19.1	20.9	21.0	20.7
Republic of Korea			23.7	23.8			25.4	27.2
Luxembourg	3.4	3.4	6.2	7.1	4.9	4.6	6.6	8.2
Netherlands	7.6	14.0	18.2	18.4	10.2	17.2	20.0	19.6
Norway		9.3	9.0	7.9		11.5	11.1	9.4
Poland c		11.7	27.0	27.0		10.9	27.7	26.2
Portugal	18.3	20.4	22.8	22.2	20.5	22.7	24.2	22.4
Slovakia		4.8	4.7	6.6		4.6	4.8	6.9
Slovenia [d]		14.3	17.4	18.2		16.1	19.7	20.0
Spain	29.8	32.1	29.3	25.3	34.2	34.6	31.4	26.6
Sweden		15.2	16.1	16.4		17.4	18.7	18.3
Switzerland		11.5	13.2	12.9		12.8	13.1	13.3
Turkey	14.4	20.3	11.2	12.3	16.0	12.6	11.6	11.8
United Kingdom	5.2	6.8	5.4	6.2	7.0	7.7	6.0	6.5
United States [c]		4.0				4.2		
All OECD countries	10.0	11.3	12.0	12.0	11.0	12.0	12.7	12.5

Source: OECD. Stat Extracts.

Notes: Definitions of temporary employment tend to vary slightly in different countries; for definitions, see OECD. Stat Extracts.
[a] 1991 [b] 1992 [c] 2001 [d] 2002

2000 and 2011. In some of the countries – Denmark, Greece, Iceland, Spain and Turkey – the incidence of temporary employment declined between 2 and 5 percentage points.

In most of these countries, a higher proportion of women than men are in temporary employment, the exception being Poland. In Japan, the Republic of Korea and Finland, women's temporary employment is also much higher than that of men. In only four countries – Poland, Spain, the Republic of Korea and Portugal – is the incidence of temporary employment amongst men higher than 20 per cent, ranging from 21 per cent to 28 per cent of wage and salary workers.

In recent years, a distinction has been made between voluntary and involuntary temporary employment.[38] Estimates for the EU as a whole show that involuntary temporary employees accounted for 60 per cent of all temporary employees in 2007, and this increased to 62 per cent in 2010.[39]

---

[38] Eurostat provides information that helps to differentiate between voluntary and involuntary part-time and temporary work. Workers are considered to be engaged in involuntary work when they cannot find either full-time or permanent jobs.

[39] ILO, *World of Work Report 2012: Better jobs for a better economy*, International Institute for Labour Studies, Geneva, 2012.

Women and men in the informal economy: A statistical picture

(a) Earnings

Information on hourly earnings of workers in fixed-term contracts for a subset of countries provides an indication of pay differentials.[40] In many of the countries, hourly earnings are of temporary workers are lower than those of workers on "indefinite" or regular contracts (an employment arrangement with no end date established ex ante). In some cases this may be due, at least partly, to differences in jobs. Temporary arrangements are more prevalent in certain job categories (often entry level) and in certain industries than in others. New labour force entrants (particularly youth), because they are in entry-level jobs, are more likely to be in temporary employment and to have lower earnings. As noted below, country-level studies have found that, once controls for individual characteristics are included, there remain hourly pay differentials between temporary workers and those in indefinite employment. In some countries, specifically Estonia, Latvia and Lithuania, hourly earnings are higher for workers with fixed-term contracts. The differential is smaller for women than for men, possibly because women generally tend to have lower and less varied earnings (women are concentrated in a few occupational levels), and their earnings are less affected by the nature of their employment contracts.

In the United States in 2005, workers in varied types of temporary employment had lower median hourly earnings than the average for the workforce. For example, the median wage for short-term workers was $9.00 compared with $11.12 for the workforce as a whole, a difference due in part to their holding different types of jobs. More striking was the difference in weekly earnings, which was probably due to working fewer hours over a year; median weekly earnings for short-term workers were $300 compared with $572 for the average of all workers.[41]

In Canada, there are consistent differences in hourly earnings between permanent/standard jobs and temporary jobs (contract, seasonal, casual and other temporary).[42] In 1997, compared with the average hourly earnings in permanent jobs, earnings in seasonal jobs were 34 per cent lower, contract jobs were 12 per cent lower, and "casual and other" jobs were 32 per cent lower. In 2009, compared with hourly earnings of 22.7 Canadian dollars (C$), seasonal jobs were 34 per cent lower (C$15.0), contract jobs were 14 per cent lower (C$19.6) and "casual and other" jobs were 33 per cent lower (C$15.3). Controlling for personal characteristics of workers[43] mitigates these differences to some extent and for some worker groups, but gaps still remain overall. The average hourly earnings of women in seasonal jobs are 35 per cent lower than those of comparable women in permanent jobs. Compared to women in permanent jobs, the average hourly earnings of women in contract work are eight per cent lower and those in "casual and other temporary" jobs are 25 per cent lower.[44]

(b) Benefits

Member states of the EU mandate parity in wages and benefits for workers in most forms of temporary employment, whether through direct hire or through a temporary employment

---

[40] Eurostat, *Structure of Earnings Survey*, 2006; available at: http://epp.eurostat.ec.europa.eu/cache/ITY_SDDS/en/earn_ses06_esms.htm.

[41] Carré, F.; Heintz J, "The United States: Different sources of precariousness in a mosaic of employment arrangements, in Vosko, L; MacDonald, M.; Campbell, I., eds., *Cross-national perspectives on precarious employment: Developing common understandings across space, scale, and social location* (London, Routledge), 2009, p. 51, table 3.2, based on Current Population Survey.

[42] In the labour force survey of Statistics Canada, temporary agency workers are counted among the "casual and other temporary" sub-category of temporary workers.

[43] Those characteristics are gender, age, education, student status, family type, recent immigrant status, province, and CMA (Census Metropolitan Area) versus non-CMA (Galarneau, 2010, op. cit., pp. 5-17, "Temporary employment in the downturn," in *Perspectives* No. 75-001-X, pp. 5-17, Nov. 2010 (Ottawa, Statistics Canada).

[44] Some would argue that, given that labour markets are stratified and even segregated, a number of characteristics are closely correlated with greater odds of ending up in temporary work, so that controlling for these characteristics effectively diminishes the differences in the labour market. Nevertheless, after controlling for personal characteristics, pay differentials remain in this case (Galarneau, op. cit., p. 14, tables 6 and 7, based on the Labour Force Surveys, 1997, 2005 and 2009).

Chapter 3 – Statistics on developed countries

agency.[45] Although such workers remain eligible for all socially administered employment-based benefits, they may not meet some of the working hours, seniority and earnings thresholds necessary for eligibility due to the instability of their employment.

In Canada, temporary or contract workers were less likely than full-time workers to be entitled to employer pensions, health plans, dental plans, paid sick leave and paid vacation leave. According to the 2000 Survey of Labour and Income Dynamics, workers in temporary/non-permanent jobs had lower rates of employer-sponsored benefits than workers in permanent jobs. Only 14 per cent had insurance (extended medical, dental and life/disability) compared with 57 per cent of permanent workers. Only 19 per cent had an employer-sponsored retirement plan compared with 52 per cent of permanent workers.[46]

In the United States, where core benefits are employer-based, temporary workers are much less likely than regular, full-time workers to have health insurance and private pension plans. In 2005, only 17 per cent of workers in temporary employment (including short-term hires, temporary agency workers, on-call workers and day labourers) received some health benefit coverage through their employer; 41 per cent had no health insurance from any source. This contrasts with only 14 per cent of regular full-time workers without health insurance from any source. Within temporary employment, there were differences in coverage: 34 per cent of on-call workers, 58 per cent of temp agency workers, and 61 per cent of day labourers had no health insurance from any source.[47]

Regarding mandates for paid time off, the situation in the United States contrasts with that of many countries. It has no federal mandate concerning a minimum period of paid time off (for sick time or holidays), though state legislatures can pass a mandate, nor provisions that are available to full-time regular workers mandated to apply to workers in temporary (or part-time) employment. Other countries extend some guaranteed paid time off to workers in temporary employment. For example, in Australia, casual workers receive a "casual loading" on top of their usual salary to compensate for not receiving paid annual leave.[48] In Sweden, a "holiday pay" mandate (12 per cent of wages) applies to all workers, including "replacement staff, short-term employees, and those on probation who have worked more than 60 hours for an employer".[49]

3.1.2 Part-time employment

In OECD statistics, part-time work is defined as working less than 30 hours per week in a main job. Part-time work is often associated with lesser coverage under employer-based, and even socially provided, insurance and other forms of social protection. In many countries it can also be associated with lower hourly pay. OECD reports that in part-time jobs there are lower hourly wages, slower advancement and less long-term employment than in full-time jobs, even after taking into account individual and job characteristics.[50] Limited working hours are source of economic risk for the

---

[45] European Council Directive EU311999L0070 (Council of Ministers 1999) covers parity for fixed-term direct hires, as described in Michon, F., *Temporary agency work in Europe* (Brussels and Dublin, European Foundation for the Improvement of Living and Working Conditions), 1999; available at: http://www.eurofound.europa.eu/eiro/1999/01/study/tn9901201s.htm (accessed 13 Dec 2001). EU Directive 2008/104/EC covers temporary agency work. ILO Convention No. 181 sets standards for private employment agencies (Eurociett, *Adapting to change*, Brussels, 2011).

[46] Marshall, K., "Benefits of the job", in *Perspectives on Labour and Income*, Vol. 4, No. 5, May 2003, table 2 (Ottawa, Statistics Canada); available at: http://www.statcan.gc.ca/pub/75-001-x/00503/6515-eng.html (accessed 12 January 2012).

[47] Carré and Heintz, "The United States: Different sources of precariousness in a mosaic of employment arrangements", op. cit., p. 53, table 3.3.

[48] Ray, R; Schmitt, J., "No-vacation nation USA – A comparison of leave and holiday in OECD countries", *European Economic and Employment Policy Brief*, No. 3, 2007, p. 8.

[49] Ibid, p. 12.

[50] OECD, *How good is part-time work?*, Position paper (Paris, OECD), 2010, p. 3. Also, in OECD countries as a whole, involuntary part-time employment accounted for an average of 2.5 per cent of total employment in 2008 (Source: OECD. Stat Extracts, Incidence of involuntary part-time workers; available at: http://stats.oecd.org/Index.aspx?DatasetCode=INVPT_I (accessed on 24 Sept. 2009).

Women and men in the informal economy: A statistical picture

Table 3.2 Part-time employment as share of total employment in selected OECD countries, 1990, 2000, 2008 and 2011

	All persons				Women			
	1990	2000	2008	2011	1990	2000	2008	2011
Australia [b]		23.7	23.8	24.7		38.8	37.7	38.5
Austria		12.2	17.7	18.9		24.4	31.3	32.8
Belgium	13.5	19.0	18.3	18.8	28.8	34.5	32.5	32.4
Canada	17.0	18.1	18.5	19.9	26.7	27.2	26.6	27.2
Czech Republic		3.2	3.5	3.9		5.4	5.8	6.6
Denmark	19.2	16.1	17.8	19.2	29.7	24.0	23.3	25.2
Estonia		7.1	6.2	8.8		9.9	8.9	12.4
Finland	7.6	10.4	11.5	12.7	10.6	13.9	15.1	16.0
France	12.2	14.2	12.9	13.6	22.5	24.9	21.9	22.1
Germany	13.4	17.6	21.8	22.1	29.8	33.9	38.5	38.0
Greece	6.7	5.5	7.9	9.0	11.6	9.5	13.6	14.0
Hungary		2.9	3.1	4.7		4.5	4.3	6.4
Iceland [a]	22.2	20.4	15.1	17.0	39.7	33.7	23.6	24.1
Ireland	10.0	18.1	20.8	25.7	21.2	33.0	35.6	39.3
Israel		14.6	14.7	13.7		24.1	23.1	21.1
Italy	8.9	12.2	15.9	16.7	18.4	23.4	30.6	31.3
Japan [c]		17.7	19.6	20.6		30.9	33.2	34.8
Republic of Korea	4.5	7.0	9.3	13.5	6.5	9.8	13.2	18.5
Luxembourg	7.6	12.4	13.4	16.0	19.1	28.4	28.9	30.2
Netherlands	28.2	32.1	36.1	37.2	52.5	57.2	59.8	60.5
New Zealand	19.7	22.2	22.2	22.0	34.8	35.7	34.6	34.3
Norway	21.8	20.2	20.3	20.0	39.8	33.4	30.8	30.0
Poland		12.8	9.3	8.3		17.9	14.1	12.4
Portugal	7.6	9.4	9.7	11.5	12.8	14.9	14.3	14.4
Slovakia		1.9	2.7	4.0		2.9	4.1	5.7
Slovenia [c]		4.9	7.5	8.6	6.1	9.6	10.9	
Spain	4.6	7.7	11.1	12.9	11.5	16.5	21.0	21.9
Sweden	14.5	14.0	14.4	13.8	24.5	21.4	19.6	18.4
Switzerland [a]	22.1	24.4	25.9	25.9	42.6	44.7	45.9	45.5
Turkey	9.3	9.4	8.5	11.7	19.0	19.3	19.0	24.3
United Kingdom	20.1	23.0	23.0	24.6	39.5	40.8	37.8	39.3
United States	14.1	12.6	12.8	12.6	20.2	18.0	17.8	17.1
All OECD countries	**10.8**	**11.9**	**15.6**	**16.5**	**19.1**	**20.2**	**25.3**	**26.0**

Source: OECD. Stat Extracts.

Notes: The common OECD definition for part-time work is less than 30 hours in the main job.
[a] 1991 [b] 2001 [c] 2002

self-employed as well as for wage earners. While a distinction between involuntary and voluntary part-time employment would be useful in order to assess the extent of greater hardship associated with some types of part-time work as compared with others, in the context of measuring informal employment it does not matter whether part-time employment is voluntary or involuntary.

Part-time employment as share of total employment has grown in many OECD countries since the 1990s (table 3.2). In the OECD countries as a whole, the incidence of part-time employment in total employment increased from 10.8 per cent in 1990 to 16.5 per cent in 2011. The increase in the share of part-time workers has been observed in most OECD countries: for example, it grew by nearly 9 percentage points in Germany between 1990 and 2011 (from 13.4 per cent to 22.1 per cent). There are however some important exceptions, such as the United States, where it fell by 1.5 percentage point, and Iceland (down by 5.2 percentage points).

Chapter 3 – Statistics on developed countries

In 2011, part-time employment as a percentage of total employment was higher than 25 per cent in the following countries: the Netherlands (37 per cent), Switzerland (26 per cent), Ireland (26 per cent), the United Kingdom (25 per cent) and Australia (25 per cent).

Recent estimates show that the incidence of involuntary part-time employment has increased in a majority of the OECD countries since the global financial crisis.[51] The share of part-time employment increased by an average of 0.9 per cent from 2008 to 2011 for OECD countries as a whole, and it increased from 2008 to 2011 in most countries for which data were available (25 out of 32). The highest increases were registered in Ireland (nearly 5 per cent) and the Republic of Korea (4 per cent).

Part-time work affects employment for women to a greater degree than for men. For women, part-time employment is often considered as a choice, as limiting their working hours gives them time for their care-giving responsibilities, and is thus deemed to be "voluntary". However the social context, social norms and the extent of public support for child care determine the degree to which women actually "choose" their working hours. In some countries, part-time work (and thus reduced earnings) is the only way women are able to hold a job and meet their care-giving responsibilities. Furthermore, given the gender-related segregation of jobs, including stereotyping of part-time jobs as "women's jobs", some women who would like to work full-time may only find part-time job opportunities.

In 2011, the rate of women in part-time employment as percentage of total women in employment was the highest in the Netherlands (60.5 per cent) and Switzerland (45.5 per cent). In 2011, in all selected OECD countries, the share of part-time work was higher among women's employment as compared to total employment.

During the global financial crisis from 2008 to 2011, women's share in part-time employment increased slightly in the majority of countries, except Ireland, the Republic of Korea and Turkey, where it increased by four to five per cent. In some of the countries where the proportion of women in part-time employment was quite high, there was no change during the global crisis.

(a) Earnings

In all but five European countries for which information was available, average hourly earnings of part-time workers are lower than for full-time workers.[52] This disparity exists in spite of an EU directive for member countries to implement equal pay for part-time and full-time workers in the same jobs. However, part-time workers may not be in the same jobs as full-time workers, thus weakening the impact of a pay parity mandate. Part-time workers are more likely to be in service jobs which tend to have lower hourly pay.[53] Canada and the United States do not have a national mandate for pay parity between part-time and full-time workers. The majority of full-time workers in the United States earn more per hour than part-time workers.[54] Even after controlling for observable differences in workers' characteristics, a pay differential remains.[55] Also, involuntary part-time workers – those who would prefer full-time work – had lower hourly wages in 2005, at $8, than the average of all employed, at $11.12.[56]

---

[51] ILO, 2012, op.cit.

[52] European Commission, Eurostat, *Labour market statistics,* Structure of earnings survey (Brussels) 2006. Countries where hourly earnings are not lower are: Belgium, Greece, Hungary, Portugal and Turkey.

[53] 2006 Eurostat data, at: http://epp.eurostat.ec.europa.eu/cache/ITY_SDDS/en/earn_ses06_esms.htm.

[54] Pongrace, D.M.; Zilberman, A.P., "A comparison of hourly wage rates for full- and part-time workers by occupation, 2007", in Compensation and Working Conditions Online (posted 23 July2009; accessed on 27 May 2011; available at: http://www.bls.gov/opub/mlr/cwc/a-comparison-of-hourly-wage-rates-for-fulland-part-time-workers-by-occupation-2007.pdf.

[55] Kalleberg, A.L.; Reskin, B.; Hudson, K.., "Bad jobs in America: Standard and non-standard employment relations and job quality in the United States", in *American Sociological Review*, 65, April, 2000, pp. 256-278.

[56] Carré and Heintz, "The United States: Different sources of precariousness in a mosaic of employment arrangements", op.cit., p. 53.

(b) Benefits

Part-time workers tend to receive fewer benefits than full-time workers. However, part-time workers in Europe are more likely to be eligible for benefits than part-time workers in North America, Japan and the Republic of Korea. The EU issued in 1997 a directive proscribing discrimination by employers against part-time workers in terms of pay, certain benefits and working conditions.[57] In some countries, however, these protections do not apply to part-time workers who work for less than a given number of hours. For example, public health, old age pension and unemployment benefits in France, Germany, Ireland, Japan and Sweden require a minimum number of working hours or earnings for eligibility, which part-time workers may not meet.[58]

Regarding paid time off, Ireland mandates compensation for holidays (pay, time off, or premium for working on a public holiday) for part-time workers if they have worked "at least 40 hours in the five weeks before the public holiday."[59] In the United Kingdom, part-time workers, as all other workers, are guaranteed at least four weeks of annual leave.[60]

In Canada, part-time workers are less likely than full-time workers to be entitled to company pensions, health and dental plans, paid sick leave and paid vacation leave.[61] Data from the 2000 Survey of Labour and Income Dynamics show that only 17 per cent of part-time workers had employer-sponsored insurance (extended medical, dental and life/disability) compared with 58 per cent of full-time workers. Similarly, 22 per cent had an employer-based pension plan, compared with 52 per cent of full-time workers.[62] In the United States, where part-time work is less common than in most of the other OECD countries, part-time workers are offered very few benefits. For example, in 2005, 72 per cent of part-time workers were not offered or were not eligible for a job-based retirement plan.[63]

Japanese employers are not obligated to pay social security, disability and unemployment insurance for many part-time and temporary workers.[64] With regard to health insurance, Japan has a universal programme, with everyone enrolled in some form of health insurance.

3.1.3 Own-account self-employment

Since the self-employed do not have access to employer-based benefits, and often have limited access to systems of social protection, they can be considered as being in non-standard employment. But the self-employed are not a homogeneous group.[65] Within self-employment, some proportion of own-account workers face similar conditions as workers in the informal economy, such

---

[57] EU Directive on Part-time Work (97/81/EC), December 1997.

[58] Ray and Schmitt, 2007, op.cit.

[59] Ibid, p. 10.

[60] Ibid, p.13.

[61] Lipsett, B.; Reesor, M., *Flexible work arrangements: Evidence from the 1991 and 1995 Survey of Work Arrangements*, Human Resources Development Canada Research Paper R-97 (Quebec), 1997.

[62] Marshall, 2003, op.cit. table 2.

[63] Ditsler and Fisher, 2006 254. in Mishel, L.; Bernstein, J.; Shierholz, H., eds., *The state of working America: 2008–09* (Washington, DC and Ithaca: Economic Policy Institute and Cornell University Press), 2009.

[64] Houseman, S.; Osawa, M., "The growth of nonstandard employment in Japan and the United States: A comparison of causes and consequences", in Houseman, S; Machiko Osawa, M., eds., *Nonstandard work in developed economies: Causes and consequences* (Kalamazoo, MI, Upjohn Institute for Employment Research), 2003.

[65] Statistics on self-employment distinguish three main sub-categories: a) self-employed with employees (i.e. employers); b) self-employed without employees (i.e. own-account operators including independent contractors and freelancers); and c) unpaid family workers. Unpaid family workers are usually excluded from compilations of the self-employed because they are considered entrepreneurial assistants and not entrepreneurs. OECD data show this would underestimate the real level of women's entrepreneurship because some women classified as unpaid family workers would be better considered as partners of self-employed persons.

as relatively lower earnings, poorer working conditions and weaker attachments to formal structures. In OECD countries, for example, compared with both self-employed employers and regular employees, own-account workers tend to report poorer working conditions, longer and irregular working hours, less access to training, less autonomy and greater job insecurity – in short, own-account workers tend to be exposed to higher economic risk.[66]

Recent changes in labour market structures have made it harder to draw a clear distinction between wage work and self-employment. This is because it is often difficult to verify whether a worker is *economically* independent or dependent. For example, a self-employed worker may have only one customer and may even work on the customer's work site. Such self-employed workers are similar to dependent wage workers. A number of governments have been increasingly concerned with the rise of "false self-employment" as a means for firms to avoid tax liabilities. In many such cases, the customer firms try to avoid or bypass obligations, such as payroll taxes that cover unemployment insurance, worker compensation insurance, pensions and (except in the United States) health insurance, by declaring that their workers are self-employed.[67]

In 2008, own-account self-employment ranged from about 20 per cent of total employment in Greece, the Republic of Korea and Turkey to a low of 4 per cent in Luxembourg (table 3.3). These rates were relatively stable for most countries. From 1990 to 2008, own-account self-employment declined significantly in only four (of the 28) countries for which data were available: Belgium, Greece, Ireland and Spain, while in France, Japan and Luxembourg there was a steady but small decline. The Czech Republic and Slovakia reported a significant increase over the whole period. During the recent period, 2000 to 2008, the rates of own-account self-employment declined by two to four per cent in Greece, Hungary, Iceland, the Republic of Korea, Poland and Turkey, while they increased slightly in 6 countries and significantly in Slovakia.

Compared to men, women's rates of self-employment are lower, but, *within* self-employment, they are more likely to be own-account workers and less likely to be employers.[68] In 2008, women's own-account self-employment was relatively high in Greece, Portugal and the Republic of Korea, accounting for over 12 per cent of total women's employment. Women's own-account self-employment declined significantly from 1990 to 2008 in Belgium, Japan and Spain, but from 2000 to 2008, it changed little in most countries, except for an increase of three per cent in Slovakia and a decrease of four per cent in Poland.

(a) Benefits

Self-employed workers are, by definition, responsible for their own contributions to national retirement plans (in countries with universal systems where they are eligible to enroll), health insurance schemes and other protection. In some countries, enrolment and payment of a premium out of a person's resources are mandatory. For example, most developed countries have a tax-financed old age pension system with mandatory contributions. Generally, self-employed workers are not eligible for government-run unemployment insurance, as they are considered to be responsible for their own jobs.

Conditions concerning "false" self-employed workers may vary across countries and across parts of social protection systems. Some workers may receive access to some aspects of social protection selectively, and, if they submit requests and complaints, they may be reclassified as wage workers.

---

[66] OECD, OECD Employment Outlook 2000 (Paris, OECD).
[67] Ibid.
[68] Authors' calculations based on ILO LABORSTATA and Eurostat online databases.

Table 3.3: Own-account self-employment as a share of total employment in selected OECD Countries, 1990, 2000, 2008 (per cent)

	Total			Women		
	1990 j/	2000	2008	1990 j/	2000	2008
Australia b/	9.5	9.6	8.8	7.3	6.9	6.6
Austria c/	5.5	5.0	6.6	5.4%	4.6	6.0
Belgium a/	14.4	9.4	8.4	10.2	7.3	6.2%
Canada a/	7.4	10.3	10.2	6.1	8.7	8.3
Czech Republic	6.3	10.3	11.9	4.4	7.0	7.7
Denmark a/	5.1	4.0	4.5	1.9	2.4	2.8
Finland a/	n.a	8.5	8.5	n.a	6.0	6.2
France a/	8.1	5.8	4.9	5.0	3.9	3.5
Germany a/	4.1	5.0	6.0	3.0	3.8	4.8
Greece c/	27.4	24.4	20.9	17.0	17.9	16.9
Hungary c/	6.0	10.0	6.7	4.7	5.8	5.2
Iceland b/, c/	10.9	10.2	8.0	5.9	6.3	4.9
Ireland	17.2	11.7	10.9	5.7	4.4	4.3
Italy i/	n.a	11.6	10.6	n.a	7.9	7.0
Japan	11.0	8.5	7.0	9.4	6.5	4.6
Republic of Korea b/, c/	n.a	20.8	18.8	n.a	16.2	14.5
Luxembourg a/, g/	6.5	5.1	3.9	5.0	4.7	4.6
Netherlands a/	6.8	7.1	9.0	6.7	6.1	7.5
New Zealand b/	11.4	12.7	11.1	7.7	8.8	8.1
Norway	n.a	5.4	5.4	n.a	3.3	2.9
Poland a/	n.a	18.6	14.7	n.a	15.7	11.8
Portugal	17.4	17.5%	17.5	18.4	17.5	17.9
Slovakia c/, d/	4.3	5.3	10.4	2.3	2.9	6.0
Spain e/	16.1	12.2%	10.5	13.5	9.6	8.1
Sweden a/	n.a	6.7	6.4	n.a	3.8	4.1
Switzerland b/, f/	5.5	8.4	7.7	4.5	7.9	7.4
Turkey b/, h/	n.a	24.7%	20.4	n.a	11.8	11.0
United Kingdom a/	9.2	8.7	10.2	5.3	5.6	6.4
United States	n.a	n.a	n.a	n.a	n.a	n.a

Sources and notes:

Unless otherwise indicated, ILO – LABORSTA database, Main statistics (annual); available at http://laborsta.ilo.org/, table 2D, Employment by status in employment.

[a] Eurostat, *Labour Force Survey* series (annual), Employment by sex, age group and economic activity; available at: http://epp.eurostat.ec.europa.eu/portal/page/portal/employment_unemployment_lfs/data/database; and for Canada, Statistics Canada, Labour Force Survey estimates, table 282-0012, employment by class of worker, System (NAICS) and sex, annual North American Industry Classification (accessed: February 21, 2012). [b] Excluding armed forces. [c] Excluding conscripts; in Austria, excluding conscripts in military service. [d] Excluding persons on child-care leave. [e] Excluding compulsory military service. [f] Excluding seasonal border workers. [g] 2001. [h] 2002. [i] Revisions of national labor force survey provided April 2011. 2004 instead of 2000. Data prior to 2004 not included due to change in series. [j] 1991 for Iceland, New Zealand, and Switzerland; 1992 for Hungary and Portugal; 1993 for the Czech Republic and Greece; for Austria and Slovakia.

Sources of data

- Eurostat 2006 for Earnings of part-time and full-time workers. http://epp.eurostat.ec.europa.eu/cache/ITY_SDDS/en/earn_ses06_esms.htm.
- Eurostat, Labor Force Survey, Annual.
- http://epp.eurostat.ec.europa.eu/portal/page/portal/employment_unemployment_lfs/data/database.
- Federal Statistical Office of Germany, 2010, *Atypical employment decreasing in crisis year 2009*. https://www.destatis.de/EN/PressServices/Press/pr/2010/07/PE10_257_132.html.
- Gautié, Jerôme and John Schmitt, Eds. 2010, *Low-Wage Work in the Wealthy World*, New York: Russell Sage Foundation.
- IILS, 2012, World of Work Report 2012: Better Jobs for a Better Economy, Geneva, ILO.
- ILO, Laborst online, Main Statistics (annual), Table 1C, Economically active population by industry and status in employment. http://laborsta.ilo.org.
- ILO, 2002, *Men and Women in the Informal Economy*, Geneva, Switzerland: International Labour Organization.
- OECD online, "Employment by Permanency of the Job". (Accessed in 2010) http://stats.oecd.org/Index.aspx?DataSetCode=TEMP_D.
- Organisation for Economic Co-operation and Development (OECD) online, OECD.Stat, "Incidence of Involuntary Part-time Workers". (Data extracted on 24 Sep 2009)
- Organisation for Economic Co-operation and Development (OECD), 2010, "How good is part-time work?", Position Paper, Paris: OECD.
- Organisation for Economic Co-operation and Development (OECD), 2000, *OECD Employment Outlook*, (Paris: OECD).
- Organisation for Economic Co-operation and Development (OECD), 2004, *Employment Outlook*, (Paris: OECD).
- Organisation for Economic Co-operation and Development (OECD), 2008, *Employment Outlook*, (Paris: OECD).
- UN Statistics Division, 2010, *The World's Women 2010: Trends and Statistics*, New York: United Nations.

Chapter 4

Specific Groups of Urban Informal Workers

Domestic work, home-based work, street vending and waste picking are all age-old occupations in which large number of workers around the world are still employed, especially in developing countries. Few have secure work, most have low and erratic earnings and few are protected against loss of work and income. Most operate outside the reach of government regulations and protection, and the four groups remain largely invisible in official statistics. Only one of the four groups of workers – domestic workers – is routinely identified in official national statistics, although this group is often undercounted[69] and misclassified.[70] The recent ILO global and regional estimates on domestic work, which suggest at least 52.6 million domestic workers across the world in 2010, are therefore conservative.[71]

The statistical challenge is not so much to capture informal workers as employed, but rather to identify which category of work they are employed in. In part, this challenge is due to the fact that these groups tend to be informally employed, and informal employment arrangements are generally more difficult to measure than formal ones. Often, countries may not include all the relevant questions which are necessary for identifying the respective groups. For example, some countries do not include a question on the place of work, which is a key indicator for distinguishing domestic workers between (employer's home), home-based workers (own home) and street vendors (public space). The challenge also stems from the need to revise existing classifications to capture and describe the full range of work arrangements today. The ICSE-93, as adopted by the 15th ICLS in 1993, mentions the need to identify several specific groups – including casual day labourers and industrial outworkers – which are sub-categories or disaggregations of the six main categories for status in employment but do not fit neatly under them.[72] National statistical services often do not ask enough questions or do not have sufficient pre-coded response categories to identify these groups. Also, international and national classification codes for industries and occupations are not sufficiently detailed at digit levels that would capture all types of informal employment, especially informal employment of women.

The WIEGO network is working with the ILO and others to improve identification of these workers in official statistics (box 4.1). This has already resulted in a better picture of the significant number of women and men in these often forgotten segments of the urban workforce. For exam-

---

[69] This issue of misclassification and under-enumeration of domestic workers is discussed extensively in ILO, *Domestic workers across the world: Global and regional statistics and the extent of legal protection*, chapter 2 (Geneva), 2013.

[70] Of the 47 countries for which data are in the annex tables, 32 identify domestic workers in their official statistics: all 16 countries from Latin America and the Caribbean, eight (out of 12) from Africa, five (out of seven) from Asia, two (out of six) from Eastern Europe and Central Asia, and one (out of three) from the Middle East and North Africa. It is difficult to determine how many of these countries underestimate or misclassify domestic workers. In the case of India, the country table indicates that 2 per cent of informal non-agricultural workers are domestic workers but a further analysis of the Indian data detailed in this section found that 4 per cent of all urban workers are domestic workers.

[71] See ILO, 2013, op.cit.

[72] In Latin America, many countries use an amended version of ICSE-93, which classifies domestic workers separately from other wage employees. In line with this, the ILO's regional statistical publication, *Panorama Laboral*, usually lists domestic workers as a separate category of employment (see also ILO, 2013, op.cit., chapter 2).

ple, in India in 2009–2010, the four groups combined – domestic workers, home-based workers, street vendors and waste pickers – accounted for 33 per cent of *total* urban employment (35 per cent of male and 24 per cent of female urban workers) and 41 per cent of urban *informal* employment (44 per cent of male and 29 per cent of female urban informal workers). Virtually all workers in each of these groups were informally employed.

> **Box 4.1 Recent initiatives to improve estimates of domestic workers, home-based workers, street vendors and waste pickers**
>
> Most countries collect and tabulate data on domestic workers, though not on the other categories of workers considered in this section. Some, but not all, of these data are reported to the ILO and recorded in the ILO database, LABORSTA. For its global and regional estimates on domestic work, the ILO also consults a broad range of national sources and has been able to trace data from 117 countries and territories worldwide.[73] However, to better identify domestic workers, statistical methods need to be further refined.[74] For example, in the work commissioned by the WIEGO network, G. Raveendran, the former Additional Director General of the Central Statistical Organisation of India, found that there was a significant underestimation of domestic workers based on what was generally regarded as the nearest classification code for their identification. This code – Division 95 of the National Industrial Code – defined domestic work "as any type of work performed in or for a private household and a domestic worker as any person engaged in domestic work within an employment relationship."
>
> However in practice, those who work for multiple households for fixed time periods are often not classified as domestic workers. Further, in many cases, the industry code used in recording persons employed by households is that of the specific work performed instead of domestic work. For example, a person tutoring children in the household for wages is categorized in the industry code of primary teacher or secondary teacher instead of domestic worker. Similarly, a driver employed by a private household is categorized in the industry code of non-scheduled passenger land transport. The consequent lack of consistency between industry classification and occupational classification thus leads to an underestimation of domestic workers. By using a combination of national occupational codes, place of work and informal employment codes, an additional one million domestic workers who work but do not reside in their employer's home were identified, leading to a revised total for domestic workers in India of 5.2 million in 2004/05.
>
> In India, the Self-Employed Women's Association (SEWA) has worked for many years with national research organizations, government commissions and the national statistical system to develop statistics on working poor women in the informal economy. Together with Jeemol Unni, a labour economist, SEWA collaborated closely with the National Sample Survey Organization (NSSO) in the design of the 1999–2000 Survey of Employment and Unemployment. This was the first official survey in India that included questions for identification of the informal sector in both urban and rural areas. In addition, the survey enabled the classification of home-based workers, both self-employed and industrial outworkers (called homeworkers), and of street vendors. Subsequently, SEWA proposed that the Government of India established an Independent Group on Home-based Workers in India. This Group of statisticians, researchers and advocates met during 2007–2008 to address concepts and definitions of home-based workers and categories for data collection; develop a plan for tabulation and analysis of data from various official sources; and identify data needs and make recommendations for filling the gaps.[75]

---

[73] Data for a further 17 small jurisdictions (mainly small island states) were compiled, but not used for the estimates.

[74] See WIEGO, *Challenges of measuring domestic workers*, at: http://wiego.org/informal-economy/challenges-measuring-domestic-workers-1.

[75] See: Report of the Independent Group on Home-based Workers, 31 March 2008 (New Delhi), at: http://www.unwomensouthasia.org/assets/Home-based-Workers-Report-india-unifem-.pdf.

Chapter 4 – Specific groups of urban informal workers

In Brazil, along with efforts to organize waste pickers and help them secure better livelihoods, there has been improved measurement of these workers. "Waste picking" is now a category with its own distinct code in the Brazilian Classification of Occupations. The definition was developed in consultations between representatives of waste picker cooperatives, the national statistical service and municipal environmental groups. Since its adoption in 2002, the waste picker category – and the related classification code – has been used in all relevant data collection efforts in the country, including both the national household surveys and administrative data on enterprises.

As part of a global project called Inclusive Cities for the Working Poor, WIEGO has placed special importance on measuring urban informal employment and specific categories of urban informal workers. Under this project, WIEGO has commissioned data analysts to generate estimates of urban informal employment, including estimates of domestic workers, home-based workers, street vendors and waste pickers, in a number of cities and countries. Among others, DIAL, a research unit of the French Institut de Recherche pour le Developpement (IRD), was commissioned to analyse its database. For many years DIAL has assisted countries in carrying out and processing statistical surveys on the informal sector and poverty. These surveys, mainly in capital cities, provided data for 11 cities in 10 countries. In addition, tabulations and briefing notes were prepared on urban informal employment, including on special categories of workers in Brazil, Ghana, Kenya and South Africa. Together, these provide the main source of data for the Statistical Picture (See "Sources of Data" at the end of this section.) Based on this work, WIEGO has also prepared a guide aiming at advocates and statisticians for the preparation of data on categories of informal workers.[76]

Box 4.2 Cities and countries with data on four urban informal groups, as compiled by WIEGO

Asia
- India: national urban/rural
- Viet Nam: Hanoi and Ho Chi Minh City

Africa

East Africa
- Kenya: national urban/rural
- Madagascar: Antananarivo

West Africa:
- Benin: Cotonou
- Burkina Faso: Ouagadougou
- Côte d'Ivoire: Abidjan
- Ghana: national

West Africa (cont.):
- Mali: Bamako
- Niger: Niamey
- Senegal: Dakar
- Togo: Lome

*Southern Africa**
- South Africa: national

Latin America
- Argentina: Buenos Aires
- Brazil: national
- Peru: Lima

Data sources: Reports on the methods used and findings from each of these different analyses have been published by WIEGO and are available on the WIEGO website at: www.wiego.org. See also "Sources of data" at the end of this chapter for a list of these reports.

* South Africa is reported separately from the other countries of sub-Saharan Africa because it has substantially higher rates of formal employment and unemployment, and lower rates of informal employment.

---

[76] Vanek, J.; Chen, M.; Raveendran, G., *A guide to obtaining data on types of informal workers in official statistics*, WIEGO Statistical Brief No. 8; available at: http://wiego.org/sites/wiego.org/files/publications/files/Vanek_WIEGO_SB8.pdf.

The efforts described in box 4.1 provide data on the four categories of urban workers in major cities or in national urban employment in 16 countries (box 4.2). At this early stage of work, the estimates cannot be combined in a harmonized table because of differences in the classification codes and populations surveyed (see technical note at the end of the Report).[77] However, the data provide useful information on the significance of these categories of workers in urban employment, the differences between women and men in such employment, the extent of informality and other characteristics.[78]

4.1 Domestic Workers

Domestic workers work in the homes of others for pay, providing a range of domestic services: they sweep, clean, wash clothes and dishes, shop, cook, care for children or the elderly, sick and disabled, and/or provide such services as gardening, driving and security. In June 2011, the ILC approved, by an overwhelming majority vote, ILO Convention No. 189 on Domestic Workers, 2011, which calls for national policies to promote fair treatment and decent working conditions for domestic workers.[79] In the accompanying Recommendation, paragraph 25(2) states:

> Members should, after consulting with the most representative organizations of employers and workers and, where they exist, with organizations representative of domestic workers and those of representative employers of domestic workers, develop appropriate indicators and measurement systems in order to strengthen the capacity of national statistical offices to effectively collect data necessary to support policymaking regarding domestic work.[80]

Domestic work is an important occupation, involving a significant and, at least in some countries and regions, a growing proportion of the workforce worldwide. According to recent estimates by the ILO, their number grew from 33.2 million in 1995 to 52.6 million in 2010 (table 4.1). The latter figure is equivalent to 3.6 per cent of global wage employment, and represents a far higher share in regions such as Latin America (11.9 per cent) and the Middle East (8 per cent).[81] Since domestic workers are often undercounted in labour force surveys, these figures are conservative estimates and are likely to understate the true extent of domestic work. Moreover, the figures do not include the estimated 7.4 million children below the age of 15 years who are engaged as domestic workers.[82]

Domestic work is mostly, but not exclusively, performed by women (as much as 83 per cent in 2010),[83] many of whom are migrants. Female domestic workers are concentrated in cleaning and care services, while male domestic workers tend to have better paying jobs as gardeners, drivers or security guards. In many regions, domestic work is a primary source of wage employment for female workers: in the Middle East, one out of three female wage employees is domestic worker, and in Latin America and the Caribbean, the figure is one in four.[84]

---

[77] In presenting data on these urban occupational groups, urban agricultural and non-agricultural employment are not distinguished. Agriculture accounts for, at best, a small share of employment in most cities.

[78] Reports on the methods used and findings from each of these different analyses have been published by WIEGO and are available on the WIEGO website at: www.wiego.org. See "Sources of data" at the end of this section for a list of these reports, including the names of the analysts and authors and the sources of the data they analysed. See also an earlier version of this publication (ILO, 2002) and the section on "Informal economy/occupational groups" on the WIEGO website at: www.wiego.org.

[79] See: http://www.ilo.org/dyn/normlex/en/f?p=NORMLEXPUB:12100:0::NO:12100:P12100_INSTRUMENT_ID:2551460:NO.

[80] See: http://www.ilo.org/dyn/normlex/en/f?p=NORMLEXPUB:12100:0::NO:12100:P12100_INSTRUMENT_ID:2551502:NO.

[81] ILO, 2013, op.cit.

[82] Ibid.

[83] Ibid.

[84] Ibid.

Chapter 4 – Specific groups of urban informal workers

Table 4.1 Global and regional estimates by the ILO of the number of domestic workers, by sex, 1995 and 2010

Panel A – Women and men

	Domestic workers 1995	Domestic workers 2010	Domestic workers as a percentage of total employment 1995	Domestic workers as a percentage of total employment 2010
Developed countries	3 245 000	3 555 000	0.8	0.8
Eastern Europe and the CIS	477 000	595 000	0.2	0.3
Asia and the Pacific	13 826 000	21 467 000	1.0	1.2
(excluding China)	7 116 000	12 077 000	1.0	1.2
Latin America and the Caribbean	10 402 000	19 593 000	5.7	7.6
Africa	4 178 000	5 236 000	1.7	1.4
Middle East	1 101 000	2 107 000	5.0	5.6
Total	**33 229 000**	**52 553 000**	**1.5**	**1.7**

Panel B – Women

	Female domestic workers 1995	Female domestic workers 2010	Female domestic workers as a percentage of total female employment 1995	Female domestic workers as a percentage of total female employment 2010
Developed countries	2 868 000	2 597 000	1.7	1.3
Eastern Europe and the CIS	289 000	396 000	0.3	0.4
Asia and the Pacific	12 194 000	17 464 000	2.3	2.5
(excluding China)	5 305 000	9 013 000	2.3	2.6
Latin America and the Caribbean	9 623 000	18 005 000	14.6	17.4
Africa	3 121 000	3 835 000	3.3	2.5
Middle East	745 000	1 329 000	22.6	20.5
Total	28 840 000	43 628 000	3.4	3.5

Panel C – Men

	Male domestic workers 1995	Male domestic workers 2010	Male domestic workers as a percentage of total male employment 1995	Male domestic workers as a percentage of total male employment 2010
Developed countries	377 000	958 000	0.2	0.4
Eastern Europe and the CIS	188 000	199 000	0.2	0.2
Asia and the Pacific	2 172 000	4 003 000	0.4	0.4
(excluding China)	1 811 000	3 064 000	0.4	0.5
Latin America and the Caribbean	779 000	1 588 000	0.7	1.0
Africa	1 057 000	1 400 000	0.7	0.6
Middle East	356 000	778 000	1.9	2.5
Total	5 961 000	8 925 000	0.4	0.5

Source: ILO 2013, *Domestic workers across the world: Global and regional statistics and the extent of legal protection* (Geneva), in particular, Appendix I, p. 109 for regional groupings. The figures in the table above are ILO estimates based on data from official sources.

Women and men in the informal economy: A statistical picture

The ILO's global and regional estimates cited above draw on official sources that are mainly national in coverage and do not disaggregate by urban and rural. Data compiled by WIEGO focuses on urban areas. Nonetheless, both sources point in the same direction, that domestic workers can be found in all parts of the world, and that the sector is a significant source of employment in many countries, especially for women.

Domestic work[85] is an important occupation, involving a sizeable proportion of the urban workforce.

- *As share of total urban employment*
    - Africa: 3-9 per cent in 7 West African cities and in 1 East African city
    - India: 4 per cent
    - Latin America: 6 per cent in Lima, 8 per cent in Buenos Aires.

- *As share of urban informal employment*
    - Brazil: 9 per cent
    - India: 5 per cent
    - South Africa: 23 per cent
    - Buenos Aires: 16 per cent

- *As share of urban employees/wage workers*
    - Buenos Aires: 10 per cent

Everywhere in the urban workforce, a much higher percentage of women than men perform domestic work.

- *As share of total urban employment*
    - Africa (in 8 cities): 4-20 per cent of women compared with 2-3 per cent of men
    - India: 8 per cent of women compared with 3 per cent of men
    - Latin America: in Lima, 13 per cent of women compared with 1 per cent of men; in Buenos Aires 18 per cent compared with 0.5 per cent; and in Brazil, 19 per cent of women compared with 1 per cent of men.

- *As share of urban informal employment*
    - India: 10 per cent of women compared with 4 per cent of men.
    - Buenos Aires: 35 per cent of women compared with 1 per cent of men.

- *As share of urban employees/wage workers*
    - Buenos Aires: 22 per cent of women compared with 0.7 per cent of men.

Expressed differently, most urban domestic workers are women: 82 per cent in Kenya, 95 per cent in Brazil, 96 per cent in South Africa and 97 per cent in Buenos Aires.

Everywhere, the majority – in some countries the vast majority – of domestic workers are in informal employment. In the eight African cities (excluding those in South Africa), 91–97 per cent of domestic workers are informal and in Buenos Aires, 97 per cent are informal. In South Africa and Brazil, however, roughly a quarter of domestic workers are considered formal because their

---

[85] In Hanoi and Ho Chi Minh City, domestic workers cannot be distinguished from home-based workers because the national statistical office classifies work carried out in both "employer's home" and "own home" as "home-based work".

> **Box 4.3 Immigrant Domestic Workers in and from Latin America**[a]
>
> In Latin America domestic service is an important occupation, involving a significant proportion of the workforce. Domestic work is mostly, but not exclusively, performed by women, and increasingly by migrants.
>
> - Domestic work is an important source of employment for immigrants in Latin America, involving 16-21 per cent of immigrants in Costa Rica, Chile and Argentina.
>
>   – The proportions of women immigrants in domestic work are: 10 per cent (Dominican Republic), 19 per cent (Paraguay), 37 per cent (Chile), 47 per cent (Costa Rica) and 78 per cent (Argentina).
>
>   – Most immigrants employed in domestic work are women: 70-74 per cent in Costa Rica, the Dominican Republic and Honduras, and 90-96 per cent in Argentina, Brazil, Chile and Paraguay.
>
> - In the United States in 2000, 58 per cent of workers in personal and related services (including domestic) were immigrants from Latin America.
>
> [a] This box is based on Tokman, V., *Domestic services in Latin America: Statistical profile for regulations*, WIEGO Working Paper No. 17, 2010, prepared at the request of the International Union of Food and Allied Workers (IUF) and (WIEGO); available at: www.wiego.org. The data are from the United Nations Economic Commission for Latin America and the Caribbean (ECLAC), *Social panorama of Latin America*, 2009, (Santiago), Statistical appendix; available at: www.eclac.org/publications. The surveys covered 10 countries in 2008, two countries in 2007, three countries in 2006 and one country in 2004.

employers contribute to their health insurance or old age pensions (South Africa), or they have a worker identity card (*Carteira de Trabalho*) that entitles them to various workers' benefits (Brazil).[86]

In early 2010, as part of their joint support of the campaign for an international convention on domestic work, WIEGO and the International Union of Food and Allied Workers (IUF) commissioned an analysis of data on domestic workers in urban Latin America. These data include estimates of the percentage of women immigrants who are domestic workers, the percentage of immigrant domestic workers who are women, and the percentage of workers involved in personal and related services in the United States who are immigrants from Latin America (see box 4.3 for a summary of the findings).

4.2 Home-Based Workers[87]

Home-based workers carry out remunerative work in their own homes, or in adjacent grounds or premises. Home-based work does not include unpaid housework or paid domestic work. The general term, home-based workers, refers to two broad categories: self-employed and subcontracted. The more specific term, "homeworkers", refers to the subcontracted home-based workers who carry out paid work for firms/businesses or their intermediaries, typically on a piece-rate basis.

---

[86] Brazil has already managed to substantially increase the proportion of domestic workers who are contributing to the Social Security Institute, from 18.2 per cent in 1993 to 30.6 per cent in 2007 (Instituto Brasileiro de Geografia e Estatística (IBGE), FDT240 - Contribuintes de instituto de previdência no trabalho principal, na população de 10 anos ou mais de idade, ocupada – Serviços domésticos (accessed June 2012).

[87] As noted earlier, in Hanoi and Ho Chi Minh City, home-based workers cannot be distinguished from domestic workers because the national statistical office classifies work carried out in both "employer's home" and "own home" as "home-based work". But other studies show that there is a relatively high prevalence of home-based work in Asia compared to Africa and Latin America, as the figures from India suggest.

Women and men in the informal economy: A statistical picture

This important distinction between self-employed and subcontracted home-based workers reflects differences that have policy implications.[88]

Home-based work, which cuts across different branches of industry, accounts for a significant share of urban employment in some countries.

- *As share of urban employment*
    - India: 18 per cent
    - Buenos Aires: 3 per cent
    - South Africa: 6 per cent

- *As share of urban informal employment*
    - Africa: 11-25 per cent in 8 cities, 21 per cent in Ghana
    - India: 23 per cent
    - Latin America: 3 per cent in Lima, 5 per cent in Buenos Aires

The vast majority of home-based workers are women: 62 per cent in South Africa;[89] 70 per cent in Brazil and 88 per cent in Ghana.

The majority of home-based workers are informally employed: 60 per cent in Buenos Aires and 75 per cent in South Africa.

A significant proportion of home-based workers are to be found in manufacturing and trade. In South Africa, 24 per cent of all home-based workers are involved in manufacturing (mainly crafts and related trades) and 37 per cent in trade. Of those in trade, some operate in small convenience stores (spaza shops) or informal pubs (shibeen). Also, some subcontracted home-based workers are engaged in various trades, such as brick making, stone masonry, construction and hand-packing. Traditional medicine practitioners account for three per cent of all home-based workers and four per cent of self-employed home-based workers in the country. In Buenos Aires, 33 per cent of all home-based workers are in manufacturing, while 23 per cent are in trade; a higher share of women home-based workers are in manufacturing (42 per cent) and a higher share of men home-based workers are in trade (35 per cent).

In India and the eight African cities, excluding South Africa, the majority of home-based workers are self-employed, mainly as own-account workers. In the 8 African cities, only 2-12 per cent of home-based workers are subcontracted workers. The rest are self-employed: 74-91 per cent are own-account workers, 4-7 per cent are contributing family workers, and 3-9 per cent are employers. By contrast, in South Africa, around 27 per cent of home-based workers are homeworkers, that is, persons carrying out work within their home under a subcontract from a firm or its contractors. As noted above, many of these are brick-makers, stonemasons, construction workers or hand packers.

In India in 2009–2010, nearly two-thirds (62 per cent) of all home-based workers – 65 per cent of men and 40 per cent of women – were own-account workers. A far larger percentage of women (39 per cent) than men (19 per cent) were unpaid, contributing family workers. A small percentage of home-based workers were wage workers: nine per cent of all, eight per cent of men, and 18 per cent of women; and a somewhat smaller percentage (except of men) were employers: eight of all, eight per cent of men and three per cent of women.

---

[88] In 1996, the International Labour Conference approved an international Convention (C177) on home work that calls for national policies to promote equality of treatment between homeworkers and other wage earners. It also specifies areas where such equality of treatment should be promoted, including inclusion in labour force statistics. For the full text of this convention, see: http://actrav.itcilo.org/actrav-english/telearn/global/ilo/law/iloc177.htm.

[89] In South Africa, unlike other developing countries, women account for less than one quarter of home-based workers. In part, this is because some subcontracted taxi drivers and truck drivers report that they are home-based.

4.3 Street vendors

Around the world, a significant share of the informal workforce operates on streets, sidewalks and other public spaces. The term "street vendor" is used in both a narrow sense to refer to those who sell goods in public space but also in a broader sense to refer to those who provide or sell services in public spaces, such as: hairdressers or barbers; shoe shiners and shoe repairers; and bicycle, motorcycle, car or truck mechanics.

Even when considered in the narrow and more precise sense of informal traders who sell goods on the street or other public spaces, street vending is a large and diverse activity: from high-income vendors who sell luxury goods at flea markets and those who sell electronics and other consumer durables, to those who sell fruit, vegetables and cooked food on city streets. Those who sell a single product or range of products as street vendors also often do so under quite different economic arrangements: some are truly self-employed and independent, others are semi-dependent (e.g. agents who sell products for firms against a commission), while still others are paid employees and fully dependent. Some sell from a fixed spot while other are mobile hawkers.

Street vendors constitute a significant proportion of urban employment in Africa, including South Africa, but less so in India and Viet Nam and even less so in Latin America.

- *proportion of urban employment*
  - India: 11 per cent
  - Latin America: 3 per cent in Brazil, 1 per cent in Buenos Aires
  - South Africa: 15 per cent

- *As proportion of urban informal employment*
  - Africa: 12-24 per cent in 8 African cities, 14 per cent in Ghana
  - India: 14 per cent
  - Viet Nam: 11 per cent each in Hanoi and Ho Chi Minh City
  - Latin America: 2 per cent in Buenos Aires, 9 per cent in Lima

- *As proportion of the urban self-employed*
  - Buenos Aires: 4 per cent

In many countries, especially in Africa, the majority of street vendors are women: 63 per cent in Kenya, 68 per cent in South Africa and 88 per cent in Ghana. In Buenos Aires, by contrast, only 29 per cent of street vendors are women.

Everywhere, the majority of street vendors are informal: 94 per cent in Buenos Aires.

Street vendors sell a variety of goods, not just food items. In South Africa, 67 per cent of all street vendors sell food items: 54 per cent of men street vendors and 73 per cent of women street vendors.

4.4 Waste pickers

The term "waste picker" refers to those who do the primary collecting and sorting of waste. The derogatory term, "scavenger", was replaced by the term "waste picker" at the First International Conference of Waste Pickers in Bogota, Colombia, in 2008. Waste pickers extract and reclaim reusable and recyclable materials from mixed types of waste that others have cast aside. They may collect or sort household waste from the curbside, litter from streets and urban waterways, or commercial and industrial waste from dumpsters. Some work at municipal dumps or landfills, and some may also be involved in the processing of recyclable waste.

Waste pickers are especially well organized in Brazil. As noted in box 4.1, they have advocated for a distinct code for waste picking in the Brazilian Classification of Occupations as well as the use of this code in all relevant data collection efforts in the country. The resulting data show the diverse work arrangements within this occupation and the significance of waste picking as a source of employment.[90] Three types of waste pickers can now be identified: (i) unorganized or autonomous waste pickers who make a living picking or buying recyclable material on the streets or in waste dumps and selling in junk shops; (ii) organized waste pickers who work through cooperatives and associations, many of them for more than 10 years, rather than recently during the economic downturn; and (iii) waste pickers with a contract who work mainly in junkyards or in metallurgical industries, but some also in the public municipal sector. The third category of waste pickers is considered to be formally employed. In Brazil there are over a quarter million waste pickers, 33 per cent of whom are women. While perhaps small in number, considering the size of the country, waste pickers are responsible for the high rates of recycling in Brazil: nearly 92 per cent of aluminium and 80 per cent of cardboard was recycled in 2008.

In the recent estimations presented here, no waste pickers were identified in one country (Ghana) and in four cities (Antananarivo, Buenos Aires, Hanoi and Ho Chi Minh City), although there were specific occupational or industrial codes for waste or garbage collecting in Ghana and the four cities. The sample size of these surveys was probably not large enough to capture waste pickers. At least one of the four cities, Buenos Aires, is known for its active cooperatives of waste pickers.

Where waste pickers were identified, they represented less than one per cent of the urban workforce.

- *As share of urban employment*
    - Africa: 0.1-0.4 per cent in 7 West African cities
    - South Africa: 0.7 per cent (both formal and informal waste pickers)
    - India: 0.1 per cent

- *As share of urban informal employment*
    - India: 0.1 per cent
    - Latin America: 0.6 per cent in Lima, 0.5 per cent in Brazil

In South Africa, of the 0.7 per cent of the workforce who reported being involved in garbage collection, only 29 per cent are informal (assumed to be waste pickers) and 71 per cent are formal (i.e. working for municipal governments).

Among informal workers, in five (of the seven) West African cities, a larger percentage of men than women are waste pickers; in one of these (Cotonou), all waste pickers identified are men. In Lima, the figures are 0.8 per cent of men and 0.3 per cent of women. In two cities in Africa – Bamako and Ouagadougou – a higher percentage of women than men informal workers are waste pickers, as also in urban India, where the figures are 0.2 per cent of women and 0.1 per cent of men.

4.5 Characteristics of the four groups (based on available data)

For all four groups, it is important to have estimates not only of their size and significance, but also of their earnings, poverty rates, social protection coverage and working conditions. In urban Latin America, domestic workers earn, on average, 41 per cent of what other urban workers earn, and they are more likely to be from households with incomes below the poverty line (box 4.4).

---

[90] Based on Dias, S., *Statistics on waste pickers in Brazil*, WIEGO Statistical Brief no. 2; available at: http://wiego.org/sites/wiego.org/files/publications/files/Dias_WIEGO_SB2.pdf.

Chapter 4 – Specific groups of urban informal workers

> ### Box 4.4 Domestic Workers in Latin America[a]
>
> In Latin America, domestic service is an important occupation, involving a significant proportion of the workforce. Most domestic work, especially by women, is informal (i.e. performed without labour contracts and social protection) and is associated with low earnings.
>
> **Earnings and poverty**
>
> - Domestic workers' average earnings are about 41 per cent of average earnings of the urban workforce
>   - Women domestic workers' earnings are 73 per cent of those of their male counterparts
>   - Women's earnings in domestic work are 76 per cent of those of all women working in the informal sector,, 84 per cent of female own-account workers, and 83 per cent of female wage workers in informal enterprises.
>   - Men's earnings in domestic work are more than those of men in self-employment in the informal sector: only 56 per cent of earnings of all male workers in the informal sector, 94 per cent of male wage workers in informal enterprises, but 118 per cent of male own-account workers
>   - Thirty-six per cent of domestic workers are from households below the poverty line compared with 26 per cent of the total urban workforce and 36 per cent of wage workers in informal enterprises.
>
> **Social protection and labour contracts [b]**
>
> - Regarding labour contracts, 20 per cent of domestic workers have such contracts compared with 58 per cent of the total urban workforce;
> - Regarding pension schemes, 19 per cent of domestic workers contribute to such schemes compared with 47 per cent of the total urban workforce and 25 per cent of wage workers in informal enterprises;
>   - A lower percentage of female domestic workers (19 per cent), than their male counterparts (31 per cent) contribute to pension schemes;
> - There are significantly fewer domestic workers *with contracts* who contribute to pension schemes (43 per cent) compared with all urban workers with contracts (83 per cent);
>   - Among domestic workers with *permanent contracts*, a lower percentage of women (38 per cent) than men (54 per cent) contribute to a pension scheme
> - Again there are far fewer domestic workers contributing to pension and/or health schemes (44 per cent) compared with the total urban workforce who contribute to such schemes (64 per cent);
>   - Of female domestic workers, 44 per cent contribute to pension and/or health schemes compared with 47 per cent of their male counterparts.
>
> **Notes:** [a] This box is based on Tokman, V., op cit. (see box 4.3 above). [b] Social protection coverage is higher and gender differences lower when health and pensions are included, as there is near universal health coverage in some of the countries.

In Kenya, domestic workers reported extremely low wages, equivalent to around one third of the average earnings of all non-agricultural, urban informal workers. Street vendors earn more, on average, than domestic workers in Kenya, but their earnings are only a little over three quarters of the average for all non-agricultural, urban informal workers.

In Brazil, the poverty rate is highest among waste pickers, at 56 per cent (66 per cent of women and 51 per cent of men). The next highest poverty rate is among domestic workers, at 30 per cent, with similar rates for women and men. Street vendors do only slightly better than domestic

Women and men in the informal economy: A statistical picture

Figure 4.1 Protection of domestic workers under national legislation, 2010

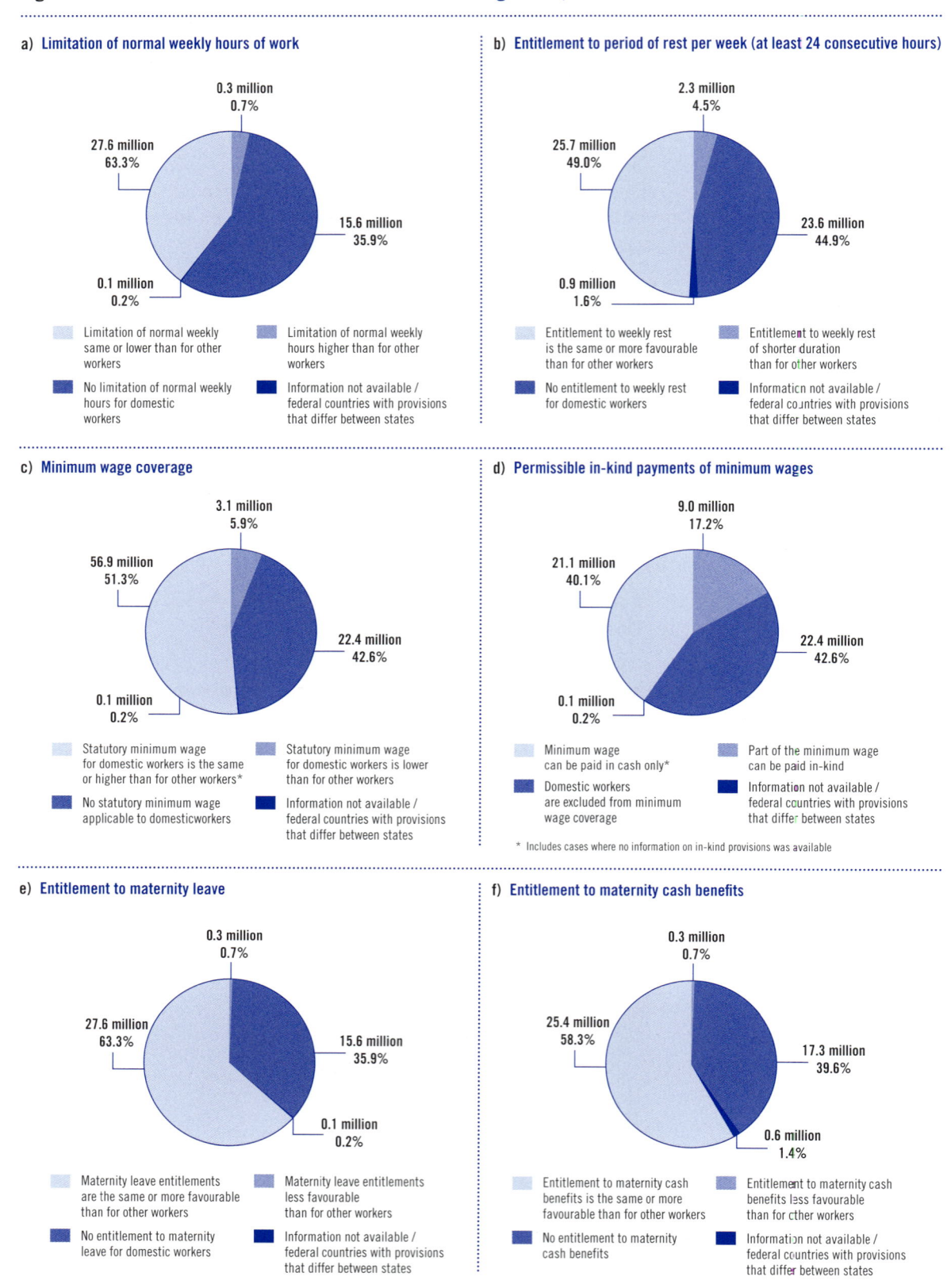

a) Limitation of normal weekly hours of work

- 0.3 million — 0.7%
- 27.6 million — 63.3%
- 15.6 million — 35.9%
- 0.1 million — 0.2%

Legend:
- Limitation of normal weekly same or lower than for other workers
- Limitation of normal weekly hours higher than for other workers
- No limitation of normal weekly hours for domestic workers
- Information not available / federal countries with provisions that differ between states

b) Entitlement to period of rest per week (at least 24 consecutive hours)

- 2.3 million — 4.5%
- 25.7 million — 49.0%
- 23.6 million — 44.9%
- 0.9 million — 1.6%

Legend:
- Entitlement to weekly rest is the same or more favourable than for other workers
- Entitlement to weekly rest of shorter duration than for other workers
- No entitlement to weekly rest for domestic workers
- Information not available / federal countries with provisions that differ between states

c) Minimum wage coverage

- 3.1 million — 5.9%
- 56.9 million — 51.3%
- 22.4 million — 42.6%
- 0.1 million — 0.2%

Legend:
- Statutory minimum wage for domestic workers is the same or higher than for other workers*
- Statutory minimum wage for domestic workers is lower than for other workers
- No statutory minimum wage applicable to domestic workers
- Information not available / federal countries with provisions that differ between states

d) Permissible in-kind payments of minimum wages

- 9.0 million — 17.2%
- 21.1 million — 40.1%
- 22.4 million — 42.6%
- 0.1 million — 0.2%

Legend:
- Minimum wage can be paid in cash only*
- Part of the minimum wage can be paid in-kind
- Domestic workers are excluded from minimum wage coverage
- Information not available / federal countries with provisions that differ between states

* Includes cases where no information on in-kind provisions was available

e) Entitlement to maternity leave

- 0.3 million — 0.7%
- 27.6 million — 63.3%
- 15.6 million — 35.9%
- 0.1 million — 0.2%

Legend:
- Maternity leave entitlements are the same or more favourable than for other workers
- Maternity leave entitlements less favourable than for other workers
- No entitlement to maternity leave for domestic workers
- Information not available / federal countries with provisions that differ between states

f) Entitlement to maternity cash benefits

- 0.3 million — 0.7%
- 25.4 million — 58.3%
- 17.3 million — 39.6%
- 0.6 million — 1.4%

Legend:
- Entitlement to maternity cash benefits is the same or more favourable than for other workers
- Entitlement to maternity cash benefits less favourable than for other workers
- No entitlement to maternity cash benefits
- Information not available / federal countries with provisions that differ between states

Source: ILO, *Domestic workers across the world: Global and regional statistics and the extent of legal protection* (Geneva), 2013.

Note: The data presented are ILO estimates based on data from official sources.

workers, with a poverty rate of 28 per cent of all street vendors (25 per cent of the women and 31 per cent of the men). There are some differences in the poverty rate between categories of street vendors: around 20 per cent of those who trade from their homes are poor compared with about 30 per cent of mobile traders and those who sell from a kiosk. Home-based workers are the least likely of the four groups to be poor in Brazil, but even among this group 21 per cent are poor.

In early 2010, as part of their joint support of the campaign for an international convention on domestic work, WIEGO and the International Union of Food and Allied Workers (IUF) commissioned an analysis of data on domestic workers in urban Latin America. These data include estimates of the earnings and poverty levels of domestic workers as well as the percentage that have social protection coverage and/or labour contracts (see box 4.4 for a summary of the findings).

An ILO report on domestic workers published in 2013,[91] examines the extent to which they are covered by labour protection. It found that in 2010 only 5.3 million domestic workers (or 10 per cent) were covered by general labour legislation, while some 15.7 million (or 29.9 per cent) were completely excluded from the scope of national labour legislation. More than half of all domestic workers were not covered by any national legislation setting limits on their normal working hours per week, and approximately 45 per cent had no entitlement to weekly rest periods (figure 4.1). With regard to minimum wages, just over half of all domestic workers enjoyed such protection on an equal basis with other workers, and for some 5.9 per cent the statutory minimum wage rate was lower. This leaves some 22.4 million domestic workers that lacked this protection (or 42.6 per cent of the total). Maternity protection is another area where there were large gaps in coverage: more than a third of all women domestic workers were not entitled to maternity leave and associated maternity cash benefits.

TECHNICAL NOTE: Classification codes used to identify specific groups of workers in the statistical picture analysis (WIEGO data)

Domestic workers

- Brazil: specific employment status code ("domestic workers")
- Ghana: not available
- India: industry code 950 + place of work codes 13 or 23 (employer's dwelling) and one of the following occupation codes: 159, 510, 520, 521, 529, 530, 531, 539, 540, 541, 542, 549, 574, 652, 986, or 999.
- Kenya: occupation code ("cleaner/domestic worker") + industry code ("domestic services")
- South Africa: occupation code 9131 ("unskilled general domestic workers") – narrow definition that excludes housekeepers and child-care workers
- Greater Buenos Aires: specific place of work code ("working for a household") + occupation code ("domestic service")
- 11 cities: production unit code ("household") + employment status code ("employee")

Home-based workers

- Brazil: place of work code ("own residence")
- Ghana: place of work code ("own residence")
- India: place of work codes 11 and 21 (own dwelling)

---

[91] ILO, Domestic workers across the world: Global and regional statistics and the extent of legal protection, (Geneva), 2013.

Women and men in the informal economy: A statistical picture

- Kenya: not available
- South Africa: place of work code ("owner's home or farm") – but question no longer asked in quarterly surveys
- Greater Buenos Aires: place of work code ("own home") in answer to the question "Where do you perform your work most of the time?" + disaggregation by industry/economic sector
- 11 cities: place of work code ("own home")

Street vendors

- Brazil: occupational codes 5441-5423 (including home-based vendors, kiosk vendors and mobile vendors)
- Ghana: occupation code ("street vending") + industry code ("retail trade") + place of work code ("street at a fixed or non-fixed location")
- India: occupation code 431 + industry code ("retail trade") with employment status codes 11 or 21 (own account workers & unpaid family workers) and place of work codes 10, 11, 15, 19, 21, 25, or 29.
- Kenya: occupation code 911 ("street vendors and related")
- South Africa: occupation codes 9111 and 9112 ("street vendors of food and non-food products, respectively")
- Greater Buenos Aires: occupation code ("trade") + place of work code ("public spaces") + production unit codes ("formal" or "informal")
- 11 cities: industry code ("trade") + place of work code ("public spaces")

Waste pickers

- Brazil: specific occupation code ("collector of recyclables")
- Ghana: occupation code ("garbage collection") OR industry code ("sewage", "refuge disposal", or "recycling") + employment status code ("self-employed")
- India: industry code 90001
- Kenya: n.a
- South Africa: occupation code 9161 ("garbage collectors") + employment status code ("self-employed") to exclude garbage collectors hired by municipalities
- Greater Buenos Aires: not available
- 11 cities: occupation code ("waste pickers/informal recycling")

Sources of data

Budlender, D. 2011, *Statistics on informal employment in South Africa*, WIEGO

Statistical Brief No. 1 (Data source: Quarterly labour force survey conducted in the second quarter of 2010 by Statistics South Africa).

—. 2011, *Statistics on informal employment in Brazil*, WIEGO Statistical Brief No. 2 (Data source: James Heintz's analysis of the 2007 Pesquisa Nacional per Amostra de Domicilios (PNAD) survey conducted by Brasileiro de Geografia e Estatistica).

—. 2011, *Statistics on informal employment in Kenya*, WIEGO Statistical Brief No. 3 (Data source: James Heintz's analysis of the 2004/06 Kenya Integrated Household Budget Survey conducted by the National Bureau of Statistics (formerly called the Central Bureau of Statistics).

—. 2011, *Informal employment in Ghana: Some statistics*, WIEGO Statistical Brief No. 4 (Data source: James Heintz's analysis of the 2006 Ghana Living Standard Survey conducted by the Ghana Statistical Service.

Chen, M.A.; Raveendran, G. 2012, "Urban employment in India: Recent trends and future prospects", In *Margin*, Special Issue on Informality (new Delhi, National Council for Applied Economics Research).

Esquivel, V., 2010, *The informal economy in Greater Buenos Aires: A statistical profile*, WIEGO Working Paper No. 9 (Data source: Informal Labour Module (ILM) of the Encuesta Permanente de Hogares, the Argentinean urban labour force survey, last quarter of 2006).

Herrera, J.; Kuepie, M.; Nordman, C. J.; Oudin, X.; Roubaud, F., 2011, *Informal sector and informal employment: Overview of data for eleven cities in ten developing countries*, WIEGO Working Paper No. 9 Data sources:
- West Africa: 1-2-3 Household surveys carried out between 2001 and 2003 by the relevant national statistics institutes, AFRISTAT and DIAL, as part of the multilateral support programme for regional statistics, Programme d'appui régional statistique à la surveillance multilatéral (PARSTAT).
- Madagascar: 1-2-3 Household survey carried out in 2006 by INSTAT and DIAL; only data from phase I have been used in the analysis.
- Peru: 2008 National Household Survey (ENAHO) in the Lima metropolitan area carried out by the National Institute of Statistics of Peru
- Viet Nam: 2007 Labor force survey for Hanoi and Ho Chi Minh City carried out at the national level by the General Statistics Office of Viet Nam

Wills, G. 2009, *South Africa's informal economy: A statistical profile*, WIEGO Working Paper No. 6 (Primary data source: 2007 Labour force survey, conducted in September Source; for trend data: 2005, 2006 and 2007 Labour force surveys).

Chapter 5

Future Directions for Measuring the Informal Economy

It is a major achievement that an increasing number of countries are now collecting and tabulating data on informal employment, both inside and outside the informal sector. Much of that data have been compiled and analyzed in this publication. The data presented here show that informal employment continues to be an important part of all employment, accounting for half to three quarters of non-agricultural employment in most developing countries. When informal employment in the agricultural sector is also measured, which is a goal for future work, the share of informal employment in total employment is likely to be even greater. When informal employment is disaggregated by employment status and into specific occupational groups, as was done for this publication, a refined picture of informal employment emerges. Four groups of informal workers – paid domestic workers, home-based workers, street vendors, and waste pickers – taken together account for a significant share of urban employment. In developed countries, the various non-standard employment arrangements, some of which show similarities with what is defined as informal employment in the developing-country context, constitute a significant proportion of total employment.

Although substantial progress has been made in collecting and providing data on the size and composition of informal employment and the informal economy in recent years, this needs to be done by more countries. It is also crucial that such data be collected and disseminated on a regular basis to enable an analysis of the dynamics and changes in this important segment of the economy. Additional data on informal workers and their households are also needed, for example, the ages of persons informally employed, the earnings of informal workers, including the self-employed, and the types of employment and sources of income of other members of their households. It would be useful for policy-makers to have additional data that provide information on aspects such as the cost-benefits and risks of being informally employed, the current extent of social protection coverage of informal workers and types of protection schemes, if any (e.g. employment-based, universal coverage, a group-based scheme or a rotating saving fund) which offer them coverage. Other useful information is whether persons are informally employed by choice, necessity, social conditioning or tradition. The data for such analyses are not necessarily complex, but require regular collection of basic data.

While the producers of statistics should try to generate more and better statistics on informal employment, the users of statistics – data analysts and policy-makers – need to recognize that there are official international definitions of the *informal sector* and *informal employment* as agreed at the ICLS in 1993 and 2003 respectively. Indeed, these agreed definitions prompted many countries to begin collecting data on the informal economy. This is reflected in the growing number of countries for which data are now available (see country-specific tables in annex 2). However, there are still various other definitions of informal employment which coexist with the latest international recommendation, and very often this is a source of confusion, for both data producers and analysts. Widespread adoption of the internationally recognized definitions would enable a better policy dialogue and a common understanding of the phenomena involved in informality. The ILO's recently published manual, *Measuring Informality: A New Statistical Manual on the Informal Sector and Informal Economy*,[92] should greatly help this process.

---

[92] See: http://www.ilo.org/global/statistics-and-databases/WCMS_182299/lang--en/index.htm.

Women and men in the informal economy: A statistical picture

A proposed plan of action

A detailed plan of action to improve statistics on informal employment and their dissemination and analysis was outlined in the previous issue of *Women and Men in the Informal Economy* in 2002, and it was also discussed during recent meetings of the International Expert group on informal sector statistics, (also known as the Delhi Group). Because the development of statistics is a long-term and continuous process, the broad goals and activities of the plan of action proposed in this chapter are essentially those outlined in the earlier edition. However, this new plan also reviews efforts over the past 10 years to improve official statistics on informal employment. These efforts, as described in chapter 1 and as reflected in the new data presented in this report, give a sharper focus to the goals and key elements of what is needed to further improve official statistics on informal employment and its constituent elements.

The following are the broad goals of the proposed plan of action:

- To institutionalize the collection, tabulation, dissemination and use of data on informal employment and on the informal sector and its contribution to GDP as part of the regular work programme of statistical offices at the national, regional and international levels.

- To further develop statistical concepts and methods in order to identify separately all types of informal employment and all categories of informal workers inside and outside the informal sector, and collect data on related aspects such as wages and earnings.

- To make statistics and analyses readily accessible to researchers, policy-makers and advocates in user-friendly formats, through, for example, the greater availability of micro-data datasets. This should be supported by the international statistical system in order to enable a better and more transparent way of analysing national cases, thereby improving comparability across regions.

These objectives could be best achieved through the continued joint action of national, regional and international statistical services of relevant governmental and international agencies, as well as activists and researchers working on the informal economy. The joint action of producers and informed users of data on informal employment led to the first edition of this report and to the progress that enabled the compilation of this new and improved report. Regarding the producers of statistics, the ILO Department of Statistics, with responsibility for labour statistics and the United Nations Statistics Division with responsibility for national accounts statistics and gender statistics, were and will continue to be key along with other relevant partners. This should lead to increasing attention to such an important concept in labour market studies. The following additional institutions have contributed to the progress made so far: the Asian Development Bank, the United Nations regional commissions, especially ESCAP, the ILO Information System for Latin America and the Caribbean (SIALC), the IRD, the Andean Community, and the Delhi Group. As for users, many were involved in the progress made, including the ILO Employment Policy Department as well as other units of the ILO, and the many advocates and researchers who have worked with WIEGO. A special group of informed users of data are the national, regional and international alliances and networks of informal workers which request data. They helped to specify what activities and workers should be included in data collection and dissemination, and in their advocacy efforts. In addition, in March 2011, WIEGO held a conference in Cape Town with the aim of identifying a critical new research agenda on the informal economy. The conference helped crystallize a research agenda around informality which included ideas for future statistical analyses and related data collection.

The following are the identified goals for a proposed plan of action:

Goal 1 – *Institutionalizing the collection, tabulation, dissemination and use of data on informal employment and the informal sector*

- Provide technical assistance and training for national statistical offices on the collection, processing and analysis of data on the informal economy. The publication in 2012 of the manual, *Measuring Informality: A New Statistical Manual on the Informal Sector and Informal Economy*,

Chapter 5 – Future directions for measuring the informal economy

prepared by the ILO Department of Statistics in cooperation with the members of the Delhi Group and the WIEGO network, could provide both an impetus and a resource for training. Such training should be provided as part of a programme of technical assistance to advise national statistical offices on the development of statistics on the informal economy through: (i) the use of relevant information already collected in surveys, and/or (ii) the inclusion of new survey questions, if necessary. The programme should also aim at improving the quality of data on the informal economy, as well as their international comparability.

- Promote the importance of collecting data on informal employment and informal sector employment in labour force surveys, rather than promoting multipurpose surveys or surveys tailored to the priorities of international funding agencies. Strong international coordination among different international donors and agencies would be needed in order to reach a common understanding on the matter, leading to the provision of coherent support and technical advice to countries.

- Highlight the need to give special attention in labour force surveys or other household surveys to collecting data on the earnings of both wage workers and self-employed workers, and types of social protection received through employment, place of work, seasonality and other temporal patterns, and through multiple or secondary jobs.

- Raise awareness of the fact that there exist several methods and types of surveys for collecting information on informal enterprises, each of which has its strengths and limitations; there is no single method that is universally applicable.

- Encourage countries to use data on the informal sector and informal employment in the preparation of national accounts in order to improve inclusion of the contribution to GDP of the informal economy. This would be a natural way of aligning with the 2008 System of National Accounts.

Goal 2 – Improving statistical concepts and methods

- Review and revise the International Classification of Status in Employment (ICSE) to identify all categories of informal employment in today's globalized economy, including relevant categories in developed countries. The 18th ICLS (2008) suggested the need for a review of the ICSE in order to make recommendations on how the ICSE should be modified and expanded to reflect contemporary realities of work as well as related social and economic concerns. A review and revision of the ICSE is crucial for the improvement of data on informal employment for several reasons. For instance, the current ICSE does not include adequate mutually exclusive categories for casual day labourers, temporary or part-time workers, or the various categories of contracted and subcontracted workers. While labour force surveys generally count these workers as employed, it is often not possible to identify them as distinct categories in data tabulations or analyses. Similarly, they are generally included in informal employment, but cannot be identified as distinct sub-categories of informal employment inside or outside the informal sector.

- Improve the methods for identifying categories of informal workers, such as paid domestic workers, home-based workers, street vendors and waste pickers. The three major classifications by economic characteristics of employment – kind of economic activity as identified in the International Standard Industrial Classification (ISIC), status in employment and occupations – are not sufficient, as they describe employment in the formal economy but not in the informal economy. Since informal employment continues to constitute a significant segment of the labour force, efforts should be made to better identify and describe these categories in the three classification systems, not only at the international and national levels, but also in the tabulation and dissemination of data on these workers.

- Improve the methods for measuring informal employment in agriculture. While the international definition of informal wage employment is suitable for agricultural as well as non-agricultural employees, the international definition of informal self-employment (other than those of contributing family workers and producers of goods exclusively for own final use by their households) refers only to non-agricultural activities. This is because employers, own-account workers and members of producers' cooperatives are considered to have informal jobs if their enterprise/cooperative belongs to the informal sector (defined by the 15th ICLS in respect of non-agricultural activities). The criteria of enterprise registration or size, which form part of the definition of informal enterprises agreed at the 15th ICLS, are not meaningful with respect to agricultural holdings; other criteria would need to be specified if the measurement of informal self-employment were to be extended to cover agricultural activities. Further methodological work is needed to develop such criteria.

- Undertake the methodological, analytic and awareness-raising work required to apply the concept of informal employment to developed countries. Given the changes that are occurring in labour markets and the structure of employment worldwide, understanding employment dynamics, trends in labour market structures and patterns of work mobility has become increasingly important. A crucial step is the revision of the ICSE so that it captures the type of economic risk (i.e. the degree of attachment of persons to their jobs) and the type of the job holder's authority over establishments and other workers across all forms of employment in developed countries. Another step is a comparison of informal employment and non-standard or atypical work in order to gauge how these concepts compare in existing survey instruments and data. This information would make it possible to determine what can be done with the existing data and what is needed to enable more comprehensive estimates of informal employment in developed countries.

Goal 3 – Making data available, encouraging data analysis and disseminating analysed data

- Develop, maintain and update at regular intervals a comprehensive international database on the informal economy, incorporating existing data on informal employment and total employment from as many countries as possible. As noted in chapter 1, the ILO Department of Statistics, working with the ILO Information System for Latin America and the Caribbean (SIALC) and the WIEGO network, compiled data on informal employment, both outside and inside the informal sector, from nearly 50 countries using a common template. A number of additional countries in the Asian and African regions had collected data on informal employment and/or informal sector employment, but they either did not respond to the ILO request for information or did not complete the questionnaire fully and thus may need technical assistance in providing data for inclusion in the international database.

- Encourage countries to prepare and make available public-access micro-data files of labour force surveys or similar household surveys. At the research conference organized by WIEGO in Cape Town in March 2011, many researchers identified difficulty in accessing micro-data files as a major problem that prevented them from working on the informal economy. To overcome this problem, a compilation of the available micro-data sets and information on how to obtain them should be prepared and regularly updated. Micro-data archives of national household survey data (i.e. archives containing the Up-to date data) should also be established and maintained at the regional level for all regions, similar to what has already been done in Latin America. Such archives could then be used to process data on the informal economy for inclusion in an international database on the topic for use by researchers.

- Encourage national, regional and international statistical agencies to analyse the data they have collected on the informal economy, and to disseminate the findings in reports, articles, press releases and websites in user-friendly formats.

Annex 1

Availability of data by region

Data coverage on informal employment and employment both within and outside the informal sector varies significantly across regions, as highlighted in table A.1. In Latin America and the Caribbean, the data coverage is very extensive, both in terms of number of countries and working age population. Sixteen countries in the region (out of 24), which accounted for more than 89 per cent of the working age population (WAP) in 2010, reported data on informal employment and informal sector employment (ISE). The extent of coverage was somewhat different in the other regions..

In South and East Asia (excluding China), the data coverage is high in terms of WAP, with around 80 per cent coverage of WAP for informal employment and 77 per cent for ISE. This is primarily explained by good coverage for India, but in other countries there is room for improvement: only seven countries out of 27 reported data on informal employment. Importantly, China is considered separately since the data on China are limited to six urban areas (see notes Table 2.1).

For Eastern Europe and the CIS, there are not much data on informal employment, with only 5.5 per cent of data coverage in terms of WAP. For ISE, the data coverage is much higher (62 per cent), as the two largest countries, the Russian Federation and Ukraine, have reported data.

For sub-Saharan Africa, the data coverage is relatively low: for WAP in informal employment and ISE it is 28 per cent and 30.5 per cent respectively. There are 12 countries (out of 46) that reported either informal employment or ISE.

For North Africa and the Middle East, the data coverage is very low for ISE with only one country reporting data (west Bank and Gaza). For informal employment, the situation is a little better as two large countries (Egypt and Turkey) reported data. Only three countries/territories (out of 23) reported either informal employment or ISE.

Table A.1: Data coverage by region

Country (Year)	Working Age Population (WAP, 15+) Total	Working Age Population (WAP, 15+) Nb countries	Available data on Informal Employment Coverage in terms of WAP	Available data on Informal Employment Nb countries	Available data on Employment in the Informal Sector Coverage in terms of WAP	Available data on Employment in the Informal Sector Nb countries	Available data on Informal Employment Outside the Informal Sector Coverage in terms of WAP	Available data on Informal Employment Outside the Informal Sector Nb countries
Southern and Eastern Asia */	1,669,127	27	80.0%	7	76.9%	7	76.7%	6
Eastern Europe and CIS countries	284,052	21	5.4%	4	61.9%	6	5.4%	4
Latin America and the Caribbean	425,178	35	89.1%	16	89.1%	16	89.1%	16
Northern Africa	143,334	7	38.7%	1	0.0%	0	0.0%	0
Sub Saharan Africa **/	418,443	46	27.9%	10	30.6%	11	25.7%	8
Western Asia ***/	152,721	16	36.6%	2	1.5%	1	1.5%	1

Coverage by region

Notes: The geographical subregions are based on United Nations definitions (see: unstats.un.org).

* Excluding China (urban data).   ** Excluding Ethiopia (urban data).   *** Excluding Armenia and Georgia, which are included in Eastern Europe and the CIS.

Source: United Nations Population estimates (revision 2010); ILO Department of Statistics for calculations and other data

Annex 2

Country-Specific Tables

Explanatory notes

The statistics presented in this annex were based on data obtained from a range of sources, including: responses to a questionnaire, which the ILO Department of Statistics had sent to countries to request data and meta-data on employment in the informal economy; special tabulations of national survey data accessible to the ILO, including the household survey micro-data database held by the ILO/SIALC (Panama) for Latin American countries; and extracts from survey reports, among others. The primary data sources were mainly national labour force surveys, but also some informal sector surveys, living standard measurement surveys and other household surveys.

Conceptual framework for measuring informal employment

Production units	Informal jobs	Formal jobs
Informal enterprises	A	B
Other units of production	C	D

The conceptual framework for the statistical measurement of informal employment adopted by the ICLS distinguishes between informality from the perspective of production units as *observation units*, on the one hand, and that of jobs as observation units on the other. Thus two concepts are involved: employment in the informal sector, which refers to employment in informal enterprises, and informal employment, which refers to employment in informal jobs.

This annex presents country-specific data on the following:

(i) *Employment within the informal sector* (A+B), including *formal employment in the informal sector* (if any) (B), i.e. employees holding formal jobs in informal enterprises.

(ii) *Informal employment outside the informal sector* (C), i.e. employees holding informal jobs in formal enterprises (including government units and non-profit institutions), as paid domestic workers employed by households or as contributing family workers in formal enterprises. Some countries/territories[93] include own-account workers producing goods exclusively for own final use by their households in their national definition of employment, and identify them separately. In such cases, these workers are also considered as informal workers outside the informal sector.

(iii) Total *informal employment* (A+C), excluding employees with formal jobs in informal enterprises.[94]

---

[93] Armenia, Brazil, Indonesia, the Philippines, the United Republic of Tanzania, Uruguay, Viet Nam and the West Bank and Gaza Strip.

[94] The 17th ICLS definition of informal employment includes contracted work and subcontracted work for formal firms if they meet the criteria of the definition. However, workers under contracts or subcontracts cannot yet be identified separately because of the lack of internationally accepted definitions and survey questions for them. In other words, they are likely to be included among persons in informal employment, but it is unclear in which category they should be included. The classification of status in employment needs to be revised to include these and other workers for whom there are no internationally accepted definitions, survey questions or classification codes so far.

Women and men in the informal economy: A statistical picture

The *informal sector* was defined by the 15th ICLS (1993) as private unincorporated enterprises that are unregistered or small in terms of the number of employed persons (e.g. less than five employees). An enterprise is unincorporated if it is not constituted as a separate legal entity, independently of its owner(s), and does not maintain a complete set of accounts. Units engaged in the production of goods or services exclusively for own final use by the household are excluded, as are enterprises engaged in agriculture, hunting, forestry and fishing. National statistical definitions of the informal sector vary to some extent; however, the countries for which data are presented in the annex have all used the international definition of informal sector. *Informal employment* was defined by the 17th ICLS (2003) as encompassing the following:

(a) Own-account workers and employers employed in their own informal enterprises;

(b) Members of informal producers' cooperatives (not established as legal entities), if any;

(c) Own-account workers producing goods exclusively for final use by their households (if considered employed, given that their production comprises an important contribution to total household consumption and is included in the national definition of employment);

(d) Contributing family workers in formal or informal enterprises; and

(e) Employees holding informal jobs in formal enterprises (including government units and non-profit institutions), informal enterprises or as paid domestic workers employed by households.

In line with the international definition, countries for which data are shown in the annex, define employees holding informal jobs as employees not covered by social security, as employed persons, or as employees not entitled to other employment benefits such as paid annual or sick leave.

The data refer to *non-agricultural employment*, i.e. they exclude employment in agriculture, hunting, forestry and fishing activities (ISIC, Rev. 3, tabulation categories A-B). Employment in non-agricultural activities is classified as: *manufacturing*, including mining and quarrying, and electricity, gas and water supply (ISIC, Rev. 3, tabulation categories C-E); *construction* (ISIC, Rev. 3, tabulation category F); *trade*, including hotels and restaurants (ISIC, Rev. 3, tabulation categories G-H); *transportation* (ISIC, Rev. 3, tabulation category I); and *services other than trade and transportation* (ISIC, Rev. 3, tabulation categories J-Q).

Wage employment refers to employees, and *self-employment* refers to the sum of employers, own-account workers, members of producers' cooperatives (if any) and contributing family workers.

For the tables presented in annex 2, persons holding more than one job during the survey reference period were classified as being employed in the informal sector or in an informal job on the basis of the characteristics of their main job. The same applies to their classification by kind of economic activity (industry) or by status in employment.

Roman numerals in parentheses refer to quarters. Example: 2010 (II) means that the data refer to the second quarter of 2010.

Depending upon the availability of data, up to 10 indicators have been computed for each of the countries/territories presented in annex 2.

Indicator 1 shows the number of persons in: (i) informal employment; (ii) employment in the informal sector; (iii) formal employment in the informal sector (if any); and (iv) informal employment outside the informal sector. The numbers presented are in absolute figures (thousands) and as a percentage of non-agricultural employment.

Indicator 2 provides the percentage distribution by status in employment of persons employed in the informal sector.

Indicator 3 provides the percentage distribution by status in employment and type of production unit of persons in informal employment.

Indicators 4 and 5 show the informality rates of different categories of self-employed persons and employees.

Indicator 6 provides the percentage distribution by status in employment/type of production unit of persons in informal employment outside the informal sector.

All indicators 1 to 6 are broken down by sex and by urban versus rural areas.

Indicators 7 and 8 indicate the percentage of women in various types of employment.

Indicator 9 shows the informality rates of employment in the different branches of non-agricultural economic activity (industries), disaggregated by sex.

Indicator 10 compares the percentage distribution by branch of non-agricultural economic activity of formal and informal employment, againdisaggregated by sex.

Countries/territories

- Argentina
- Armenia
- Bolivia (Plurinational State of)
- Brazil
- China (six cities)
- Colombia
- Costa Rica
- Côte d'Ivoire
- Dominican Republic
- Ecuador
- Egypt
- El Salvador
- Ethiopia (Urbana areas)
- Honduras
- India
- Indonesia
- Kyrgyzstan
- Lesotho
- Liberia
- Madagascar
- Mali
- Mauritius
- Mexico
- Republic of Moldova
- Namibia
- Nicaragua
- Pakistan
- Panama
- Paraguay
- Peru
- Philippines
- Russian Federation
- Serbia
- South Africa
- Sri Lanka
- Thailand
- The former Yugoslav Republic of Macedonia
- Turkey
- Uganda
- United Republic of Tanzania
- Ukraine
- Uruguay
- Venezuela (Bolivarian Republic of)
- Viet Nam
- West Bank and Gaza Strip
- Zambia
- Zimbabwe

WOMEN AND MEN IN THE INFORMAL ECONOMY – A STATISTICAL PICTURE COUNTRY-SPECIFIC TABLES

The data presented in this file are part of the activities jointly undertaken by the ILO and WIEGO.

Roman numbers in parentheses refer to quarters. Example: 2010 (II) means that the data refer to the second quarter of 2010.

Depending upon the availability of data, up to ten indicators have been computed for each of the countries/territories included here:

- **Indicator 1** shows the number of persons in: (i) informal employment; (ii) employment in the informal sector; (iii) formal employment in the informal sector (if any); and (iv) informal employment outside the informal sector. The numbers are given in absolute figures (thousands) and as a percent of non-agricultural employment.

- **Indicator 2** provides the percentage distribution by status in employment of persons employed in the informal sector.

- **Indicator 3** provides the percentage distribution by status in employment and type of production unit of persons in informal employment.

- **Indicators 4 and 5** show the informality rates of different categories of self-employed persons and employees.

- **Indicator 6** provides the percentage distribution by status in employment/type of production unit of persons in informal employment outside the informal sector. All indicators I to 6 are broken down by sex and by urban vs. rural areas.

- **Indicators 7 and 8** indicate the share of women in various types of employment.

- **Indicator 9** shows the informality rates of employment in the different branches of non-agricultural economic activity (industries), disaggregated by sex.

- **Indicator 10** compares the percentage distribution by branch of non-agricultural economic activity of formal and informal employment, distinguishing between women and men.

Women and men in the informal economy: A statistical picture

Country: Argentina   Year: 2009 (IV)

Source: Encuesta Permanente de Hogares Continua

1. Informal non-agricultural employment and its components

	Total	Women	Men	Urban	Rural
in 1,000					
Persons in informal employment	5'138.2	2'189.1	2'949.1	5'138.2	
Persons employed in the informal sector	3'317.2	1'131.3	2'185.9	3'317.2	
Persons in formal employment in the informal sector	29.3	13.5	15.8	29.3	
Persons in informal employment outside the informal sector	1'850.3	1'071.3	779.0	1'850.3	
as % of non-agricultural employment					
Persons in informal employment	49.7	49.6	49.8	49.7	
Persons employed in the informal sector	32.1	25.7	36.9	32.1	
Persons in formal employment in the informal sector	0.3	0.3	0.3	0.3	
Persons in informal employment outside the informal sector	17.9	24.3	13.2	17.9	

2. Employment in the informal sector by status in employment (%)

Status in employment	Total	Women	Men	Urban	Rural
Employers, own-account workers and MPCs*	68.3	68.7	68.0	68.3	
Contributing family workers	2.2	4.3	1.1	2.2	
Employees	29.5	27.0	30.8	29.5	
Total	100.0	100.0	100.0	100.0	

* Members of producers' cooperatives

3. Informal non-agricultural employment by status in employment (%)

Status in employment	Total	Women	Men	Urban	Rural
Employers, own-account workers and MPCs*	44.1	35.5	50.4	44.1	
Owners of informal sector enterprises	44.1	35.5	50.4	44.1	
Producers of goods exclusively for own final use					
Contributing family workers	1.6	2.4	1.0	1.6	
Employees	54.3	62.1	48.6	54.3	
Formal sector employees	23.3	20.3	25.5	23.3	
Informal sector employees	18.5	13.3	22.3	18.5	
Domestic workers employed by households	12.5	28.5	0.7	12.5	
Total	100.0	100.0	100.0	100.0	

* Members of producers' cooperatives

4. Informal non-agricultural self-employment as % of total non-agricultural self-employment by status in employment

Status in employment	Total	Women	Men	Urban	Rural
Employers & members of producers' co-operatives	70.1	67.1	71.2	70.1	
Own-account workers	98.9	98.5	99.1	98.9	
Enterprise owners	98.9	98.5	99.1	98.9	
Total self-employment (incl. contributing family workers)	93.7	94.3	93.4	93.7	

5. Informal wage employment as % of total wage employment by type of employees

Type of employees	Total	Women	Men	Urban	Rural
Agricultural employees	46.2	51.7	45.1	46.2	
Non-agricultural employees	35.7	38.5	33.3	35.7	
Formal sector employees	19.6	17.8	20.9	19.6	
Informal sector employees	97.0	95.6	97.7	97.0	
Domestic workers employed by households	86.3	86.1	95.5	86.3	
Total employees	35.8	38.6	33.5	35.8	

6. Informal non-agricultural employment outside the informal sector by type (%)

Type of employment	Total	Women	Men	Urban	Rural
Producers of goods exclusively for own final use					
Contributing family workers: formal sector	0.5	0.3	0.7	0.5	
Employees	99.5	99.7	99.3	99.5	
Employees: formal sector	64.7	41.4	96.6	64.7	
Employees: domestic work	34.8	58.3	2.7	34.8	
Total	100.0	100.0	100.0	100.0	

7. Share of women in employment by type

Share of women in …	%
1. Total employment	42.2
2. Agricultural employment	14.2
2.1 Agricultural wage employment	16.0
2.1.1 Formal agricultural wage employment	14.3
2.1.2 Informal agricultural wage employment	17.9
2.2 Agricultural self-employment	12.7
3. Non-agricultural employment	42.7
3.1 Non-agricultural wage employment*	45.1
3.1.1 Formal non-agricultural wage employment	43.1
3.1.2 Informal non-agricultural wage employment	48.7
3.2 Non-agricultural self-employment	35.1
3.2.1 Formal non-agricultural self-employment	31.8
3.2.2 Informal non-agricultural self-employment	35.3

* = MDG Indicator No. 3.2: Share of women in wage employment in the non-agricultural sector

8. Share of women in informal non-agricultural employment by component

Share of women in …	%
1. Informal employment	42.6
1.1 Self-employment	35.3
1.2 Wage employment	48.7
2. Employment in the informal sector	34.1
2.1 Self-employment	35.3
2.2 Wage employment	31.2
3. Informal employment outside the informal sector	57.9
3.1 Self-employment	38.5
3.2 Wage employment	58.0
3.2.1 Formal sector	37.1
3.2.2 Domestic work	96.8

Women and men in the informal economy: A statistical picture

9. Share of informal employment (%) by kind of non-agricultural activity

Share of informal employment in total employment in ...	Total	Women	Men
All non-agricultural actitvities	49.7	49.6	49.8
Manufacturing	42.9	57.6	37.2
Construction	77.6	30.4	78.8
Trade	64.4	65.8	63.4
Transportation	48.2	37.4	50.1
Services other than trade or transportation	39.4	43.7	32.6

10. Non-agricultural employment by sex, formal/informal nature and kind of activity (%)

A. Both sexes

Kind of activity	Total	Formal	Informal
All non-agricultural actitvities	100.0	100.0	100.0
Manufacturing	14.6	16.6	12.6
Construction	8.9	4.0	13.9
Trade	23.4	16.6	30.3
Transportation	6.7	6.9	6.5
Services other than trade or transportation	46.4	56.0	36.7

B. Women

Kind of activity	Total	Formal	Informal
All non-agricultural actitvities	100.0	100.0	100.0
Manufacturing	9.6	8.1	11.1
Construction	0.5	0.7	0.3
Trade	21.7	14.8	28.8
Transportation	2.3	2.8	1.7
Services other than trade or transportation	65.9	73.6	58.1

C. Men

Kind of activity	Total	Formal	Informal
All non-agricultural actitvities	100.0	100.0	100.0
Manufacturing	18.4	23.0	13.7
Construction	15.2	6.4	24.0
Trade	24.7	18.0	31.4
Transportation	10.0	9.9	10.0
Services other than trade or transportation	31.8	42.7	20.9

Country: Argentina Year: 2009 (IV)

Non-agricultural employment

Activity	Female informal employment: share in total employment of the activity	Informal employment: share in total employmen of the activity	Share of employment in all activities
Transportation	37.4	48.2	6.7
Construction	30.4	77.6	8.9
Manufacturing	57.6	42.9	14.6
Trade	65.8	64.4	23.4
Services other than trade or transportation	43.7	39.4	46.4
All non-agricultural activities	49.6	49.7	100.0

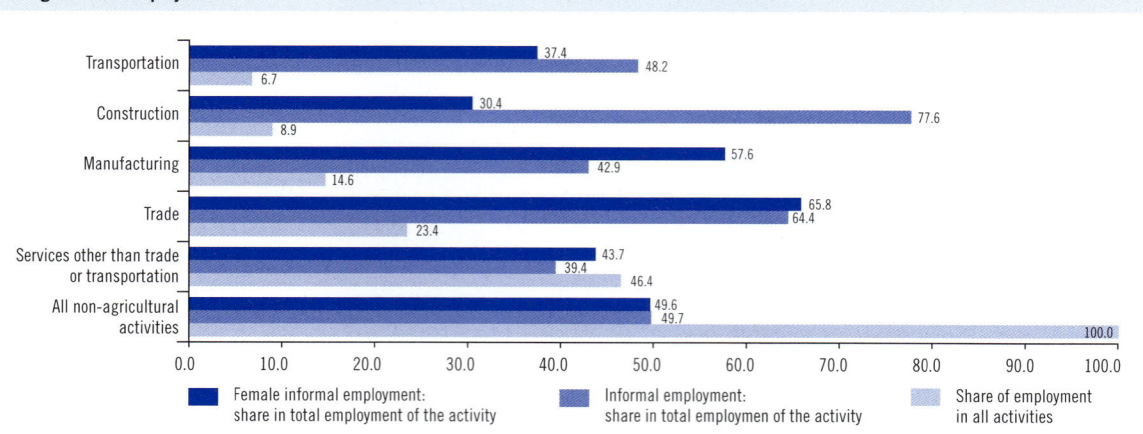

Annex II

Country: Armenia **Year: 2009**

Source: Integrated Living Conditions Survey

1. Informal non-agricultural employment and its components

	Total	Women	Men	Urban	Rural
in 1,000					
Persons in informal employment	138.0	36.8	101.2	101.3	36.5
Persons employed in the informal sector	71.0	15.1	56.0	44.1	26.9
Persons in formal employment in the informal sector	0.0	0.0	0.0	0.0	0.0
Persons in informal employment outside the informal sector	67.0	21.8	45.2	57.2	9.8
as % of non-agricultural employment					
Persons in informal employment	19.8	12.7	24.8	18.0	27.1
Persons employed in the informal sector	10.2	5.2	13.7	7.8	20.0
Persons in formal employment in the informal sector	0.0	0.0	0.0	0.0	0.0
Persons in informal employment outside the informal sector	9.6	7.5	11.1	10.2	7.3

2. Employment in the informal sector by status in employment (%)

Status in employment	Total	Women	Men	Urban	Rural
Employers, own-account workers and MPCs*	48.2	53.6	46.8	48.1	48.5
Contributing family workers	3.3	6.0	2.6	3.1	3.6
Employees	48.5	40.4	50.6	48.8	47.9
Total	100.0	100.0	100.0	100.0	100.0

* Members of producers' cooperatives

3. Informal non-agricultural employment by status in employment (%)

Status in employment	Total	Women	Men	Urban	Rural
Employers, own-account workers and MPCs*	30.0	24.4	32.0	26.2	40.6
Owners of informal sector enterprises	24.8	21.9	25.9	20.9	35.8
Producers of goods exclusively for own final use	5.1	2.5	6.1	5.3	4.8
Contributing family workers	3.1	4.7	2.6	3.1	2.7
Employees	66.9	70.9	65.4	70.7	56.7
Formal sector employees	36.8	46.8	33.2	45.4	13.4
Informal sector employees	24.9	16.5	28.0	21.2	35.4
Domestic workers employed by households	5.1	7.6	4.2	4.1	7.9
Total	100.0	100.0	100.0	100.0	100.0

* Members of producers' cooperatives

4. Informal non-agricultural self-employment as % of total non-agricultural self-employment by status in employment

Status in employment	Total	Women	Men	Urban	Rural
Employers & members of producers' co-operatives	5.8	0.0	6.3	6.8	0.0
Own-account workers	73.5	63.6	76.8	69.2	81.3
Enterprise owners	69.6	61.1	72.8	64.2	80.6
Total self-employment (incl. contributing family workers)	68.7	65.5	69.7	63.9	78.3

Women and men in the informal economy: A statistical picture

5. Informal wage employment as % of total wage employment by type of employees

Type of employees	Total	Women	Men	Urban	Rural
Agricultural employees	63.1	64.3	62.2	41.8	72.2
Non-agricultural employees	14.6	9.5	18.5	13.9	18.1
Formal sector employees	8.6	6.5	10.4	9.4	4.9
Informal sector employees	100.0	100.0	100.0	100.0	100.0
Domestic workers employed by households	100.0	100.0	100.0	100.0	100.0
Total employees	16.0	11.0	19.8	14.2	23.4

6. Informal non-agricultural employment outside the informal sector by type (%)

Type of employment	Total	Women	Men	Urban	Rural
Producers of goods exclusively for own final use	10.6	4.2	13.7	9.3	17.8
Contributing family workers: formal sector	3.0	3.8	2.6	3.0	2.7
Employees	86.5	92.1	83.8	87.6	79.5
Employees: formal sector	75.9	79.2	74.3	80.3	50.0
Employees: domestic work	10.6	12.8	9.5	7.3	29.5
Total	100.0	100.0	100.0	100.0	100.0

7. Share of women in employment by type

Share of women in …	%
1. Total employment	46.5
2. Agricultural employment	53.8
2.1 Agricultural wage employment	41.9
2.1.1 Formal agricultural wage employment	40.6
2.1.2 Informal agricultural wage employment	42.7
2.2 Agricultural self-employment	54.3
3. Non-agricultural employment	41.6
3.1 Non-agricultural wage employment*	43.4
3.1.1 Formal non-agricultural wage employment	46.0
3.1.2 Informal non-agricultural wage employment	28.3
3.2 Non-agricultural self-employment	24.6
3.2.1 Formal non-agricultural self-employment	27.1
3.2.2 Informal non-agricultural self-employment	23.4

* = MDG Indicator No. 3.2: Share of women in wage employment in the non-agricultural sector

8. Share of women in informal non-agricultural employment by component

Share of women in …	%
1. Informal employment	26.7
1.1 Self-employment	23.4
1.2 Wage employment	28.3
2. Employment in the informal sector	21.2
2.1 Self-employment	24.5
2.2 Wage employment	17.7
3. Informal employment outside the informal sector	32.5
3.1 Self-employment	19.0
3.2 Wage employment	34.6
3.2.1 Formal sector	33.9
3.2.2 Domestic work	39.4

Annex II

9. Share of informal employment (%) by kind of non-agricultural activity

Share of informal employment in total employment in …	Total	Women	Men
All non-agricultural actitvities	19.8	12.7	24.8
Manufacturing	22.2	35.0	16.9
Construction	57.8	30.3	58.3
Trade	38.6	37.7	39.3
Transportation	20.7	6.0	23.5
Services other than trade or transportation	6.2	5.8	6.8

10. Non-agricultural employment by sex, formal/informal nature and kind of activity (%)

A. Both sexes

Kind of activity	Total	Formal	Informal
All non-agricultural actitvities	100.0	100.0	100.0
Manufacturing	10.0	9.7	11.2
Construction	11.8	6.2	34.5
Trade	13.9	10.7	27.2
Transportation	9.2	9.1	9.7
Services other than trade or transportation	55.0	64.3	17.4

B. Women

Kind of activity	Total	Formal	Informal
All non-agricultural actitvities	100.0	100.0	100.0
Manufacturing	7.0	5.2	19.2
Construction	0.6	0.5	1.4
Trade	14.7	10.5	43.9
Transportation	3.6	3.9	1.7
Services other than trade or transportation	74.1	80.0	33.7

C. Men

Kind of activity	Total	Formal	Informal
All non-agricultural actitvities	100.0	100.0	100.0
Manufacturing	12.2	13.5	8.3
Construction	19.8	11.0	46.5
Trade	13.4	10.8	21.2
Transportation	13.3	13.5	12.6
Services other than trade or transportation	41.3	51.2	11.4

Country: Armenia **Year: 2009**

Non-agricultural employment

Activity	Female informal employment: share in total employment of the activity	Informal employment: share in total employmen of the activity	Share of employment in all activities
Transportation	6.0	20.7	9.2
Manufacturing	35.0	22.2	10.0
Construction	30.3	57.8	11.8
Trade	37.7	38.6	13.9
Services other than trade or transportation	5.8	6.2	55.0
All non-agricultural activities	12.7	19.8	100.0

71

Women and men in the informal economy: A statistical picture

Country: Bolivia   **Year: 2006**

Source: Encuesta de Hogares

1. Informal non-agricultural employment and its components

	Total	Women	Men	Urban	Rural
in 1,000					
Persons in informal employment	2'068.7	972.1	1'096.6	1'791.7	277.0
Persons employed in the informal sector	1'435.6	663.6	772.0	1'217.2	218.3
Persons in formal employment in the informal sector	13.9	3.0	10.9	12.2	1.7
Persons in informal employment outside the informal sector	647.0	311.5	335.6	586.6	60.4
as % of non-agricultural employment					
Persons in informal employment	75.1	78.5	72.4	74.5	79.6
Persons employed in the informal sector	52.1	53.6	51.0	50.6	62.8
Persons in formal employment in the informal sector	0.5	0.2	0.7	0.5	0.5
Persons in informal employment outside the informal sector	23.5	25.2	22.1	24.4	17.4

2. Employment in the informal sector by status in employment (%)

Status in employment	Total	Women	Men	Urban	Rural
Employers, own-account workers and MPCs*	62.2	70.8	54.7	62.6	60.1
Contributing family workers	12.7	16.7	9.3	12.4	14.3
Employees	25.1	12.5	36.0	25.0	25.5
Total	100.0	100.0	100.0	100.0	100.0

* Members of producers' cooperatives

3. Informal non-agricultural employment by status in employment (%)

Status in employment	Total	Women	Men	Urban	Rural
Employers, own-account workers and MPCs*	43.2	48.4	38.5	42.5	47.4
Owners of informal sector enterprises	43.2	48.4	38.5	42.5	47.4
Producers of goods exclusively for own final use					
Contributing family workers	10.5	13.7	7.6	10.3	11.6
Employees	46.4	37.9	53.9	47.2	41.0
Formal sector employees	24.4	19.1	29.1	25.6	16.7
Informal sector employees	16.7	8.2	24.3	16.3	19.5
Domestic workers employed by households	5.2	10.6	0.4	5.3	4.8
Total	100.0	100.0	100.0	100.0	100.0

* Members of producers' cooperatives

4. Informal non-agricultural self-employment as % of total non-agricultural self-employment by status in employment

Status in employment	Total	Women	Men	Urban	Rural
Employers & members of producers' co-operatives	55.3	59.3	54.2	51.2	91.8
Own-account workers	90.5	91.9	88.9	89.5	97.4
Enterprise owners	90.5	91.9	88.9	89.5	97.4
Total self-employment (incl. contributing family workers)	87.5	91.8	82.8	86.0	97.3

5. Informal wage employment as % of total wage employment by type of employees

Type of employees	Total	Women	Men	Urban	Rural
Agricultural employees	85.5	95.6	83.9	75.4	92.2
Non-agricultural employees	64.6	63.5	65.3	64.8	63.1
Formal sector employees	50.1	47.7	51.6	50.9	43.4
Informal sector employees	96.1	96.4	96.1	96.0	96.9
Domestic workers employed by households	92.4	95.0	58.7	95.2	76.2
Total employees	65.7	64.1	66.6	65.1	69.2

6. Informal non-agricultural employment outside the informal sector by type (%)

Type of employment	Total	Women	Men	Urban	Rural
Producers of goods exclusively for own final use					
Contributing family workers: formal sector	5.3	7.3	3.4	5.7	1.4
Employees	94.7	92.7	96.6	94.3	98.6
Employees: formal sector	78.0	59.6	95.2	78.2	76.8
Employees: domestic work	16.7	33.2	1.4	16.2	21.9
Total	100.0	100.0	100.0	100.0	100.0

7. Share of women in employment by type

Share of women in …	%
1. Total employment	44.9
2. Agricultural employment	44.9
2.1 Agricultural wage employment	14.0
2.1.1 Formal agricultural wage employment	4.3
2.1.2 Informal agricultural wage employment	15.7
2.2 Agricultural self-employment	46.3
3. Non-agricultural employment	45.0
3.1 Non-agricultural wage employment*	39.1
3.1.1 Formal non-agricultural wage employment	40.3
3.1.2 Informal non-agricultural wage employment	38.4
3.2 Non-agricultural self-employment	51.8
3.2.1 Formal non-agricultural self-employment	33.9
3.2.2 Informal non-agricultural self-employment	54.4

* = MDG Indicator No. 3.2: Share of women in wage employment in the non-agricultural sector

8. Share of women in informal non-agricultural employment by component

Share of women in …	%
1. Informal employment	47.0
1.1 Self-employment	54.4
1.2 Wage employment	38.4
2. Employment in the informal sector	46.2
2.1 Self-employment	54.0
2.2 Wage employment	22.9
3. Informal employment outside the informal sector	48.1
3.1 Self-employment	66.6
3.2 Wage employment	47.1
3.2.1 Formal sector	36.7
3.2.2 Domestic work	95.5

Women and men in the informal economy: A statistical picture

9. Share of informal employment (%) by kind of non-agricultural activity

Share of informal employment in total employment in …	Total	Women	Men
All non-agricultural actitvities	75.1	78.5	72.4
Manufacturing	81.7	92.6	75.2
Construction	92.3	71.3	92.5
Trade	87.6	90.1	83.2
Transportation	81.7	73.1	83.0
Services other than trade or transportation	52.5	59.9	44.0

10. Non-agricultural employment by sex, formal/informal nature and kind of activity (%)

A. Both sexes

Kind of activity	Total	Formal	Informal
All non-agricultural actitvities	100.0	100.0	100.0
Manufacturing	19.8	14.6	21.6
Construction	9.0	2.8	11.0
Trade	30.3	15.2	35.3
Transportation	9.1	6.7	9.9
Services other than trade or transportation	31.8	60.7	22.2

B. Women

Kind of activity	Total	Formal	Informal
All non-agricultural actitvities	100.0	100.0	100.0
Manufacturing	16.4	5.6	19.3
Construction	0.2	0.3	0.2
Trade	42.7	19.7	49.0
Transportation	2.7	3.4	2.5
Services other than trade or transportation	37.9	70.9	28.9

C. Men

Kind of activity	Total	Formal	Informal
All non-agricultural actitvities	100.0	100.0	100.0
Manufacturing	22.6	20.3	23.5
Construction	16.1	4.4	20.6
Trade	20.1	12.3	23.1
Transportation	14.3	8.8	16.4
Services other than trade or transportation	26.8	54.3	16.3

Country: Bolivia   **Year: 2006**

Non-agricultural employment

- Female informal employment: share in total employment of the activity
- Informal employment: share in total employmen of the activity
- Share of employment in all activities

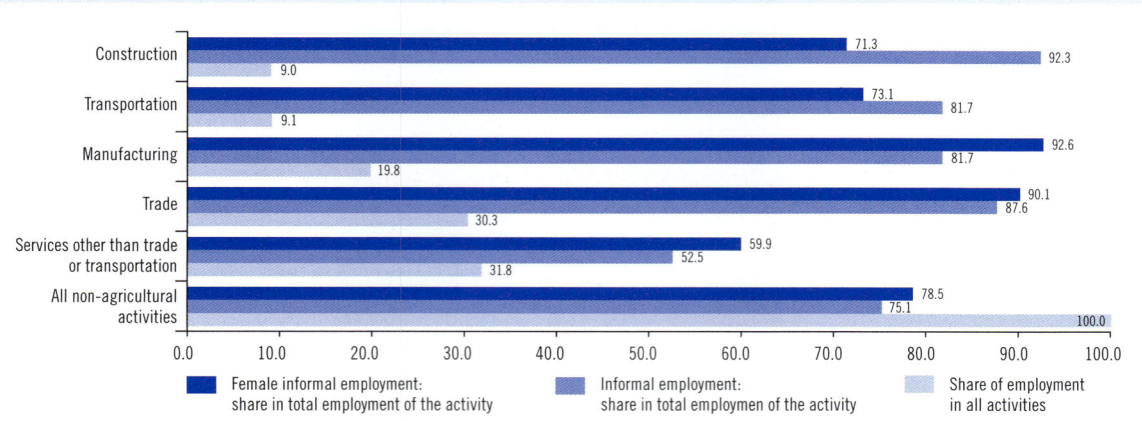

Source: China Urban Labor Survey (six cities)

Country: Brazil
Source: Pesquisa Nacional por Amostra de Domicilios

Year: 2009

1. Informal non-agricultural employment and its components

	Total	Women	Men	Urban	Rural
in 1,000					
Persons in informal employment	32'493.3	15'908.5	16'584.8	29'663.1	2'830.3
Persons employed in the informal sector	18'688.2	6'982.3	11'705.9	17'187.5	1'500.7
Persons in formal employment in the informal sector	56.5	17.6	38.9	53.5	3.0
Persons in informal employment outside the informal sector	13'861.6	8'943.8	4'917.9	12'529.1	1'332.5
as % of non-agricultural employment					
Persons in informal employment	42.2	45.9	39.2	41.3	55.1
Persons employed in the informal sector	24.3	20.1	27.7	23.9	29.2
Persons in formal employment in the informal sector	0.1	0.1	0.1	0.1	0.1
Persons in informal employment outside the informal sector	18.0	25.8	11.6	17.4	25.9

2. Employment in the informal sector by status in employment (%)

Status in employment	Total	Women	Men	Urban	Rural
Employers, own-account workers and MPCs*	71.4	74.4	69.6	71.6	69.2
Contributing family workers	2.3	3.9	1.4	2.2	3.9
Employees	26.3	21.7	29.0	26.2	26.9
Total	100.0	100.0	100.0	100.0	100.0

* Members of producers' cooperatives

3. Informal non-agricultural employment by status in employment (%)

Status in employment	Total	Women	Men	Urban	Rural
Employers, own-account workers and MPCs*	41.4	32.7	49.7	41.8	37.2
Owners of informal sector enterprises	41.1	32.7	49.2	41.5	36.7
Producers of goods exclusively for own final use	0.3	0.1	0.5	0.3	0.5
Contributing family workers	4.9	6.5	3.5	4.8	6.4
Employees	53.7	60.8	46.8	53.4	56.4
Formal sector employees	22.6	20.3	24.9	22.7	22.3
Informal sector employees	14.9	9.4	20.2	15.0	14.2
Domestic workers employed by households	16.1	31.1	1.7	15.7	19.9
Total	100.0	100.0	100.0	100.0	100.0

* Members of producers' cooperatives

4. Informal non-agricultural self-employment as % of total non-agricultural self-employment by status in employment

Status in employment	Total	Women	Men	Urban	Rural
Employers & members of producers' co-operatives	24.6	21.0	26.0	24.0	39.2
Own-account workers	83.5	85.4	82.3	83.0	90.5
Enterprise owners	83.4	85.3	82.2	82.8	90.4
Total self-employment (incl. contributing family workers)	74.5	79.0	71.5	73.5	87.2

Women and men in the informal economy: A statistical picture

5. Informal wage employment as % of total wage employment by type of employees

Type of employees	Total	Women	Men	Urban	Rural
Agricultural employees	64.9	61.8	65.2	56.8	71.0
Non-agricultural employees	30.7	36.1	25.9	29.9	42.9
Formal sector employees	16.5	17.4	15.8	16.0	24.7
Informal sector employees	98.8	98.8	98.9	98.8	99.3
Domestic workers employed by households	72.4	73.7	55.2	72.2	74.1
Total employees	33.4	36.6	30.8	30.9	54.8

6. Informal non-agricultural employment outside the informal sector by type (%)

Type of employment	Total	Women	Men	Urban	Rural
Producers of goods exclusively for own final use	0.7	0.2	1.8	0.7	1.0
Contributing family workers: formal sector	8.5	8.4	8.6	8.4	9.2
Employees	90.8	91.4	89.6	90.9	89.7
Employees: formal sector	53.1	36.1	84.0	53.7	47.4
Employees: domestic work	37.7	55.3	5.7	37.2	42.3
Total	100.0	100.0	100.0	100.0	100.0

7. Share of women in employment by type

Share of women in ...	%
1. Total employment	42.6
2. Agricultural employment	30.7
2.1 Agricultural wage employment	11.3
2.1.1 Formal agricultural wage employment	12.3
2.1.2 Informal agricultural wage employment	10.8
2.2 Agricultural self-employment	39.2
3. Non-agricultural employment	45.0
3.1 Non-agricultural wage employment*	47.2
3.1.1 Formal non-agricultural wage employment	43.5
3.1.2 Informal non-agricultural wage employment	55.5
3.2 Non-agricultural self-employment	39.0
3.2.1 Formal non-agricultural self-employment	32.1
3.2.2 Informal non-agricultural self-employment	41.4

* = MDG Indicator No. 3.2: Share of women in wage employment in the non-agricultural sector

8. Share of women in informal non-agricultural employment by component

Share of women in ...	%
1. Informal employment	49.0
1.1 Self-employment	41.4
1.2. Wage employment	55.5
2. Employment in the informal sector	37.4
2.1 Self-employment	39.7
2.2 Wage employment	30.8
3. Informal employment outside the informal sector	64.5
3.1 Self-employment	60.0
3.2 Wage employment	65.0
3.2.1 Formal sector	43.9
3.2.2 Domestic work	94.7

Annex II

9. Share of informal employment (%) by kind of non-agricultural activity

Share of informal employment in total employment in …	Total	Women	Men
All non-agricultural actitvities	42.2	45.9	39.2
Manufacturing	31.7	48.6	21.8
Construction	67.5	29.5	68.6
Trade	45.0	47.2	43.4
Transportation	39.0	18.1	42.3
Services other than trade or transportation	39.9	45.6	30.0

10. Non-agricultural employment by sex, formal/informal nature and kind of activity (%)

A. Both sexes

Kind of activity	Total	Formal	Informal
All non-agricultural actitvities	100.0	100.0	100.0
Manufacturing	17.7	20.9	13.2
Construction	9.0	5.0	14.3
Trade	26.1	24.9	27.9
Transportation	5.8	6.1	5.3
Services other than trade or transportation	41.5	43.1	39.3

B. Women

Kind of activity	Total	Formal	Informal
All non-agricultural actitvities	100.0	100.0	100.0
Manufacturing	14.4	13.7	15.3
Construction	0.6	0.7	0.4
Trade	24.6	24.0	25.3
Transportation	1.8	2.7	0.7
Services other than trade or transportation	58.6	58.9	58.3

C. Men

Kind of activity	Total	Formal	Informal
All non-agricultural actitvities	100.0	100.0	100.0
Manufacturing	20.3	26.1	11.3
Construction	15.8	8.2	27.7
Trade	27.3	25.5	30.3
Transportation	9.0	8.6	9.8
Services other than trade or transportation	27.5	31.6	21.0

Country: Brazil **Year: 2009**

Non-agricultural employment

- Female informal employment: share in total employment of the activity
- Informal employment: share in total employmen of the activity
- Share of employment in all activities

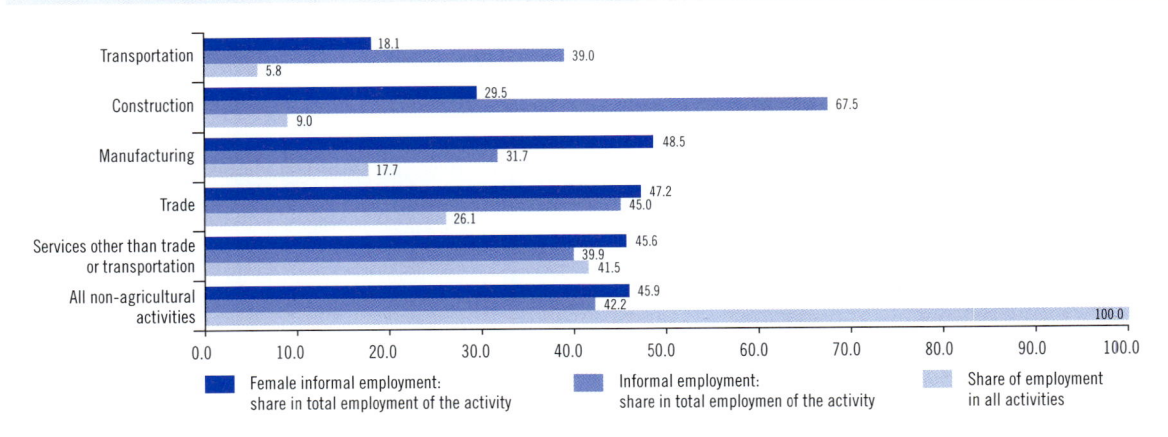

Women and men in the informal economy: A statistical picture

Country: China
Year: 2010

Source: China Urban Labor Survey (six cities)

1. Informal non-agricultural employment and its components

	Total	Women	Men	Urban	Rural
in 10,000					
Persons in informal employment	3'603.0	1'723.0	1'879.4	3'603.0	
Persons employed in the informal sector	2'422.0	1'115.0	1'306.2	2'422.0	
Persons in formal employment in the informal sector	205.0	102.0	103.0	205.0	
Persons in informal employment outside the informal sector	1'385.4	710.0	676.1	1'385.4	
as % of non-agricultural employment					
Persons in informal employment	32.6	35.7	30.1	32.6	
Persons employed in the informal sector	21.9	23.1	20.9	21.9	
Persons in formal employment in the informal sector	1.9	2.1	1.7	1.9	
Persons in informal employment outside the informal sector	12.5	14.7	10.8	12.5	

2. Employment in the informal sector by status in employment (%)

Status in employment	Total	Women	Men	Urban	Rural
Employers, own-account workers and MPCs*	68.0	61.2	73.9	68.0	
Contributing family workers	6.6	11.9	2.1	6.6	
Employees	25.4	26.9	24.1	25.4	
Total	100.0	100.0	100.0	100.0	

* Members of producers' cooperatives

3. Informal non-agricultural employment by status in employment (%)

Status in employment	Total	Women	Men	Urban	Rural
Employers, own-account workers and MPCs*	45.7	39.6	51.3	45.7	
Owners of informal sector enterprises	45.7	39.6	51.3	45.7	
Producers of goods exclusively for own final use					
Contributing family workers	5.0	8.4	1.8	5.0	
Employees	49.3	52.0	46.8	49.3	
Formal sector employees	37.7	40.0	35.5	37.7	
Informal sector employees	11.4	11.5	11.2	11.4	
Domestic workers employed by households	0.2	0.5	0.1	0.2	
Total	100.0	100.0	100.0	100.0	

* Members of producers' cooperatives

4. Informal non-agricultural self-employment as % of total non-agricultural self-employment by status in employment

Status in employment	Total	Women	Men	Urban	Rural
Employers & members of producers' co-operatives	72.4	76.0	70.6	72.4	
Own-account workers	97.2	97.1	97.1	97.2	
Enterprise owners	97.2	97.3	97.1	97.2	
Total self-employment (incl. contributing family workers)	88.0	91.2	85.4	88.0	

5. Informal wage employment as % of total wage employment by type of employees

Type of employees	Total	Women	Men	Urban	Rural
Agricultural employees	11.0	5.9	10.9	11.0	
Non-agricultural employees	19.8	22.9	17.4	19.8	
Formal sector employees	16.3	19.1	14.1	16.3	
Informal sector employees	66.6	66.0	67.2	66.6	
Domestic workers employed by households	75.0	88.9	66.7	75.0	
Total employees	19.7	22.8	17.3	19.7	

6. Informal non-agricultural employment outside the informal sector by type (%)

Type of employment	Total	Women	Men	Urban	Rural
Producers of goods exclusively for own final use					
Contributing family workers: formal sector	1.4	1.7	1.0	1.4	
Employees	98.6	98.3	99.0	98.6	
Employees: formal sector	98.0	97.2	98.7	98.0	
Employees: domestic work	0.6	1.1	0.3	0.6	
Total	100.0	100.0	100.0	100.0	

7. Share of women in employment by type

Share of women in …	%
1. Total employment	43.4
2. Agricultural employment	24.5
2.1 Agricultural wage employment	23.3
2.1.1 Formal agricultural wage employment	24.6
2.1.2 Informal agricultural wage employment	12.5
2.2 Agricultural self-employment	27.3
3. Non-agricultural employment	43.6
3.1 Non-agricultural wage employment*	43.6
3.1.1 Formal non-agricultural wage employment	41.9
3.1.2 Informal non-agricultural wage employment	50.4
3.2 Non-agricultural self-employment	43.7
3.2.1 Formal non-agricultural self-employment	31.6
3.2.2 Informal non-agricultural self-employment	45.3

* = MDG Indicator No. 3.2: Share of women in wage employment in the non-agricultural sector

8. Share of women in informal non-agricultural employment by component

Share of women in …	%
1. Informal employment	47.8
1.1 Self-employment	45.3
1.2. Wage employment	50.4
2. Employment in the informal sector	46.0
2.1 Self-employment	45.1
2.2 Wage employment	48.8
3. Informal employment outside the informal sector	51.2
3.1 Self-employment	63.2
3.2 Wage employment	51.1
3.2.1 Formal sector	50.8
3.2.2 Domestic work	88.9

Women and men in the informal economy: A statistical picture

9. Share of informal employment (%) by kind of non-agricultural activity

Share of informal employment in total employment in …	Total	Women	Men
All non-agricultural actitvities	32.4	35.5	30.0
Manufacturing	17.1	20.0	15.3
Construction	35.2	25.1	38.3
Trade	59.6	57.1	62.8
Transportation	21.8	15.8	23.1
Services other than trade or transportation	27.6	30.6	25.0

10. Non-agricultural employment by sex, formal/informal nature and kind of activity (%)

A. Both sexes

Kind of activity	Total	Formal	Informal
All non-agricultural actitvities	100.0	100.0	100.0
Manufacturing	15.2	18.7	8.0
Construction	4.1	3.9	4.4
Trade	20.7	12.4	38.0
Transportation	9.2	10.7	6.2
Services other than trade or transportation	50.8	54.4	43.3

B. Women

Kind of activity	Total	Formal	Informal
All non-agricultural actitvities	100.0	100.0	100.0
Manufacturing	13.1	16.2	7.4
Construction	2.2	2.5	1.5
Trade	26.3	17.5	42.3
Transportation	3.8	5.0	1.7
Services other than trade or transportation	54.6	58.8	47.1

C. Men

Kind of activity	Total	Formal	Informal
All non-agricultural actitvities	100.0	100.0	100.0
Manufacturing	16.8	20.4	8.6
Construction	5.6	4.9	7.1
Trade	16.3	8.7	34.1
Transportation	13.4	14.7	10.3
Services other than trade or transportation	47.9	51.3	39.9

Country: China   Year: 2010

Non-agricultural employment

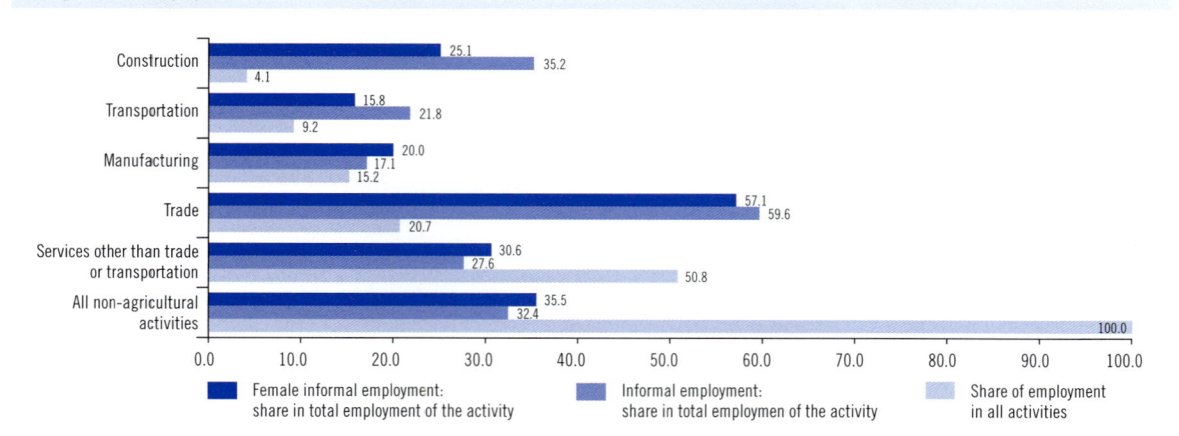

Source: China Urban Labor Survey (six cities)

Country: Colombia
Source: Gran Encuesta Integrada de Hogares Continua

Year: 2010 (II)

1. Informal non-agricultural employment and its components

	Total	Women	Men	Urban	Rural
in 1,000					
Persons in informal employment	9'307.2	4'532.5	4'774.7	8'108.7	1'198.5
Persons employed in the informal sector	8'143.6	3'701.7	4'441.9	7'087.4	1'056.2
Persons in formal employment in the informal sector	280.8	112.0	168.8	257.4	23.4
Persons in informal employment outside the informal sector	1'444.4	942.8	501.6	1'278.7	165.7
as % of non-agricultural employment					
Persons in informal employment	59.6	62.7	57.0	57.6	78.9
Persons employed in the informal sector	52.2	51.2	53.1	50.3	69.5
Persons in formal employment in the informal sector	1.8	1.5	2.0	1.8	1.5
Persons in informal employment outside the informal sector	9.3	13.0	6.0	9.1	10.9

2. Employment in the informal sector by status in employment (%)

Status in employment	Total	Women	Men	Urban	Rural
Employers, own-account workers and MPCs*	72.6	71.3	73.7	72.5	73.9
Contributing family workers	7.3	10.6	4.5	7.1	8.5
Employees	20.1	18.1	21.8	20.5	17.6
Total	100.0	100.0	100.0	100.0	100.0

* Members of producers' cooperatives

3. Informal non-agricultural employment by status in employment (%)

Status in employment	Total	Women	Men	Urban	Rural
Employers, own-account workers and MPCs*	63.6	58.2	68.6	63.3	65.1
Owners of informal sector enterprises	63.6	58.2	68.6	63.3	65.1
Producers of goods exclusively for own final use					
Contributing family workers	6.6	8.9	4.3	6.4	7.6
Employees	29.9	32.8	27.1	30.3	27.3
Formal sector employees	9.1	8.2	9.9	9.4	7.1
Informal sector employees	14.6	12.3	16.7	14.7	13.6
Domestic workers employed by households	6.2	12.4	0.4	6.2	6.7
Total	100.0	100.0	100.0	100.0	100.0

* Members of producers' cooperatives

4. Informal non-agricultural self-employment as % of total non-agricultural self-employment by status in employment

Status in employment	Total	Women	Men	Urban	Rural
Employers & members of producers' co-operatives	41.4	38.4	42.5	38.1	78.7
Own-account workers	83.7	83.5	84.0	82.9	90.1
Enterprise owners	83.7	83.5	84.0	82.9	90.1
Total self-employment (incl. contributing family workers)	81.3	82.9	80.0	80.1	90.3

Women and men in the informal economy: A statistical picture

5. Informal wage employment as % of total wage employment by type of employees

Type of employees	Total	Women	Men	Urban	Rural
Agricultural employees	69.6	58.0	71.1	45.4	76.7
Non-agricultural employees	36.7	41.8	32.2	34.9	59.0
Formal sector employees	16.0	16.5	15.7	15.2	30.7
Informal sector employees	82.8	83.3	82.6	82.3	87.4
Domestic workers employed by households	85.6	87.2	58.0	85.6	85.4
Total employees	41.5	42.4	40.8	35.4	70.4

6. Informal non-agricultural employment outside the informal sector by type (%)

Type of employment	Total	Women	Men	Urban	Rural
Producers of goods exclusively for own final use					
Contributing family workers: formal sector	1.3	1.3	1.4	1.4	0.7
Employees	98.7	98.7	98.6	98.6	99.3
Employees: formal sector	58.4	39.3	94.3	59.4	51.0
Employees: domestic work	40.3	59.4	4.2	39.2	48.3
Total	100.0	100.0	100.0	100.0	100.0

7. Share of women in employment by type

Share of women in …	%
1. Total employment	40.5
2. Agricultural employment	14.5
2.1 Agricultural wage employment	11.6
2.1.1 Formal agricultural wage employment	16.0
2.1.2 Informal agricultural wage employment	9.7
2.2 Agricultural self-employment	16.2
3. Non-agricultural employment	46.4
3.1 Non-agricultural wage employment*	47.0
3.1.1 Formal non-agricultural wage employment	43.2
3.1.2 Informal non-agricultural wage employment	53.5
3.2 Non-agricultural self-employment	45.8
3.2.1 Formal non-agricultural self-employment	41.8
3.2.2 Informal non-agricultural self-employment	46.7

* = MDG Indicator No. 3.2: Share of women in wage employment in the non-agricultural sector

8. Share of women in informal non-agricultural employment by component

Share of women in …	%
1. Informal employment	48.7
1.1 Self-employment	46.7
1.2 Wage employment	53.5
2. Employment in the informal sector	45.5
2.1 Self-employment	46.6
2.2 Wage employment	40.9
3. Informal employment outside the informal sector	65.3
3.1 Self-employment	62.2
3.2 Wage employment	65.3
3.2.1 Formal sector	43.9
3.2.2 Domestic work	96.3

Annex II

9. Share of informal employment (%) by kind of non-agricultural activity

Share of informal employment in total employment in …	Total	Women	Men
All non-agricultural actitvities	59.6	62.7	57.0
Manufacturing	54.7	67.0	45.2
Construction	76.1	29.2	77.6
Trade	70.3	74.1	66.8
Transportation	70.5	58.9	73.4
Services other than trade or transportation	45.9	53.4	33.3

10. Non-agricultural employment by sex, formal/informal nature and kind of activity (%)

A. Both sexes

Kind of activity	Total	Formal	Informal
All non-agricultural actitvities	100.0	100.0	100.0
Manufacturing	17.7	19.9	16.2
Construction	6.2	3.7	7.9
Trade	32.1	23.6	37.9
Transportation	10.1	7.3	11.9
Services other than trade or transportation	33.9	45.5	26.1

B. Women

Kind of activity	Total	Formal	Informal
All non-agricultural actitvities	100.0	100.0	100.0
Manufacturing	16.6	14.7	17.8
Construction	0.4	0.8	0.2
Trade	33.1	22.9	39.1
Transportation	4.2	4.7	4.0
Services other than trade or transportation	45.6	56.9	38.9

C. Men

Kind of activity	Total	Formal	Informal
All non-agricultural actitvities	100.0	100.0	100.0
Manufacturing	18.7	23.8	14.8
Construction	11.2	5.8	15.2
Trade	31.3	24.1	36.7
Transportation	15.1	9.4	19.4
Services other than trade or transportation	23.7	36.8	13.9

Country: Colombia **Year: 2010 (II)**

Non-agricultural employment

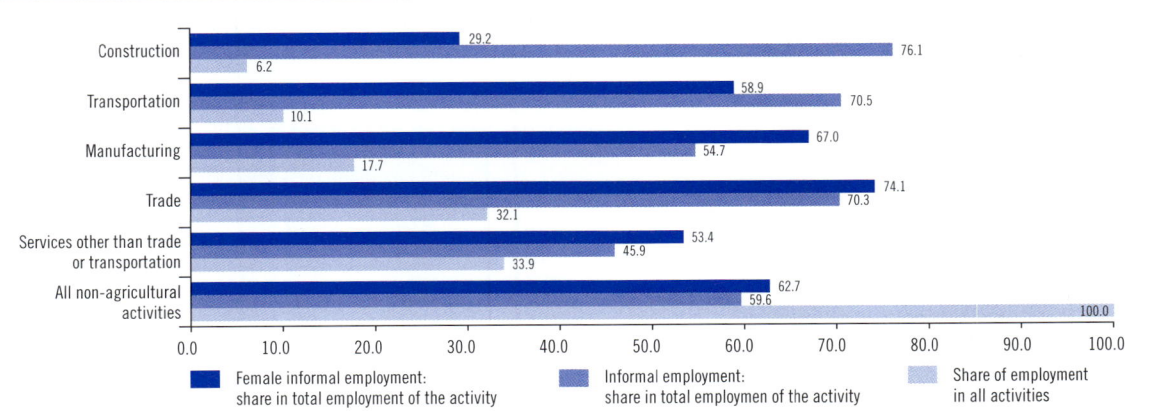

Women and men in the informal economy: A statistical picture

Country: Costa Rica
Year: 2009 (July)

Source: Encuesta de Hogares de Propósitos Múltiples

1. Informal non-agricultural employment and its components

	Total	Women	Men	Urban	Rural
in 1,000					
Persons in informal employment	754.4	322.7	431.7	478.5	275.9
Persons employed in the informal sector	638.1	246.0	392.1	407.2	230.9
Persons in formal employment in the informal sector	76.5	32.4	44.2	48.6	28.0
Persons in informal employment outside the informal sector	192.9	109.1	83.8	119.9	73.0
as % of non-agricultural employment					
Persons in informal employment	43.8	46.0	42.2	40.8	50.0
Persons employed in the informal sector	37.0	35.0	38.4	34.7	41.8
Persons in formal employment in the informal sector	4.4	4.6	4.3	4.1	5.1
Persons in informal employment outside the informal sector	11.2	15.5	8.2	10.2	13.2

2. Employment in the informal sector by status in employment (%)

Status in employment	Total	Women	Men	Urban	Rural
Employers, own-account workers and MPCs*	62.9	63.8	62.3	64.1	60.7
Contributing family workers	3.3	5.6	1.8	2.7	4.3
Employees	33.9	30.6	35.9	33.2	35.0
Total	100.0	100.0	100.0	100.0	100.0

* Members of producers' cooperatives

3. Informal non-agricultural employment by status in employment (%)

Status in employment	Total	Women	Men	Urban	Rural
Employers, own-account workers and MPCs*	53.2	48.6	56.6	54.5	50.8
Owners of informal sector enterprises	53.2	48.6	56.6	54.5	50.8
Producers of goods exclusively for own final use					
Contributing family workers	3.0	4.6	1.8	2.5	3.9
Employees	43.8	46.7	41.6	42.9	45.3
Formal sector employees	14.9	10.9	17.9	15.7	13.7
Informal sector employees	18.5	13.3	22.4	18.1	19.1
Domestic workers employed by households	10.4	22.5	1.3	9.2	12.4
Total	100.0	100.0	100.0	100.0	100.0

* Members of producers' cooperatives

4. Informal non-agricultural self-employment as % of total non-agricultural self-employment by status in employment

Status in employment	Total	Women	Men	Urban	Rural
Employers & members of producers' co-operatives	76.6	82.9	74.7	74.1	82.7
Own-account workers	100.0	100.0	100.0	100.0	100.0
Enterprise owners	100.0	100.0	100.0	100.0	100.0
Total self-employment (incl. contributing family workers)	93.7	97.3	91.5	92.5	96.1

Annex II

5. Informal wage employment as % of total wage employment by type of employees

Type of employees	Total	Women	Men	Urban	Rural
Agricultural employees	39.7	28.9	41.3	31.6	41.5
Non-agricultural employees	26.0	28.7	24.1	23.4	31.6
Formal sector employees	11.7	9.7	13.0	10.9	13.9
Informal sector employees	64.6	57.0	68.6	64.1	65.4
Domestic workers employed by households	81.4	83.0	65.3	81.2	81.7
Total employees	27.4	28.7	26.6	23.7	34.0

6. Informal non-agricultural employment outside the informal sector by type (%)

Type of employment	Total	Women	Men	Urban	Rural
Producers of goods exclusively for own final use					
Contributing family workers: formal sector	1.1	1.1	1.0	1.0	1.2
Employees	98.9	98.9	99.0	99.0	98.8
Employees: formal sector	58.4	32.3	92.4	62.5	51.7
Employees: domestic work	40.5	66.6	6.6	36.5	47.0
Total	100.0	100.0	100.0	100.0	100.0

7. Share of women in employment by type

Share of women in …	%
1. Total employment	37.2
2. Agricultural employment	10.7
2.1 Agricultural wage employment	12.3
2.1.1 Formal agricultural wage employment	14.5
2.1.2 Informal agricultural wage employment	8.9
2.2 Agricultural self-employment	7.9
3. Non-agricultural employment	40.7
3.1 Non-agricultural wage employment*	41.3
3.1.1 Formal non-agricultural wage employment	39.8
3.1.2 Informal non-agricultural wage employment	45.6
3.2 Non-agricultural self-employment	39.1
3.2.1 Formal non-agricultural self-employment	17.0
3.2.2 Informal non-agricultural self-employment	40.5

* = MDG Indicator No. 3.2: Share of women in wage employment in the non-agricultural sector

8. Share of women in informal non-agricultural employment by component

Share of women in …	%
1. Informal employment	42.8
1.1 Self-employment	40.5
1.2. Wage employment	45.6
2. Employment in the informal sector	38.5
2.1 Self-employment	40.5
2.2 Wage employment	34.8
3. Informal employment outside the informal sector	56.6
3.1 Self-employment	59.0
3.2 Wage employment	56.5
3.2.1 Formal sector	31.3
3.2.2 Domestic work	92.9

Women and men in the informal economy: A statistical picture

9. Share of informal employment (%) by kind of non-agricultural activity

Share of informal employment in total employment in ...	Total	Women	Men
All non-agricultural actitvities*	43.7	46.0	42.2
Manufacturing	35.0	45.9	30.3
Construction	62.2	40.5	63.0
Trade	54.8	59.9	51.2
Transportation	48.6	30.3	52.6
Services other than trade or transportation	34.8	39.9	28.2

10. Non-agricultural employment by sex, formal/informal nature and kind of activity (%)

A. Both sexes

Kind of activity	Total	Formal	Informal
All non-agricultural actitvities*	100.0	100.0	100.0
Manufacturing	15.2	17.5	12.1
Construction	7.4	5.0	10.6
Trade	28.8	23.1	36.0
Transportation	8.6	7.9	9.6
Services other than trade or transportation	39.7	46.0	31.5

B. Women

Kind of activity	Total	Formal	Informal
All non-agricultural actitvities*	100.0	100.0	100.0
Manufacturing	11.3	11.3	11.3
Construction	0.6	0.7	0.6
Trade	29.1	21.6	37.9
Transportation	3.8	4.9	2.5
Services other than trade or transportation	54.9	61.1	47.6

C. Men

Kind of activity	Total	Formal	Informal
All non-agricultural actitvities*	100.0	100.0	100.0
Manufacturing	17.8	21.5	12.8
Construction	12.1	7.8	18.1
Trade	28.5	24.1	34.6
Transportation	12.0	9.8	14.9
Services other than trade or transportation	29.2	36.3	19.5

* Including persons with unknown kind of activity.

Country: Costa Rica
Non-agricultural employment

Year: 2009 (July)

Activity	Female informal employment: share in total employment of the activity	Informal employment: share in total employment of the activity	Share of employment in all activities
Construction	40.5	62.2	7.4
Transportation	30.3	48.6	8.6
Manufacturing	45.9	35.0	15.2
Trade	59.9	54.8	28.8
Services other than trade or transportation	39.9	34.8	39.7
All non-agricultural activities*	46.0	43.7	100.0

* Including persons with unknown kind of activity.

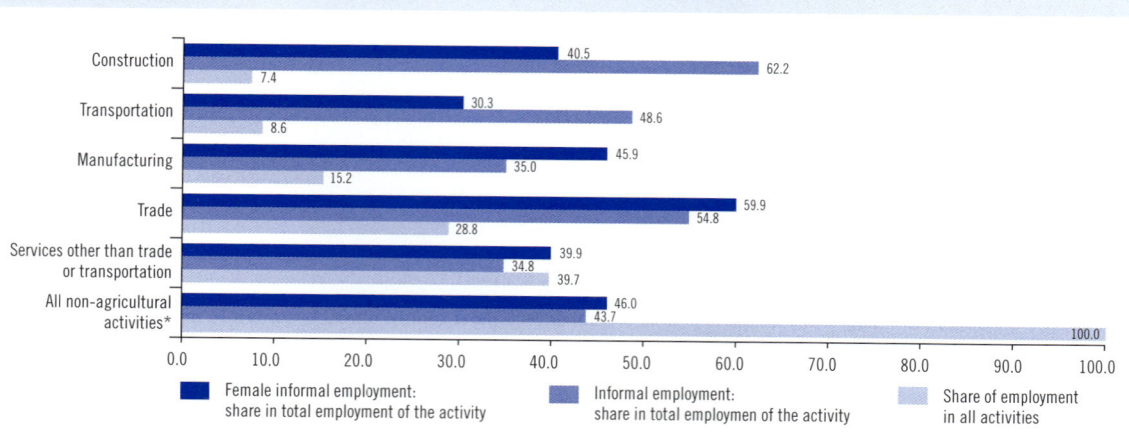

Annex II

Country: Côte d'Ivoire
Source: Enquête sur le Niveau de Vie des Ménages

Year: 2008

1. Informal non-agricultural employment and its components

	Total	Women	Men	Urban	Rural
	in 1,000				
Persons in informal employment					
Persons employed in the informal sector	2'434.4	1'194.3	1'240.1	1'853.0	581.4
Persons in formal employment in the informal sector					
Persons in informal employment outside the informal sector					
	as % of non-agricultural employment				
Persons in informal employment					
Persons employed in the informal sector	69.7	82.8	60.5	69.8	69.6
Persons in formal employment in the informal sector					
Persons in informal employment outside the informal sector					

2. Employment in the informal sector by status in employment (%)

Status in employment	Total	Women	Men	Urban	Rural
Employers, own-account workers and MPCs*	66.9	75.7	58.4	63.5	77.7
Contributing family workers	14.5	11.2	17.6	15.0	12.7
Employees	18.7	13.1	24.0	21.5	9.6
Total	100.0	100.0	100.0	100.0	100.0

* Members of producers' cooperatives

3. Informal non-agricultural employment by status in employment (%)

Status in employment	Total	Women	Men	Urban	Rural
Data not available.					

4. Informal non-agricultural self-employment as % of total non-agricultural self-employment by status in employment

Status in employment	Total	Women	Men	Urban	Rural
Employers & members of producers' co-operatives	83.0	88.5	76.6	86.1	78.3
Own-account workers	88.4	93.6	82.7	91.3	81.2
Enterprise owners	88.4	93.6	82.7	91.3	81.2
Total self-employment (incl. contributing family workers)	90.3	94.0	86.8	92.9	83.3

Women and men in the informal economy: A statistical picture

5. Informal wage employment as % of total wage employment by type of employees

Type of employees	Total	Women	Men	Urban	Rural
Data not available.					

6. Informal non-agricultural employment outside the informal sector by type (%)

Type of employment	Total	Women	Men	Urban	Rural
Data not available.					

7. Share of women in employment by type

Share of women in …	%
1. Total employment	43.9
2. Agricultural employment	45.8
2.1 Agricultural wage employment	15.7
2.1.1 Formal agricultural wage employment	
2.1.2 Informal agricultural wage employment	
2.2 Agricultural self-employment	47.4
3. Non-agricultural employment	41.3
3.1 Non-agricultural wage employment*	25.8
3.1.1 Formal non-agricultural wage employment	
3.1.2 Informal non-agricultural wage employment	
3.2 Non-agricultural self-employment	48.8
3.2.1 Formal non-agricultural self-employment	30.2
3.2.2 Informal non-agricultural self-employment	50.8

* = MDG Indicator No. 3.2: Share of women in wage employment in the non-agricultural sector

8. Share of women in informal non-agricultural employment by component

Share of women in …	%
1. Informal employment	
1.1 Self-employment	
1.2. Wage employment	
2. Employment in the informal sector	49.1
2.1 Self-employment	52.4
2.2 Wage employment	34.4
3. Informal employment outside the informal sector	
3.1 Self-employment	
3.2 Wage employment	
3.2.1 Formal sector	
3.2.2 Domestic work	

9. Share of informal employment (%) by kind of non-agricultural activity

Share of informal employment* in total employment in …	Total	Women	Men
All non-agricultural actitvities	69.7	82.8	60.5
Manufacturing	68.0	78.5	64.7
Construction	73.1	7.8	76.0
Trade	92.5	94.8	87.3
Transportation	66.8	48.5	67.6
Services other than trade or transportation	54.3	67.8	47.2

10. Non-agricultural employment by sex, formal/informal nature and kind of activity (%)

A. Both sexes

Kind of activity	Total	Formal**	Informal*
All non-agricultural actitvities	100.0	100.0	100.0
Manufacturing	14.2	15.0	13.8
Construction	2.4	2.2	2.6
Trade	31.9	7.9	42.3
Transportation	7.0	7.6	6.7
Services other than trade or transportation	44.6	67.3	34.7

B. Women

Kind of activity	Total	Formal**	Informal*
All non-agricultural actitvities	100.0	100.0	100.0
Manufacturing	8.4	10.5	7.9
Construction	0.2	1.3	0.0
Trade	53.5	16.3	61.2
Transportation	0.7	2.1	0.4
Services other than trade or transportation	37.2	69.8	30.5

C. Men

Kind of activity	Total	Formal**	Informal*
All non-agricultural actitvities	100.0	100.0	100.0
Manufacturing	18.3	16.3	19.5
Construction	4.0	2.4	5.0
Trade	16.7	5.4	24.0
Transportation	11.4	9.3	12.7
Services other than trade or transportation	49.7	66.5	38.8

* Informal sector employment   ** Formal sector employment

Country: Côte d'Ivoire

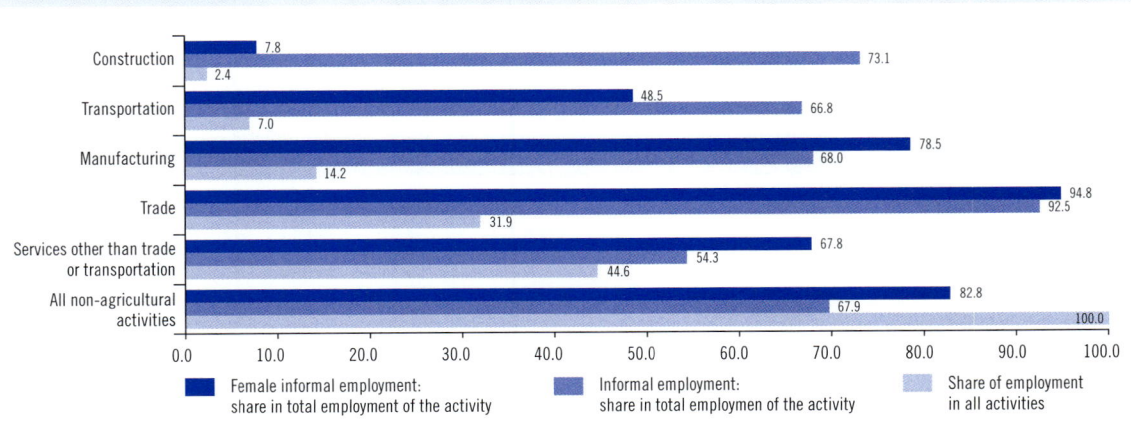

Year: 2008

Non-agricultural employment

Activity	Female informal employment: share in total employment of the activity	Informal employment: share in total employmen of the activity	Share of employment in all activities
Construction	7.8	73.1	2.4
Transportation	48.5	66.8	7.0
Manufacturing	78.5	68.0	14.2
Trade	94.8	92.5	31.9
Services other than trade or transportation	67.8	54.3	44.6
All non-agricultural activities	82.8	67.9	100.0

Women and men in the informal economy: A statistical picture

Country: Dominican Republic

Source: Encuesta de Fuerza de Trabajo

Year: 2009

1. Informal non-agricultural employment and its components

	Total	Women	Men	Urban	Rural
	in 1,000				
Persons in informal employment	1'483.8	614.7	869.0	1'044.5	439.3
Persons employed in the informal sector	898.3	282.5	615.8	616.2	282.1
Persons in formal employment in the informal sector	7.9	3.1	4.9	6.1	1.8
Persons in informal employment outside the informal sector	593.5	335.3	258.2	434.4	159.0
	as % of non-agricultural employment				
Persons in informal employment	48.5	51.4	46.7	45.0	59.5
Persons employed in the informal sector	29.4	23.6	33.1	26.6	38.2
Persons in formal employment in the informal sector	0.3	0.3	0.3	0.3	0.2
Persons in informal employment outside the informal sector	19.4	28.0	13.9	18.7	21.5

2. Employment in the informal sector by status in employment (%)

Status in employment	Total	Women	Men	Urban	Rural
Employers, own-account workers and MPCs*	89.6	85.9	91.3	89.3	90.3
Contributing family workers	2.7	5.6	1.4	2.6	2.9
Employees	7.7	8.5	7.3	8.1	6.8
Total	100.0	100.0	100.0	100.0	100.0

* Members of producers' cooperatives

3. Informal non-agricultural employment by status in employment (%)

Status in employment	Total	Women	Men	Urban	Rural
Employers, own-account workers and MPCs*	54.2	39.5	64.7	52.7	58.0
Owners of informal sector enterprises	54.2	39.5	64.7	52.7	58.0
Producers of goods exclusively for own final use					
Contributing family workers	3.6	5.6	2.2	3.9	3.0
Employees	42.1	54.9	33.1	43.4	39.0
Formal sector employees	24.7	22.5	26.3	26.5	20.6
Informal sector employees	4.1	3.4	4.6	4.2	3.9
Domestic workers employed by households	13.3	29.0	2.1	12.7	14.5
Total	100.0	100.0	100.0	100.0	100.0

* Members of producers' cooperatives

4. Informal non-agricultural self-employment as % of total non-agricultural self-employment by status in employment

Status in employment	Total	Women	Men	Urban	Rural
Employers & members of producers' co-operatives	23.6	28.3	22.1	21.0	40.6
Own-account workers	70.2	74.9	68.4	67.6	76.5
Enterprise owners	70.2	74.9	68.4	67.6	76.5
Total self-employment (incl. contributing family workers)	66.6	73.1	63.9	63.2	75.5

5. Informal wage employment as % of total wage employment by type of employees

Type of employees	Total	Women	Men	Urban	Rural
Agricultural employees	52.3	59.7	51.8	50.7	52.9
Non-agricultural employees	35.3	41.3	30.2	32.7	44.7
Formal sector employees	24.4	22.5	25.8	23.0	30.0
Informal sector employees	88.5	87.2	89.2	87.8	90.4
Domestic workers employed by households	100.0	100.0	100.0	100.0	100.0
Total employees	36.0	41.4	31.7	33.0	45.7

6. Informal non-agricultural employment outside the informal sector by type (%)

Type of employment	Total	Women	Men	Urban	Rural
Producers of goods exclusively for own final use					
Contributing family workers: formal sector	5.0	5.5	4.2	5.7	3.1
Employees	95.0	94.5	95.8	94.3	96.9
Employees: formal sector	61.9	41.2	88.7	63.7	56.8
Employees: domestic work	33.2	53.2	7.1	30.6	40.1
Total	100.0	100.0	100.0	100.0	100.0

7. Share of women in employment by type

Share of women in …	%
1. Total employment	34.0
2. Agricultural employment	4.8
2.1 Agricultural wage employment	5.5
2.1.1 Formal agricultural wage employment	4.7
2.1.2 Informal agricultural wage employment	6.3
2.2 Agricultural self-employment	4.7
3. Non-agricultural employment	39.1
3.1 Non-agricultural wage employment*	46.2
3.1.1 Formal non-agricultural wage employment	41.9
3.1.2 Informal non-agricultural wage employment	54.0
3.2 Non-agricultural self-employment	29.4
3.2.1 Formal non-agricultural self-employment	23.7
3.2.2 Informal non-agricultural self-employment	32.3

* = MDG Indicator No. 3.2: Share of women in wage employment in the non-agricultural sector

8. Share of women in informal non-agricultural employment by component

Share of women in …	%
1. Informal employment	41.4
1.1 Self-employment	32.3
1.2. Wage employment	54.0
2. Employment in the informal sector	31.5
2.1 Self-employment	31.2
2.2 Wage employment	34.8
3. Informal employment outside the informal sector	56.5
3.1 Self-employment	63.2
3.2 Wage employment	56.2
3.2.1 Formal sector	37.6
3.2.2 Domestic work	90.7

Women and men in the informal economy: A statistical picture

9. Share of informal employment (%) by kind of non-agricultural activity

Share of informal employment in total employment in …	Total	Women	Men
All non-agricultural actitvities*	48.5	51.4	46.7
Manufacturing	35.3	31.7	36.6
Construction	74.9	62.4	75.4
Trade	60.5	66.3	57.1
Transportation	44.1	33.1	45.2
Services other than trade or transportation	38.7	47.0	26.3

10. Non-agricultural employment by sex, formal/informal nature and kind of activity (%)

A. Both sexes

Kind of activity	Total	Formal	Informal
All non-agricultural actitvities*	100.0	100.0	100.0
Manufacturing	13.7	17.2	10.0
Construction	7.3	3.6	11.3
Trade	32.7	25.1	40.8
Transportation	9.0	9.8	8.2
Services other than trade or transportation	37.2	44.3	29.7

B. Women

Kind of activity	Total	Formal	Informal
All non-agricultural actitvities*	100.0	100.0	100.0
Manufacturing	9.0	12.7	5.6
Construction	0.6	0.5	0.8
Trade	31.0	21.5	40.0
Transportation	2.1	2.9	1.4
Services other than trade or transportation	57.2	62.3	52.3

C. Men

Kind of activity	Total	Formal	Informal
All non-agricultural actitvities*	100.0	100.0	100.0
Manufacturing	16.7	19.8	13.1
Construction	11.7	5.4	18.8
Trade	33.8	27.2	41.4
Transportation	13.4	13.8	13.0
Services other than trade or transportation	24.4	33.8	13.8

* Including persons with unknown kind of activity.

Country: Dominican Republic   Year: 2009
Non-agricultural employment

- Female informal employment: share in total employment of the activity
- Informal employment: share in total employmen of the activity
- Share of employment in all activities

* Including persons with unknown kind of activity.

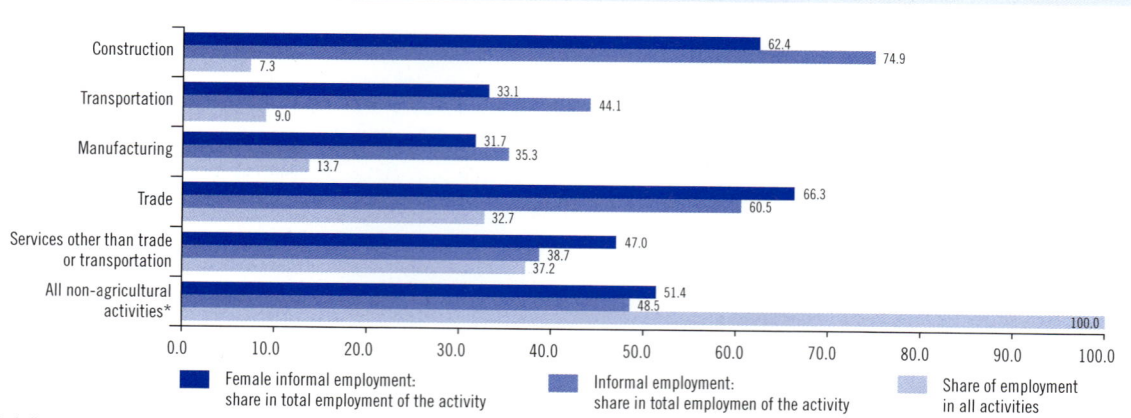

Annex II

Country: Ecuador
Source: Encuesta de Empleo, Desempleo y Subempleo

Year: 2009 (IV)

1. Informal non-agricultural employment and its components

	Total	Women	Men	Urban	Rural
in 1,000					
Persons in informal employment	2'691.4	1'213.9	1'477.4	2'192.1	499.3
Persons employed in the informal sector	1'646.2	681.9	964.3	1'310.8	335.4
Persons in formal employment in the informal sector	17.0	5.1	11.9	11.8	5.2
Persons in informal employment outside the informal sector	1'062.2	537.1	525.0	893.1	169.1
as % of non-agricultural employment					
Persons in informal employment	60.9	63.7	58.8	58.2	76.8
Persons employed in the informal sector	37.3	35.8	38.4	34.8	51.6
Persons in formal employment in the informal sector	0.4	0.3	0.5	0.3	0.8
Persons in informal employment outside the informal sector	24.0	28.2	20.9	23.7	26.0

2. Employment in the informal sector by status in employment (%)

Status in employment	Total	Women	Men	Urban	Rural
Employers, own-account workers and MPCs*	60.8	72.1	52.8	63.8	49.3
Contributing family workers	8.6	13.9	4.9	8.5	9.0
Employees	30.6	14.0	42.3	27.7	41.8
Total	100.0	100.0	100.0	100.0	100.0

* Members of producers' cooperatives

3. Informal non-agricultural employment by status in employment (%)

Status in employment	Total	Women	Men	Urban	Rural
Employers, own-account workers and MPCs*	37.2	40.5	34.5	38.1	33.1
Owners of informal sector enterprises	37.2	40.5	34.5	38.1	33.1
Producers of goods exclusively for own final use					
Contributing family workers	10.3	16.1	5.6	10.8	8.5
Employees	52.5	43.4	59.9	51.1	58.4
Formal sector employees	27.7	22.1	32.3	28.7	23.5
Informal sector employees	18.1	7.5	26.8	16.0	27.0
Domestic workers employed by households	6.7	13.9	0.8	6.4	7.9
Total	100.0	100.0	100.0	100.0	100.0

* Members of producers' cooperatives

4. Informal non-agricultural self-employment as % of total non-agricultural self-employment by status in employment

Status in employment	Total	Women	Men	Urban	Rural
Employers & members of producers' co-operatives	27.7	29.0	27.2	24.2	61.5
Own-account workers	74.3	77.7	71.2	72.7	84.1
Enterprise owners	74.3	77.7	71.2	72.7	84.1
Total self-employment (incl. contributing family workers)	73.4	80.1	66.9	71.4	85.3

Women and men in the informal economy: A statistical picture

5. Informal wage employment as % of total wage employment by type of employees

Type of employees	Total	Women	Men	Urban	Rural
Agricultural employees	87.6	80.6	88.9	76.9	91.8
Non-agricultural employees	52.8	50.3	54.4	49.4	71.7
Formal sector employees	38.0	35.4	39.7	36.2	52.1
Informal sector employees	96.6	94.7	97.1	96.7	96.3
Domestic workers employed by households	85.7	86.2	79.4	83.5	94.5
Total employees	59.7	52.9	63.3	51.5	82.6

6. Informal non-agricultural employment outside the informal sector by type (%)

Type of employment	Total	Women	Men	Urban	Rural
Producers of goods exclusively for own final use					
Contributing family workers: formal sector	12.8	18.7	6.8	13.9	7.3
Employees	87.2	81.3	93.2	86.1	92.7
Employees: formal sector	70.2	49.9	91.0	70.4	69.3
Employees: domestic work	16.9	31.4	2.2	15.7	23.4
Total	100.0	100.0	100.0	100.0	100.0

7. Share of women in employment by type

Share of women in ...	%
1. Total employment	39.6
2. Agricultural employment	31.1
2.1 Agricultural wage employment	14.9
2.1.1 Formal agricultural wage employment	23.4
2.1.2 Informal agricultural wage employment	13.7
2.2 Agricultural self-employment	40.3
3. Non-agricultural employment	43.1
3.1 Non-agricultural wage employment*	39.2
3.1.1 Formal non-agricultural wage employment	41.3
3.1.2 Informal non-agricultural wage employment	37.3
3.2 Non-agricultural self-employment	49.2
3.2.1 Formal non-agricultural self-employment	36.8
3.2.2 Informal non-agricultural self-employment	53.7

* = MDG Indicator No. 3.2: Share of women in wage employment in the non-agricultural sector

8. Share of women in informal non-agricultural employment by component

Share of women in ...	%
1. Informal employment	45.1
1.1 Self-employment	53.7
1.2. Wage employment	37.3
2. Employment in the informal sector	41.4
2.1 Self-employment	51.3
2.2 Wage employment	19.0
3. Informal employment outside the informal sector	50.6
3.1 Self-employment	73.7
3.2 Wage employment	47.2
3.2.1 Formal sector	35.9
3.2.2 Domestic work	93.7

9. Share of informal employment (%) by kind of non-agricultural activity

Share of informal employment in total employment in ...	Total	Women	Men
All non-agricultural actitvities	60.9	63.7	58.8
Manufacturing	60.9	72.0	55.3
Construction	88.5	50.6	90.0
Trade	69.5	75.1	63.4
Transportation	65.7	49.9	68.6
Services other than trade or transportation	41.7	50.9	29.1

10. Non-agricultural employment by sex, formal/informal nature and kind of activity (%)

A. Both sexes

Kind of activity	Total	Formal	Informal
All non-agricultural actitvities	100.0	100.0	100.0
Manufacturing	16.7	16.7	16.7
Construction	9.6	2.8	13.9
Trade	34.5	26.9	39.4
Transportation	8.1	7.1	8.7
Services other than trade or transportation	31.1	46.4	21.3

B. Women

Kind of activity	Total	Formal	Informal
All non-agricultural actitvities	100.0	100.0	100.0
Manufacturing	13.0	10.0	14.7
Construction	0.8	1.1	0.7
Trade	41.7	28.7	49.2
Transportation	2.9	4.1	2.3
Services other than trade or transportation	41.5	56.1	33.2

C. Men

Kind of activity	Total	Formal	Informal
All non-agricultural actitvities	100.0	100.0	100.0
Manufacturing	19.5	21.2	18.4
Construction	16.2	3.9	24.8
Trade	29.1	25.8	31.4
Transportation	12.0	9.2	14.0
Services other than trade or transportation	23.2	39.9	11.5

Country: Ecuador **Year: 2009 (IV)**

Non-agricultural employment

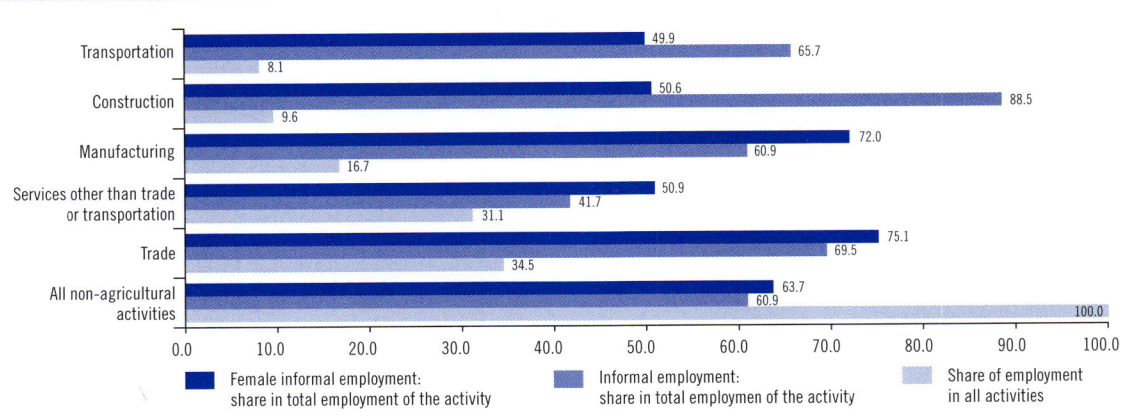

* Including persons with unknown kind of activity.

Women and men in the informal economy: A statistical picture

Country: Egypt
Source: Labour Force Sample Survey

Year: 2009

1. Informal non-agricultural employment and its components

	Total	Women	Men	Urban	Rural
	in 1,000				
Persons in informal employment	8'247.2	572.1	7'675.1		
Persons employed in the informal sector					
Persons in formal employment in the informal sector					
Persons in informal employment outside the informal sector					
	as % of non-agricultural employment				
Persons in informal employment	51.2	23.1	56.3		
Persons employed in the informal sector					
Persons in formal employment in the informal sector					
Persons in informal employment outside the informal sector					

2. Employment in the informal sector by status in employment (%)

Status in employment	Total	Women	Men	Urban	Rural
Data not available.					

3. Informal non-agricultural employment by status in employment (%)

Status in employment	Total	Women	Men	Urban	Rural
Data not available.					

4. Informal non-agricultural self-employment as % of total non-agricultural self-employment by status in employment

Status in employment	Total	Women	Men	Urban	Rural
Data not available.					

5. Informal wage employment as % of total wage employment by type of employees

Type of employees	Total	Women	Men	Urban	Rural
Data not available.					

6. Informal non-agricultural employment outside the informal sector by type (%)

Type of employment	Total	Women	Men	Urban	Rural
Data not available.					

7. Share of women in employment by type

Share of women in …	%
1. Total employment	19.9
2. Agricultural employment	30.6
2.1 Agricultural wage employment	
2.1.1 Formal agricultural wage employment	
2.1.2 Informal agricultural wage employment	
2.2 Agricultural self-employment	
3. Non-agricultural employment	15.3
3.1 Non-agricultural wage employment*	
3.1.1 Formal non-agricultural wage employment	
3.1.2 Informal non-agricultural wage employment	
3.2 Non-agricultural self-employment	
3.2.1 Formal non-agricultural self-employment	
3.2.2 Informal non-agricultural self-employment	

* = MDG Indicator No. 3.2: Share of women in wage employment in the non-agricultural sector

8. Share of women in informal non-agricultural employment by component

Share of women in …	%
1. Informal employment	6.9
1.1 Self-employment	
1.2. Wage employment	
2. Employment in the informal sector	
2.1 Self-employment	
2.2 Wage employment	
3. Informal employment outside the informal sector	
3.1 Self-employment	
3.2 Wage employment	
3.2.1 Formal sector	
3.2.2 Domestic work	

9. Share of informal employment (%) by kind of non-agricultural activity

Share of informal employment in total employment in …	Total	Women	Men
All non-agricultural actitvities	51.2	23.1	56.3
Manufacturing	49.0	48.5	49.0
Construction	92.1	39.6	92.4
Trade	84.4	84.9	84.3
Transportation	77.2	9.9	78.9
Services other than trade or transportation	19.8	11.6	23.0

Women and men in the informal economy: A statistical picture

10. Non-agricultural employment by sex, formal/informal nature and kind of activity (%)

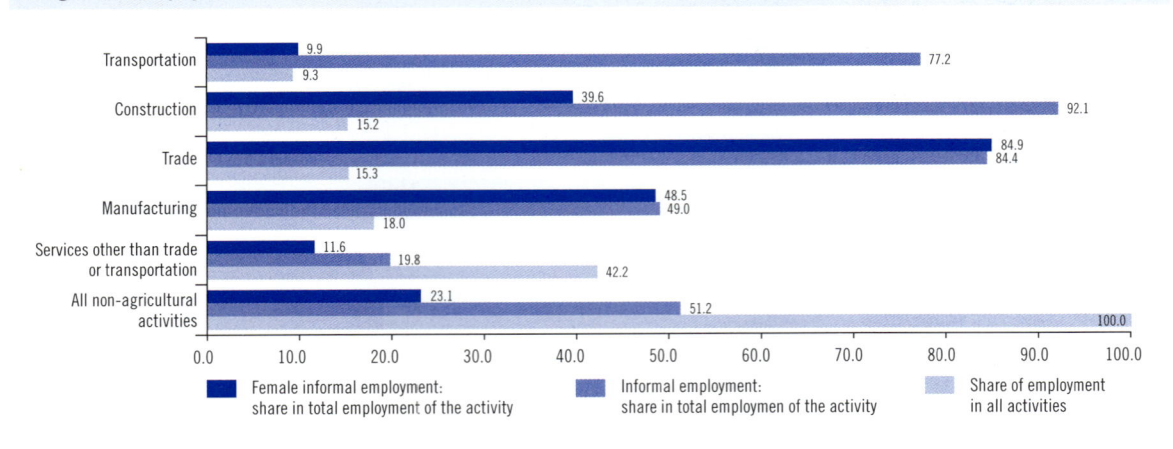

A. Both sexes

Kind of activity	Total	Formal	Informal
All non-agricultural actitvities	100.0	100.0	100.0
Manufacturing	18.0	18.8	17.2
Construction	15.2	2.4	27.3
Trade	15.3	4.9	25.2
Transportation	9.3	4.4	14.0
Services other than trade or transportation	42.2	69.5	16.3

B. Women

Kind of activity	Total	Formal	Informal
All non-agricultural actitvities	100.0	100.0	100.0
Manufacturing	8.5	5.7	17.8
Construction	0.6	0.5	1.0
Trade	11.3	2.2	41.4
Transportation	1.6	1.8	0.7
Services other than trade or transportation	78.1	89.8	39.1

C. Men

Kind of activity	Total	Formal	Informal
All non-agricultural actitvities	100.0	100.0	100.0
Manufacturing	19.7	23.0	17.1
Construction	17.8	3.1	29.2
Trade	16.0	5.7	24.0
Transportation	10.7	5.2	15.0
Services other than trade or transportation	35.8	63.0	14.6

Country: Egypt **Year: 2009**

Non-agricultural employment

Activity	Female informal employment: share in total employment of the activity	Informal employment: share in total employmen of the activity	Share of employment in all activities
Transportation	9.9	77.2	9.3
Construction	39.6	92.1	15.2
Trade	84.9	84.4	15.3
Manufacturing	48.5	49.0	18.0
Services other than trade or transportation	11.6	19.8	42.2
All non-agricultural activities	23.1	51.2	100.0

Country: El Salvador
Source: Encuesta de Hogares de Propósitos Múltiples

Year: 2009

1. Informal non-agricultural employment and its components

	Total	Women	Men	Urban	Rural
in 1,000					
Persons in informal employment	1'241.9	692.9	549.1	932.7	309.2
Persons employed in the informal sector	998.5	555.1	443.4	763.1	235.4
Persons in formal employment in the informal sector	33.1	15.4	17.6	29.7	3.4
Persons in informal employment outside the informal sector	276.5	153.2	123.3	199.4	77.1
as % of non-agricultural employment					
Persons in informal employment	66.4	72.5	60.1	63.0	79.2
Persons employed in the informal sector	53.4	58.1	48.5	51.6	60.3
Persons in formal employment in the informal sector	1.8	1.6	1.9	2.0	0.9
Persons in informal employment outside the informal sector	14.8	16.0	13.5	13.5	19.8

2. Employment in the informal sector by status in employment (%)

Status in employment	Total	Women	Men	Urban	Rural
Employers, own-account workers and MPCs*	62.7	72.2	50.7	63.7	59.4
Contributing family workers	8.7	10.6	6.3	9.0	7.6
Employees	28.7	17.2	43.1	27.3	32.9
Total	100.0	100.0	100.0	100.0	100.0

* Members of producers' cooperatives

3. Informal non-agricultural employment by status in employment (%)

Status in employment	Total	Women	Men	Urban	Rural
Employers, own-account workers and MPCs*	50.4	57.9	40.9	52.1	45.2
Owners of informal sector enterprises	50.4	57.9	40.9	52.1	45.2
Producers of goods exclusively for own final use					
Contributing family workers	7.2	8.7	5.3	7.6	5.9
Employees	42.4	33.5	53.8	40.3	48.8
Formal sector employees	13.3	7.4	20.7	13.4	12.9
Informal sector employees	20.4	11.5	31.6	19.2	24.0
Domestic workers employed by households	8.8	14.5	1.6	7.7	11.9
Total	100.0	100.0	100.0	100.0	100.0

* Members of producers' cooperatives

4. Informal non-agricultural self-employment as % of total non-agricultural self-employment by status in employment

Status in employment	Total	Women	Men	Urban	Rural
Employers & members of producers' co-operatives	90.7	92.9	89.5	89.7	98.3
Own-account workers	99.9	100.0	99.7	99.9	99.7
Enterprise owners	99.9	100.0	99.7	99.9	99.7
Total self-employment (incl. contributing family workers)	99.0	99.6	97.8	98.8	99.7

Women and men in the informal economy: A statistical picture

5. Informal wage employment as % of total wage employment by type of employees

Type of employees	Total	Women	Men	Urban	Rural
Agricultural employees	92.8	89.6	93.1	84.9	95.9
Non-agricultural employees	45.9	47.0	45.1	41.0	65.2
Formal sector employees	22.0	17.4	25.0	19.7	34.3
Informal sector employees	88.4	83.8	90.8	85.8	95.7
Domestic workers employed by households	97.4	98.4	87.1	97.1	98.1
Total employees	53.1	48.8	55.8	43.7	77.3

6. Informal non-agricultural employment outside the informal sector by type (%)

Type of employment	Total	Women	Men	Urban	Rural
Producers of goods exclusively for own final use					
Contributing family workers: formal sector	0.9	0.8	1.0	1.1	0.4
Employees	99.1	99.2	99.0	98.9	99.6
Employees: formal sector	59.7	33.6	92.0	62.7	51.7
Employees: domestic work	39.4	65.6	7.0	36.2	47.9
Total	100.0	100.0	100.0	100.0	100.0

7. Share of women in employment by type

Share of women in …	%
1. Total employment	42.5
2. Agricultural employment	9.7
2.1 Agricultural wage employment	10.3
2.1.1 Formal agricultural wage employment	14.8
2.1.2 Informal agricultural wage employment	9.9
2.2 Agricultural self-employment	9.3
3. Non-agricultural employment	51.1
3.1 Non-agricultural wage employment*	43.0
3.1.1 Formal non-agricultural wage employment	42.1
3.1.2 Informal non-agricultural wage employment	44.0
3.2 Non-agricultural self-employment	64.1
3.2.1 Formal non-agricultural self-employment	24.1
3.2.2 Informal non-agricultural self-employment	64.5

* = MDG Indicator No. 3.2: Share of women in wage employment in the non-agricultural sector

8. Share of women in informal non-agricultural employment by component

Share of women in …	%
1. Informal employment	55.8
1.1 Self-employment	64.5
1.2. Wage employment	44.0
2. Employment in the informal sector	55.6
2.1 Self-employment	64.6
2.2 Wage employment	33.3
3. Informal employment outside the informal sector	55.4
3.1 Self-employment	49.7
3.2 Wage employment	55.4
3.2.1 Formal sector	31.2
3.2.2 Domestic work	92.1

Annex II

9. Share of informal employment (%) by kind of non-agricultural activity

Share of informal employment in total employment in …	Total	Women	Men
All non-agricultural actitvities	66.4	72.5	60.1
Manufacturing	57.1	62.5	51.9
Construction	79.8	43.5	80.8
Trade	82.0	87.6	72.9
Transportation	71.9	30.1	75.5
Services other than trade or transportation	50.4	60.0	37.4

10. Non-agricultural employment by sex, formal/informal nature and kind of activity (%)

A. Both sexes

Kind of activity	Total	Formal	Informal
All non-agricultural actitvities	100.0	100.0	100.0
Manufacturing	19.7	25.1	17.0
Construction	6.4	3.8	7.7
Trade	36.9	19.8	45.5
Transportation	5.4	4.5	5.9
Services other than trade or transportation	31.6	46.7	23.9

B. Women

Kind of activity	Total	Formal	Informal
All non-agricultural actitvities	100.0	100.0	100.0
Manufacturing	18.9	25.7	16.3
Construction	0.3	0.7	0.2
Trade	44.5	20.1	53.8
Transportation	0.9	2.2	0.4
Services other than trade or transportation	35.4	51.4	29.3

C. Men

Kind of activity	Total	Formal	Informal
All non-agricultural actitvities	100.0	100.0	100.0
Manufacturing	20.6	24.7	17.8
Construction	12.7	6.1	17.2
Trade	28.9	19.6	35.0
Transportation	10.2	6.2	12.8
Services other than trade or transportation	27.6	43.3	17.2

Country: El Salvador Year: 2009

Non-agricultural employment

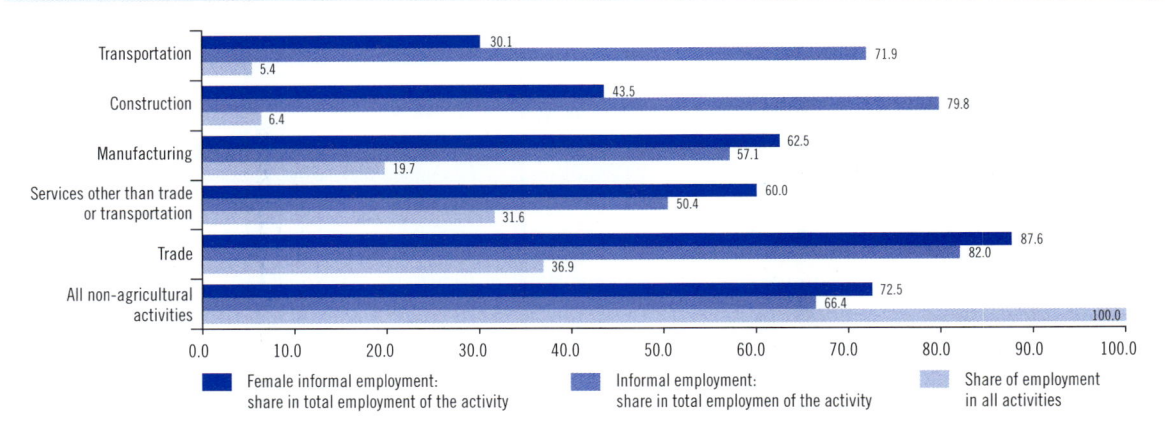

Women and men in the informal economy: A statistical picture

Country: Ethiopia (urban areas) **Year: 2004**

Source: Labour Force Survey

1. Informal non-agricultural employment and its components

	Total	Women	Men	Urban	Rural
in 1,000					
Persons in informal employment					
Persons employed in the informal sector	1'088.6	560.5	528.1	1'088.6	
Persons in formal employment in the informal sector					
Persons in informal employment outside the informal sector					
as % of non-agricultural employment					
Persons in informal employment					
Persons employed in the informal sector	41.4	47.9	36.3	41.4	
Persons in formal employment in the informal sector					
Persons in informal employment outside the informal sector					

2. Employment in the informal sector by status in employment (%)

Status in employment	Total	Women	Men	Urban	Rural
Employers, own-account workers and MPCs*	81.9	82.3	81.4	81.9	
Contributing family workers	10.1	14.5	5.4	10.1	
Employees	8.0	3.1	13.2	8.0	
Total	100.0	100.0	100.0	100.0	

* Members of producers' cooperatives

3. Informal non-agricultural employment by status in employment (%)

Status in employment	Total	Women	Men	Urban	Rural
Data not available.					

4. Informal non-agricultural self-employment as % of total non-agricultural self-employment by status in employment

Status in employment	Total	Women	Men	Urban	Rural
Employers & members of producers' co-operatives)	82.4	90.5	75.1	82.4	
Own-account workers)					
Enterprise owners					
Total self-employment (incl. contributing family workers)	84.6	92.1	77.1	84.6	

5. Informal wage employment as % of total wage employment by type of employees

Type of employees	Total	Women	Men	Urban	Rural
Data not available.					

6. Informal non-agricultural employment outside the informal sector by type (%)

Type of employment	Total	Women	Men	Urban	Rural
Data not available.					

7. Share of women in employment by type

Share of women in ...	%
1. Total employment	43.0
2. Agricultural employment	25.2
2.1 Agricultural wage employment	22.6
2.1.1 Formal agricultural wage employment	
2.1.2 Informal agricultural wage employment	
2.2 Agricultural self-employment	26.0
3. Non-agricultural employment	44.6
3.1 Non-agricultural wage employment*	42.5
3.1.1 Formal non-agricultural wage employment	
3.1.2 Informal non-agricultural wage employment	
3.2 Non-agricultural self-employment	49.7
3.2.1 Formal non-agricultural self-employment	24.7
3.2.2 Informal non-agricultural self-employment	54.2

* = MDG Indicator No. 3.2: Share of women in wage employment in the non-agricultural sector

8. Share of women in informal non-agricultural employment by component

Share of women in ...	%
1. Informal employment	
1.1 Self-employment	
1.2. Wage employment	
2. Employment in the informal sector	51.5
2.1 Self-employment	54.2
2.2 Wage employment	20.1
3. Informal employment outside the informal sector	
3.1 Self-employment	
3.2 Wage employment	
3.2.1 Formal sector	
3.2.2 Domestic work	

9. Share of informal employment (%) by kind of non-agricultural activity

Share of informal employment in total employment in ...	Total	Women	Men
Data not available.			

10. Non-agricultural employment by sex, formal/informal nature and kind of activity (%)

Kind of activity	Total	Formal	Informal
Data not available.			

Women and men in the informal economy: A statistical picture

Country: Honduras
Source: Encuesta Permanente de Hogares de Propósitos Múltiples

Year: 2009

1. Informal non-agricultural employment and its components

	Total	Women	Men	Urban	Rural
in 1,000					
Persons in informal employment	1'453.6	724.5	729.2	907.0	546.7
Persons employed in the informal sector	1'146.4	580.3	566.1	692.1	454.3
Persons in formal employment in the informal sector	26.7	14.0	12.7	22.8	3.9
Persons in informal employment outside the informal sector	334.0	158.1	175.8	237.7	96.3
as % of non-agricultural employment					
Persons in informal employment	73.9	74.8	73.0	68.2	85.6
Persons employed in the informal sector	58.3	59.9	56.6	52.1	71.1
Persons in formal employment in the informal sector	1.4	1.4	1.3	1.7	0.6
Persons in informal employment outside the informal sector	17.0	16.3	17.6	17.9	15.1

2. Employment in the informal sector by status in employment (%)

Status in employment	Total	Women	Men	Urban	Rural
Employers, own-account workers and MPCs*	62.8	71.4	54.0	63.4	61.8
Contributing family workers	13.3	18.2	8.2	12.1	15.1
Employees	23.9	10.4	37.8	24.4	23.1
Total	100.0	100.0	100.0	100.0	100.0

* Members of producers' cooperatives

3. Informal non-agricultural employment by status in employment (%)

Status in employment	Total	Women	Men	Urban	Rural
Employers, own-account workers and MPCs*	49.5	57.2	41.9	48.4	51.4
Owners of informal sector enterprises	49.5	57.2	41.9	48.4	51.4
Producers of goods exclusively for own final use					
Contributing family workers	10.7	14.9	6.5	9.4	12.8
Employees	39.8	27.9	51.6	42.2	35.8
Formal sector employees	18.0	13.0	23.0	21.4	12.4
Informal sector employees	17.0	6.4	27.6	16.1	18.5
Domestic workers employed by households	4.8	8.6	1.0	4.7	4.9
Total	100.0	100.0	100.0	100.0	100.0

* Members of producers' cooperatives

4. Informal non-agricultural self-employment as % of total non-agricultural self-employment by status in employment

Status in employment	Total	Women	Men	Urban	Rural
Employers & members of producers' co-operatives	64.8	66.1	64.1	63.5	70.9
Own-account workers	97.8	98.6	96.7	97.1	98.9
Enterprise owners	97.8	98.6	96.7	97.1	98.9
Total self-employment (incl. contributing family workers)	95.9	97.5	93.6	94.4	98.2

5. Informal wage employment as % of total wage employment by type of employees

Type of employees	Total	Women	Men	Urban	Rural
Agricultural employees	95.3	89.0	95.7	85.8	96.4
Non-agricultural employees	54.8	46.7	60.5	49.4	69.6
Formal sector employees	37.4	31.3	42.1	35.1	45.9
Informal sector employees	90.3	76.8	94.0	86.5	96.3
Domestic workers employed by households	85.2	86.0	78.8	80.1	94.7
Total employees	65.4	48.9	73.2	51.3	84.2

6. Informal non-agricultural employment outside the informal sector by type (%)

Type of employment	Total	Women	Men	Urban	Rural
Producers of goods exclusively for own final use					
Contributing family workers: formal sector	0.8	1.3	0.4	0.6	1.4
Employees	99.2	98.7	99.6	99.4	98.6
Employees: formal sector	78.4	59.5	95.4	81.6	70.7
Employees: domestic work	20.7	39.2	4.1	17.8	27.9
Total	100.0	100.0	100.0	100.0	100.0

7. Share of women in employment by type

Share of women in ...	%
1. Total employment	39.0
2. Agricultural employment	8.3
2.1 Agricultural wage employment	6.3
2.1.1 Formal agricultural wage employment	14.7
2.1.2 Informal agricultural wage employment	5.9
2.2 Agricultural self-employment	11.0
3. Non-agricultural employment	49.2
3.1 Non-agricultural wage employment*	41.1
3.1.1 Formal non-agricultural wage employment	48.5
3.1.2 Informal non-agricultural wage employment	35.0
3.2 Non-agricultural self-employment	58.7
3.2.1 Formal non-agricultural self-employment	35.1
3.2.2 Informal non-agricultural self-employment	59.7

* = MDG Indicator No. 3.2: Share of women in wage employment in the non-agricultural sector

8. Share of women in informal non-agricultural employment by component

Share of women in ...	%
1. Informal employment	49.8
1.1 Self-employment	59.7
1.2. Wage employment	35.0
2. Employment in the informal sector	50.6
2.1 Self-employment	59.6
2.2 Wage employment	22.0
3. Informal employment outside the informal sector	47.3
3.1 Self-employment	72.4
3.2 Wage employment	47.1
3.2.1 Formal sector	35.9
3.2.2 Domestic work	89.5

Women and men in the informal economy: A statistical picture

9. Share of informal employment (%) by kind of non-agricultural activity

Share of informal employment in total employment in …	Total	Women	Men
All non-agricultural actitvities*	73.9	74.8	73.0
Manufacturing	70.6	76.8	64.2
Construction	93.1	52.5	93.9
Trade	83.3	87.0	78.0
Transportation	75.9	31.1	81.8
Services other than trade or transportation	56.7	60.4	50.8

10. Non-agricultural employment by sex, formal/informal nature and kind of activity (%)

A. Both sexes

Kind of activity	Total	Formal	Informal
All non-agricultural actitvities*	100.0	100.0	100.0
Manufacturing	21.9	24.6	20.9
Construction	10.4	2.7	13.1
Trade	35.1	22.4	39.5
Transportation	5.3	4.9	5.4
Services other than trade or transportation	27.3	45.2	21.0

B. Women

Kind of activity	Total	Formal	Informal
All non-agricultural actitvities*	100.0	100.0	100.0
Manufacturing	22.5	20.7	23.1
Construction	0.4	0.8	0.3
Trade	41.8	21.5	48.6
Transportation	1.3	3.5	0.5
Services other than trade or transportation	34.0	53.4	27.5

C. Men

Kind of activity	Total	Formal	Informal
All non-agricultural actitvities*	100.0	100.0	100.0
Manufacturing	21.3	28.1	18.7
Construction	20.1	4.5	25.8
Trade	28.6	23.2	30.5
Transportation	9.2	6.2	10.3
Services other than trade or transportation	20.8	37.8	14.5

* Including persons with unknown kind of activity.

Country: Honduras
Non-agricultural employment
Year: 2009

- Female informal employment: share in total employment of the activity
- Informal employment: share in total employmen of the activity
- Share of employment in all activities

* Including persons with unknown kind of activity.

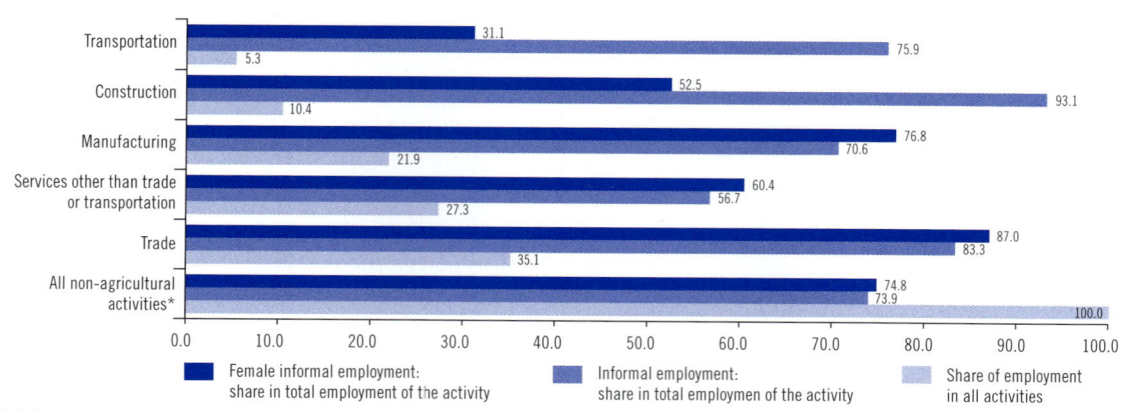

Annex II

Country: India
Source: National Sample Survey, 66th Round

Year: 2009–2010

1. Informal non-agricultural employment and its components

	Total	Women	Men	Urban	Rural
in 1,000					
Persons in informal employment	185'876.3	34'921.4	150'954.9	90'800.4	95'075.9
Persons employed in the informal sector	150'113.1	24'474.6	125'638.5	72'961.9	77'151.1
Persons in formal employment in the informal sector	1'645.5	346.5	1'299.0	1'196.8	448.7
Persons in informal employment outside the informal sector	37'408.7	10'793.3	26'615.4	19'035.3	18'373.4
as % of non-agricultural employment					
Persons in informal employment	83.6	84.7	83.3	77.5	90.3
Persons employed in the informal sector	67.5	59.4	69.4	62.3	73.3
Persons in formal employment in the informal sector	0.7	0.8	0.7	1.0	0.4
Persons in informal employment outside the informal sector	16.8	26.2	14.7	16.3	17.5

2. Employment in the informal sector by status in employment (%)

Status in employment	Total	Women	Men	Urban	Rural
Employers, own-account workers and MPCs*	47.0	41.2	48.1	48.9	45.1
Contributing family workers	11.2	26.5	8.2	11.7	10.7
Employees	41.9	32.3	43.7	39.4	44.1
Total	100.0	100.0	100.0	100.0	100.0

* Members of producers' cooperatives

3. Informal non-agricultural employment by status in employment (%)

Status in employment	Total	Women	Men	Urban	Rural
Employers, own-account workers and MPCs*	37.9	28.9	40.0	39.3	36.6
Owners of informal sector enterprises	37.9	28.9	40.0	39.3	36.6
Producers of goods exclusively for own final use					
Contributing family workers	9.3	18.9	7.1	9.8	8.9
Employees	52.8	52.3	52.9	50.9	54.5
Formal sector employees	17.8	24.1	16.3	17.6	18.0
Informal sector employees	32.9	21.7	35.5	30.4	35.3
Domestic workers employed by households	2.1	6.5	1.1	3.0	1.2
Total	100.0	100.0	100.0	100.0	100.0

* Members of producers' cooperatives

4. Informal non-agricultural self-employment as % of total non-agricultural self-employment by status in employment

Status in employment	Total	Women	Men	Urban	Rural
Employers & members of producers' co-operatives	86.1	90.0	85.9	85.5	88.7
Own-account workers	96.8	96.3	96.9	96.2	97.5
Enterprise owners	96.8	96.3	96.9	96.2	97.5
Total self-employment (incl. contributing family workers)	97.1	97.7	96.9	96.4	97.8

Women and men in the informal economy: A statistical picture

5. Informal wage employment as % of total wage employment by type of employees

Type of employees	Total	Women	Men	Urban	Rural
Agricultural employees	99.9	100.0	99.8	98.1	99.9
Non-agricultural employees	74.3	75.5	74.1	65.2	84.9
Formal sector employees	50.6	60.2	48.0	40.6	66.0
Informal sector employees	97.4	95.6	97.6	95.8	98.7
Domestic workers employed by households	100.0	100.0	100.0	100.0	100.0
Total employees	84.9	89.9	83.1	66.9	93.8

6. Informal non-agricultural employment outside the informal sector by type (%)

Type of employment	Total	Women	Men	Urban	Rural
Producers of goods exclusively for own final use					
Contributing family workers: formal sector	1.3	0.9	1.5	1.9	0.7
Employees	98.7	99.1	98.5	98.1	99.3
Employees: formal sector	88.4	78.1	92.5	84.0	92.9
Employees: domestic work	10.3	21.0	6.0	14.1	6.4
Total	100.0	100.0	100.0	100.0	100.0

7. Share of women in employment by type

Share of women in ...	%
1. Total employment	27.4
2. Agricultural employment	35.9
2.1 Agricultural wage employment	37.2
2.1.1 Formal agricultural wage employment	3.1
2.1.2 Informal agricultural wage employment	37.3
2.2 Agricultural self-employment	35.0
3. Non-agricultural employment	18.5
3.1 Non-agricultural wage employment*	18.3
3.1.1 Formal non-agricultural wage employment	17.5
3.1.2 Informal non-agricultural wage employment	18.6
3.2 Non-agricultural self-employment	18.9
3.2.1 Formal non-agricultural self-employment	14.9
3.2.2 Informal non-agricultural self-employment	19.0

* = MDG Indicator No. 3.2: Share of women in wage employment in the non-agricultural sector

8. Share of women in informal non-agricultural employment by component

Share of women in ...	%
1. Informal employment	18.8
1.1 Self-employment	19.0
1.2 Wage employment	18.6
2. Employment in the informal sector	16.3
2.1 Self-employment	19.0
2.2 Wage employment	12.6
3. Informal employment outside the informal sector	28.9
3.1 Self-employment	20.2
3.2 Wage employment	29.0
3.2.1 Formal sector	25.5
3.2.2 Domestic work	58.8

9. Share of informal employment (%) by kind of non-agricultural activity

Share of informal employment in total employment in …	Total	Women	Men
All non-agricultural actitvities	83.6	84.7	83.3
Manufacturing	87.1	94.1	84.5
Construction	97.6	99.3	97.3
Trade	97.2	97.9	97.2
Transportation	84.5	65.9	85.0
Services other than trade or transportation	59.9	67.0	57.3

10. Non-agricultural employment by sex, formal/informal nature and kind of activity (%)

A. Both sexes

Kind of activity	Total	Formal	Informal
All non-agricultural acttivities	100.0	100.0	100.0
Manufacturing	23.4	18.4	24.4
Construction	19.8	2.9	23.1
Trade	20.5	3.5	23.9
Transportation	9.3	8.8	9.4
Services other than trade or transportation	25.1	61.2	18.0

B. Women

Kind of activity	Total	Formal	Informal
All non-agricultural acttivities	100.0	100.0	100.0
Manufacturing	34.0	13.1	37.8
Construction	15.4	0.7	18.1
Trade	11.3	1.6	13.1
Transportation	1.3	2.9	1.0
Services other than trade or transportation	36.9	79.5	29.2

C. Men

Kind of activity	Total	Formal	Informal
All non-agricultural acttivities	100.0	100.0	100.0
Manufacturing	21.0	19.6	21.3
Construction	20.8	3.3	24.3
Trade	22.6	3.9	26.4
Transportation	11.1	10.1	11.4
Services other than trade or transportation	22.4	57.4	15.4

Country: India
Non-agricultural employment

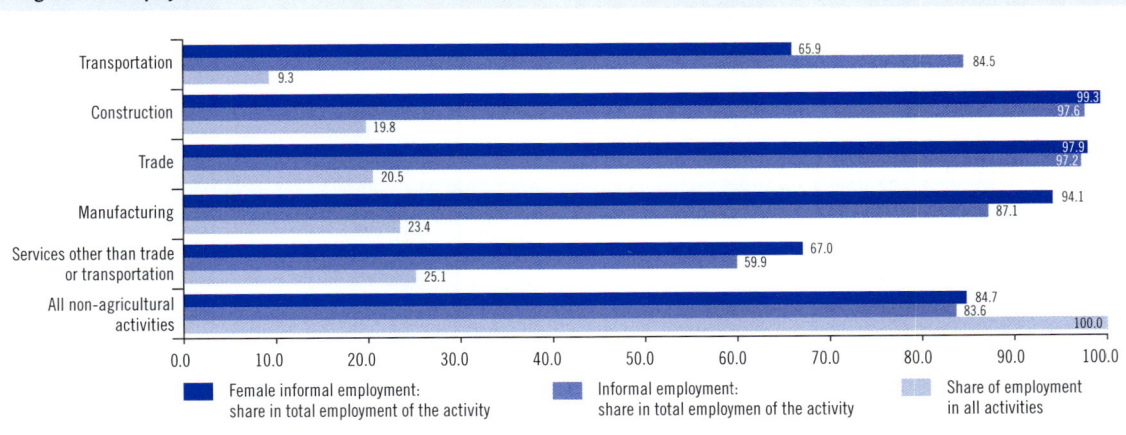

Year: 2009–2010

Women and men in the informal economy: A statistical picture

Country: Indonesia (Banten and Yogyakarta)   Year: 2009
Source: Informal Sector Survey

1. Informal non-agricultural employment and its components

	Total	Women	Men	Urban	Rural
in 1,000					
Persons in informal employment	3'156.8	1'179.6	1'977.2	2'120.0	1'036.8
Persons employed in the informal sector	2'620.5	1'034.2	1'787.5	1'855.7	966.0
Persons in formal employment in the informal sector	196.6	81.5	115.2	141.0	55.6
Persons in informal employment outside the informal sector	531.8	226.9	304.8	405.3	126.5
as % of non-agricultural employment					
Persons in informal employment	72.5	72.9	72.3	67.6	85.1
Persons employed in the informal sector	60.2	63.9	65.4	59.2	79.3
Persons in formal employment in the informal sector	4.5	5.0	4.2	4.5	4.6
Persons in informal employment outside the informal sector	12.2	14.0	11.1	12.9	10.4

2. Employment in the informal sector by status in employment (%)

Status in employment	Total	Women	Men	Urban	Rural
Employers, own-account workers and MPCs*	47.2	45.4	43.0	45.4	40.8
Contributing family workers	11.6	21.3	4.7	12.0	8.5
Employees	48.8	33.4	52.3	42.6	50.6
Total	100.0	100.0	100.0	100.0	100.0

* Members of producers' cooperatives

3. Informal non-agricultural employment by status in employment (%)

Status in employment	Total	Women	Men	Urban	Rural
Employers, own-account workers and MPCs*	39.4	40.2	38.9	39.8	38.4
Owners of informal sector enterprises	39.2	39.8	38.9	39.8	38.0
Producers of goods exclusively for own final use	0.2	0.5	0.0	0.1	0.4
Contributing family workers	9.8	19.0	4.3	10.7	7.9
Employees	50.8	40.8	56.9	49.5	53.6
Formal sector employees	13.4	11.1	14.7	15.0	10.1
Informal sector employees	34.3	22.3	41.4	30.6	41.8
Domestic workers employed by households	3.2	7.3	0.7	3.9	1.7
Total	100.0	100.0	100.0	100.0	100.0

* Members of producers' cooperatives

4. Informal non-agricultural self-employment as % of total non-agricultural self-employment by status in employment

Status in employment	Total	Women	Men	Urban	Rural
Employers & members of producers' co-operatives	94.9	97.0	93.3	93.4	98.2
Own-account workers	99.1	98.7	99.4	99.4	98.5
Enterprise owners	99.1	98.6	99.4	99.4	98.5
Total self-employment (incl. contributing family workers)	98.2	98.7	97.8	97.9	98.7

5. Informal wage employment as % of total wage employment by type of employees

Type of employees	Total	Women	Men	Urban	Rural
Agricultural employees	95.8	95.6	95.8	100.0	94.6
Non-agricultural employees	57.9	52.8	60.4	51.4	76.0
Formal sector employees	30.4	27.6	31.9	27.2	46.9
Informal sector employees	84.6	76.4	87.7	82.2	88.6
Domestic workers employed by households	96.8	96.2	100.0	97.6	92.9
Total employees	62.1	57.1	64.5	53.2	81.0

6. Informal non-agricultural employment outside the informal sector by type (%)

Type of employment	Total	Women	Men	Urban	Rural
Producers of goods exclusively for own final use	1.0	2.4	0.0	0.3	3.2
Contributing family workers: formal sector	0.8	1.8	0.0	1.0	0.0
Employees	98.2	95.8	100.0	98.7	96.8
Employees: formal sector	79.4	57.9	95.4	78.4	82.7
Employees: domestic work	18.8	37.8	4.6	20.2	14.1
Total	100.0	100.0	100.0	100.0	100.0

7. Share of women in employment by type

Share of women in …	%
1. Total employment	37.4
2. Agricultural employment	38.2
2.1 Agricultural wage employment	29.3
2.1.1 Formal agricultural wage employment	30.6
2.1.2 Informal agricultural wage employment	29.3
2.2 Agricultural self-employment	41.2
3. Non-agricultural employment	37.2
3.1 Non-agricultural wage employment*	32.9
3.1.1 Formal non-agricultural wage employment	36.8
3.1.2 Informal non-agricultural wage employment	30.0
3.2 Non-agricultural self-employment	44.8
3.2.1 Formal non-agricultural self-employment	33.0
3.2.2 Informal non-agricultural self-employment	45.0

* = MDG Indicator No. 3.2: Share of women in wage employment in the non-agricultural sector

8. Share of women in informal non-agricultural employment by component

Share of women in …	%
1. Informal employment	37.4
1.1 Self-employment	45.0
1.2. Wage employment	30.0
2. Employment in the informal sector	39.5
2.1 Self-employment	44.7
2.2 Wage employment	27.0
3. Informal employment outside the informal sector	42.7
3.1 Self-employment	100.0
3.2 Wage employment	41.6
3.2.1 Formal sector	31.1
3.2.2 Domestic work	86.0

Women and men in the informal economy: A statistical picture

9. Share of informal employment (%) by kind of non-agricultural activity

Share of informal employment in total employment in ...	Total	Women	Men
All non-agricultural actitvities	72.5	72.9	72.3
Manufacturing	56.5	50.4	60.3
Construction	91.9	60.9	92.5
Trade	90.9	92.4	89.6
Transportation	77.9	65.3	79.2
Services other than trade or transportation	65.8	73.4	59.9

10. Non-agricultural employment by sex, formal/informal nature and kind of activity (%)

A. Both sexes

Kind of activity	Total	Formal	Informal
All non-agricultural actitvities	100.0	100.0	100.0
Manufacturing	26.3	41.7	20.5
Construction	7.0	2.1	8.9
Trade	24.6	8.1	30.8
Transportation	9.6	7.7	10.3
Services other than trade or transportation	32.5	40.4	29.5

B. Women

Kind of activity	Total	Formal	Informal
All non-agricultural actitvities	100.0	100.0	100.0
Manufacturing	27.3	49.9	18.9
Construction	0.4	0.5	0.3
Trade	31.5	8.8	39.9
Transportation	2.5	3.2	2.2
Services other than trade or transportation	38.4	37.7	38.7

C. Men

Kind of activity	Total	Formal	Informal
All non-agricultural actitvities	100.0	100.0	100.0
Manufacturing	25.8	36.9	21.5
Construction	10.9	3.0	14.0
Trade	20.5	7.7	25.4
Transportation	13.8	10.3	15.1
Services other than trade or transportation	29.0	42.0	24.0

Country: Indonesia (Bantan and Yogyakarta)   Year: 2009
Non-agricultural employment

Activity	Female informal employment: share in total employment of the activity	Informal employment: share in total employmen of the activity	Share of employment in all activities
Construction	60.9	91.9	7.0
Transportation	65.3	77.9	9.6
Trade	92.4	90.9	24.6
Manufacturing	50.4	56.5	26.3
Services other than trade or transportation	73.4	65.8	32.5
All non-agricultural activities	72.9	72.5	100.0

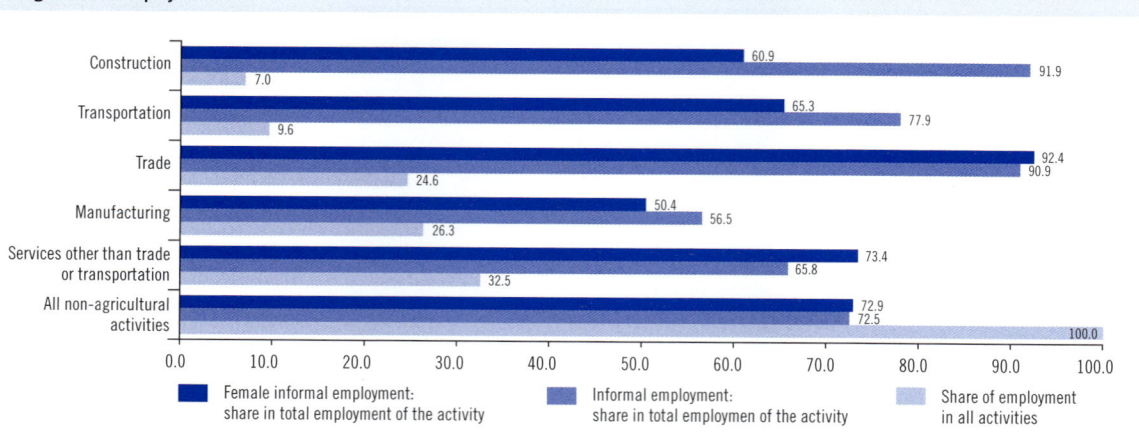

Country: Kyrgyzstan
Source: Labour Force Survey

Year: 2009

1. Informal non-agricultural employment and its components

	Total	Women	Men	Urban	Rural
in 1,000					
Persons in informal employment					
Persons employed in the informal sector	886.8	321.0	565.8	400.3	486.5
Persons in formal employment in the informal sector	43.7	21.3	22.5	8.5	35.3
Persons in informal employment outside the informal sector					
as % of non-agricultural employment					
Persons in informal employment					
Persons employed in the informal sector	59.2	50.7	65.4	54.7	63.5
Persons in formal employment in the informal sector	2.9	3.4	2.6	1.2	4.6
Persons in informal employment outside the informal sector					

2. Employment in the informal sector by status in employment (%)

Status in employment	Total	Women	Men	Urban	Rural
Employers, own-account workers and MPCs*	35.2	35.6	35.0	35.9	34.7
Contributing family workers	0.0	0.0	0.1	0.0	0.1
Employees	64.7	64.4	64.9	64.1	65.2
Total	100.0	100.0	100.0	100.0	100.0

* Members of producers' cooperatives

3. Informal non-agricultural employment by status in employment (%)

Status in employment	Total	Women	Men	Urban	Rural
Data not available.					

4. Informal non-agricultural self-employment as % of total non-agricultural self-employment by status in employment

Status in employment	Total	Women	Men	Urban	Rural
Employers & members of producers' co-operatives	95.1	97.5	95.1	98.9	85.3
Own-account workers	100.0	100.0	100.0	100.0	100.0
Enterprise owners	100.0	100.0	100.0	100.0	100.0
Total self-employment (incl. contributing family workers)	99.8	99.9	99.8	99.9	99.7

Women and men in the informal economy: A statistical picture

5. Informal wage employment as % of total wage employment by type of employees

Type of employees	Total	Women	Men	Urban	Rural
Agricultural employees	78.1	85.8	75.6	73.3	79.5
Non-agricultural employees					
Formal sector employees					
Informal sector employees	92.4	89.7	93.9	96.7	88.9
Domestic workers employed by households					
Total employees					

6. Informal non-agricultural employment outside the informal sector by type (%)

Type of employment	Total	Women	Men	Urban	Rural
Data not available.					

7. Share of women in employment by type

Share of women in ...	%
1. Total employment	41.7
2. Agricultural employment	40.6
2.1 Agricultural wage employment	24.9
2.1.1 Formal agricultural wage employment	16.2
2.1.2 Informal agricultural wage employment	27.4
2.2 Agricultural self-employment	41.6
3. Non-agricultural employment	42.3
3.1 Non-agricultural wage employment*	43.8
3.1.1 Formal non-agricultural wage employment	
3.1.2 Informal non-agricultural wage employment	
3.2 Non-agricultural self-employment	36.5
3.2.1 Formal non-agricultural self-employment	16.7
3.2.2 Informal non-agricultural self-employment	36.5

* = MDG Indicator No. 3.2: Share of women in wage employment in the non-agricultural sector

8. Share of women in informal non-agricultural employment by component

Share of women in ...	%
1. Informal employment	
1.1 Self-employment	
1.2. Wage employment	
2. Employment in the informal sector	36.2
2.1 Self-employment	36.5
2.2 Wage employment	36.0
3. Informal employment outside the informal sector	
3.1 Self-employment	
3.2 Wage employment	
3.2.1 Formal sector	
3.2.2 Domestic work	

Annex II

9. Share of informal employment (%) by kind of non-agricultural activity

Share of informal employment* in total employment in …	Total	Women	Men
All non-agricultural actitvities	56.3	47.4	62.8
Manufacturing	50.6	68.3	38.9
Construction	83.7	70.4	84.3
Trade	92.9	94.1	91.7
Transportation	70.0	11.8	77.7
Services other than trade or transportation	22.8	22.0	24.2

10. Non-agricultural employment by sex, formal/informal nature and kind of activity (%)

A. Both sexes

Kind of activity	Total	Formal**	Informal*
All non-agricultural actitvities	100.0	100.0	100.0
Manufacturing	15.1	17.1	13.6
Construction	16.3	6.1	24.2
Trade	21.1	3.4	34.8
Transportation	9.7	6.6	12.0
Services other than trade or transportation	37.8	66.8	15.3

B. Women

Kind of activity	Total	Formal**	Informal*
All non-agricultural actitvities	100.0	100.0	100.0
Manufacturing	14.2	8.6	20.5
Construction	1.7	1.0	2.5
Trade	25.3	2.8	50.3
Transportation	2.7	4.5	0.7
Services other than trade or transportation	56.2	83.2	26.1

C. Men

Kind of activity	Total	Formal**	Informal*
All non-agricultural actitvities	100.0	100.0	100.0
Manufacturing	15.7	25.9	9.8
Construction	27.0	11.4	36.2
Trade	18.0	4.0	26.4
Transportation	14.8	8.9	18.3
Services other than trade or transportation	24.4	49.8	9.4

* Informal sector employment   ** Formal sector employment

Country: Kyrgyztan   Year: 2009
Non-agricultural employment

- Female informal employment: share in total employment of the activity
- Informal employment: share in total employmen of the activity
- Share of employment in all activities

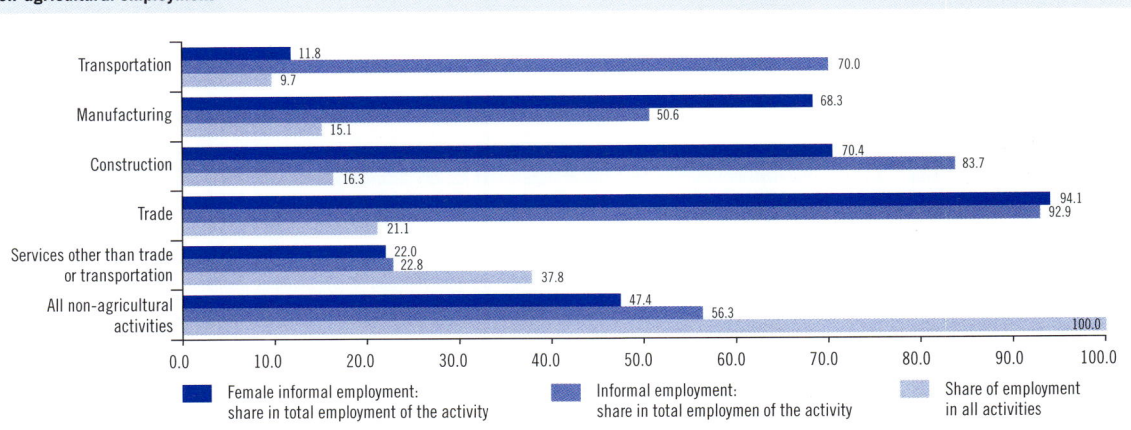

Women and men in the informal economy: A statistical picture

Country: Lesotho
Source: Lesotho Integrated Labour Force Survey

Year: 2008

1. Informal non-agricultural employment and its components

	Total	Women	Men	Urban	Rural
in 1,000					
Persons in informal employment	160.1	70.5	89.6		
Persons employed in the informal sector	225.2	94.0	131.2		
Persons in formal employment in the informal sector	164.0	69.8	94.1		
Persons in informal employment outside the informal sector	98.9	46.4	52.6		
as % of non-agricultural employment					
Persons in informal employment	34.9	36.1	34.1		
Persons employed in the informal sector	49.1	48.1	49.9		
Persons in formal employment in the informal sector	35.8	35.8	35.8		
Persons in informal employment outside the informal sector	21.6	23.7	20.0		

2. Employment in the informal sector by status in employment (%)

Status in employment	Total	Women	Men	Urban	Rural
Employers, own-account workers and MPCs*	5.4	6.4	4.6		
Contributing family workers	1.3	1.3	1.2		
Employees	93.4	92.3	94.1		
Total	100.0	100.0	100.0		

* Members of producers' cooperatives

3. Informal non-agricultural employment by status in employment (%)

Status in employment	Total	Women	Men	Urban	Rural
Employers, own-account workers and MPCs*	7.6	8.6	6.8		
Owners of informal sector enterprises	7.6	8.6	6.8		
Producers of goods exclusively for own final use					
Contributing family workers	2.5	2.7	2.4		
Employees	89.9	88.8	90.8		
Formal sector employees	16.8	14.1	19.0		
Informal sector employees	28.9	24.0	32.8		
Domestic workers employed by households	44.1	50.7	39.0		
Total	100.0	100.0	100.0		

* Members of producers' cooperatives

4. Informal non-agricultural self-employment as % of total non-agricultural self-employment by status in employment

Status in employment	Total	Women	Men	Urban	Rural
Employers & members of producers' co-operatives	59.3	60.8	58.6		
Own-account workers	75.4	78.2	72.6		
Enterprise owners	75.4	78.2	72.6		
Total self-employment (incl. contributing family workers)	78.5	81.2	76.1		

5. Informal wage employment as % of total wage employment by type of employees

Type of employees	Total	Women	Men	Urban	Rural
Agricultural employees	67.6	66.9	67.7		
Non-agricultural employees	32.9	33.7	32.3		
Formal sector employees	18.8	16.7	20.3		
Informal sector employees	22.0	19.5	23.8		
Domestic workers employed by households	84.3	91.5	78.1		
Total employees	35.0	34.3	35.5		

6. Informal non-agricultural employment outside the informal sector by type (%)

Type of employment	Total	Women	Men	Urban	Rural
Producers of goods exclusively for own final use					
Contributing family workers: formal sector	1.3	1.4	1.1		
Employees	98.7	98.6	98.9		
Employees: formal sector	27.3	21.5	32.4		
Employees: domestic work	71.5	77.1	66.5		
Total	100.0	100.0	100.0		

7. Share of women in employment by type

Share of women in …	%
1. Total employment	42.2
2. Agricultural employment	41.7
2.1 Agricultural wage employment	10.9
2.1.1 Formal agricultural wage employment	11.2
2.1.2 Informal agricultural wage employment	10.8
2.2 Agricultural self-employment	45.1
3. Non-agricultural employment	42.6
3.1 Non-agricultural wage employment*	42.4
3.1.1 Formal non-agricultural wage employment	41.8
3.1.2 Informal non-agricultural wage employment	43.5
3.2 Non-agricultural self-employment	47.4
3.2.1 Formal non-agricultural self-employment	41.5
3.2.2 Informal non-agricultural self-employment	49.0

* = MDG Indicator No. 3.2: Share of women in wage employment in the non-agricultural sector

8. Share of women in informal non-agricultural employment by component

Share of women in …	%
1. Informal employment	44.0
1.1 Self-employment	49.0
1.2. Wage employment	43.5
2. Employment in the informal sector	41.7
2.1 Self-employment	48.6
2.2 Wage employment	41.2
3. Informal employment outside the informal sector	46.9
3.1 Self-employment	53.9
3.2 Wage employment	46.8
3.2.1 Formal sector	36.9
3.2.2 Domestic work	50.5

Women and men in the informal economy: A statistical picture

9. Share of informal employment (%) by kind of non-agricultural activity

Share of informal employment* in total employment in …	Total	Women	Men
Data not available.			

10. Non-agricultural employment by sex, formal/informal nature and kind of activity (%)

Kind of activity	Total	Formal	Informal
Data not available.			

Country: Liberia

Source: Labour Force Survey

Year: 2010

1. Informal non-agricultural employment and its components

	Total	Women	Men	Urban	Rural
in 1,000					
Persons in informal employment	343	206	136	241	102
Persons employed in the informal sector	284	188	96	196	88
Persons in formal employment in the informal sector	2	0	2	1	0
Persons in informal employment outside the informal sector	62	19	42	46	14
as % of non-agricultural employment					
Persons in informal employment	60.0	72.0	47.4	59.4	61.4
Persons employed in the informal sector	49.7	65.7	33.4	48.3	53.0
Persons in formal employment in the informal sector	0.3	0.0	0.7	0.2	0.0
Persons in informal employment outside the informal sector	10.8	6.6	14.6	11.3	8.4

2. Employment in the informal sector by status in employment (%)

Status in employment	Total	Women	Men	Urban	Rural
Employers, own-account workers and MPCs*	85.9	88.3	80.2	87.2	84.1
Contributing family workers	8.8	9.6	8.3	7.7	11.4
Employees	4.9	1.6	11.5	5.1	4.5
Total	100.0	100.0	100.0	100.0	100.0

* Members of producers' cooperatives

3. Informal non-agricultural employment by status in employment (%)

Status in employment	Total	Women	Men	Urban	Rural
Employers, own-account workers and MPCs*	71.1	80.6	56.6	71.0	72.5
Owners of informal sector enterprises	71.1	80.6	56.6	71.0	72.5
Producers of goods exclusively for own final use					
Contributing family workers	11.4	11.7	11.8	10.0	14.7
Employees	17.5	7.8	31.6	19.1	12.7
Formal sector employees	12.0	4.9	22.1	12.4	7.8
Informal sector employees	3.5	1.5	6.6	3.7	3.9
Domestic workers employed by households	2.0	1.5	2.9	2.9	1.0
Total	100.0	100.0	100.0	100.0	100.0

* Members of producers' cooperatives

4. Informal non-agricultural self-employment as % of total non-agricultural self-employment by status in employment

Status in employment	Total	Women	Men	Urban	Rural
Employers & members of producers' co-operatives	22.7	25.0	14.3	21.1	66.7
Own-account workers	71.8	78.1	61.5	71.1	74.2
Enterprise owners	71.8	78.1	61.5	71.1	74.2
Total self-employment (incl. contributing family workers)	71.8	78.5	61.2	70.1	77.4

Women and men in the informal economy: A statistical picture

5. Informal wage employment as % of total wage employment by type of employees

Type of employees	Total	Women	Men	Urban	Rural
Agricultural employees	52.6	50.0	53.3	25.0	56.3
Non-agricultural employees	34.1	37.2	32.3	36.5	26.5
Formal sector employees	27.5	27.8	26.5	28.6	18.6
Informal sector employees	85.7	100.0	81.8	90.0	100.0
Domestic workers employed by households	53.8	75.0	44.4	63.6	50.0
Total employees	35.9	38.3	34.5	36.2	33.8

6. Informal non-agricultural employment outside the informal sector by type (%)

Type of employment	Total	Women	Men	Urban	Rural
Producers of goods exclusively for own final use					
Contributing family workers: formal sector	22.6	31.6	19.0	19.6	35.7
Employees	77.4	68.4	81.0	80.4	64.3
Employees: formal sector	66.1	52.6	71.4	65.2	57.1
Employees: domestic work	11.3	15.8	9.5	15.2	7.1
Total	100.0	100.0	100.0	100.0	100.0

7. Share of women in employment by type

Share of women in ...	%
1. Total employment	50.1
2. Agricultural employment	50.2
2.1 Agricultural wage employment	21.1
2.1.1 Formal agricultural wage employment	22.2
2.1.2 Informal agricultural wage employment	20.0
2.2 Agricultural self-employment	51.4
3. Non-agricultural employment	50.0
3.1 Non-agricultural wage employment*	24.4
3.1.1 Formal non-agricultural wage employment	23.3
3.1.2 Informal non-agricultural wage employment	26.7
3.2 Non-agricultural self-employment	61.4
3.2.1 Formal non-agricultural self-employment	46.8
3.2.2 Informal non-agricultural self-employment	67.1

* = MDG Indicator No. 3.2: Share of women in wage employment in the non-agricultural sector

8. Share of women in informal non-agricultural employment by component

Share of women in ...	%
1. Informal employment	60.1
1.1 Self-employment	67.1
1.2. Wage employment	26.7
2. Employment in the informal sector	66.2
2.1 Self-employment	68.4
2.2 Wage employment	21.4
3. Informal employment outside the informal sector	30.6
3.1 Self-employment	42.9
3.2 Wage employment	27.1
3.2.1 Formal sector	24.4
3.2.2 Domestic work	42.9

9. Share of informal employment (%) by kind of non-agricultural activity

Share of informal employment in total employment in …	Total	Women	Men
All non-agricultural actitvities	59.4	72.0	46.7
Manufacturing	57.1	76.2	49.0
Construction	61.5	60.0	59.1
Trade	77.0	81.4	67.1
Transportation	54.2	60.0	50.0
Services other than trade or transportation	34.8	47.5	27.1

10. Non-agricultural employment by sex, formal/informal nature and kind of activity (%)

A. Both sexes

Kind of activity	Total	Formal	Informal
All non-agricultural actitvities	100.0	100.0	100.0
Manufacturing	12.2	12.9	11.8
Construction	4.5	4.3	4.7
Trade	47.2	26.7	61.2
Transportation	4.2	4.7	3.8
Services other than trade or transportation	27.1	43.5	15.9

B. Women

Kind of activity	Total	Formal	Informal
All non-agricultural actitvities	100.0	100.0	100.0
Manufacturing	7.3	6.3	7.8
Construction	1.7	2.5	1.5
Trade	65.7	43.8	74.3
Transportation	1.7	2.5	1.5
Services other than trade or transportation	20.6	38.8	13.6

C. Men

Kind of activity	Total	Formal	Informal
All non-agricultural actitvities	100.0	100.0	100.0
Manufacturing	17.1	16.3	17.9
Construction	7.7	5.9	9.7
Trade	28.6	17.6	41.0
Transportation	7.0	6.5	7.5
Services other than trade or transportation	33.4	45.8	19.4

Country: Liberia　　　　**Year: 2010**

Non-agricultural employment

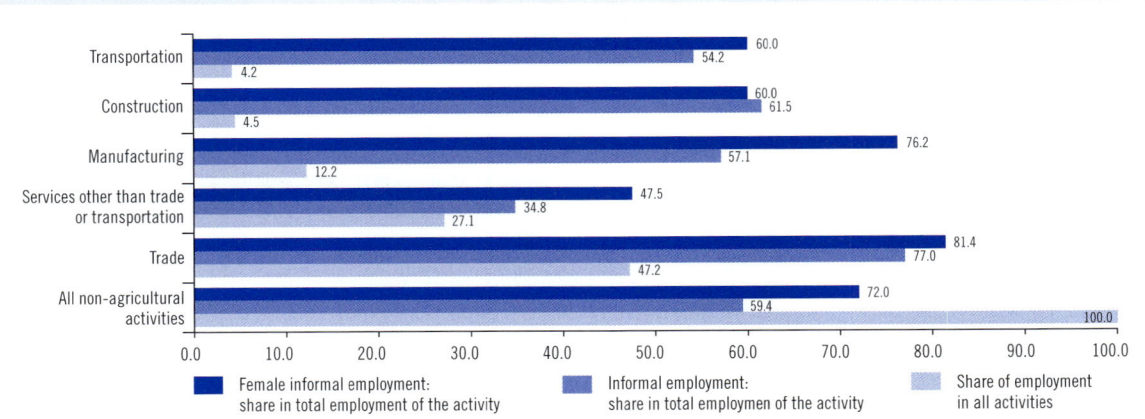

Women and men in the informal economy: A statistical picture

Country: The Former Yugoslav Republic of Macedonia
Source: Labour Force Survey

Year: 2010

1. Informal non-agricultural employment and its components

	Total	Women	Men	Urban	Rural
in 1,000					
Persons in informal employment	65	16	49	34	31
Persons employed in the informal sector	39	5	33	18	20
Persons in formal employment in the informal sector	2	1	1	1	0
Persons in informal employment outside the informal sector	27	11	16	17	11
as % of non-agricultural employment					
Persons in informal employment	12.6	8.1	15.4	9.5	19.4
Persons employed in the informal sector	7.6	2.5	10.3	5.0	12.5
Persons in formal employment in the informal sector	0.4	0.5	0.3	0.3	0.2
Persons in informal employment outside the informal sector	5.2	5.6	5.0	4.8	6.6

2. Employment in the informal sector by status in employment (%)

Status in employment	Total	Women	Men	Urban	Rural
Employers, own-account workers and MPCs*	51.3	40.0	54.5	61.1	45.0
Contributing family workers	5.1	0.0	6.1	2.8	7.5
Employees	43.6	60.0	42.4	38.9	50.0
Total	100.0	100.0	100.0	100.0	100.0

* Members of producers' cooperatives

3. Informal non-agricultural employment by status in employment (%)

Status in employment	Total	Women	Men	Urban	Rural
Employers, own-account workers and MPCs*	30.8	12.5	36.7	32.4	29.0
Owners of informal sector enterprises	30.8	12.5	36.7	32.4	29.0
Producers of goods exclusively for own final use					
Contributing family workers	9.2	6.3	10.2	5.9	12.9
Employees	60.0	81.3	53.1	61.8	58.1
Formal sector employees	35.4	62.5	26.5	44.1	25.8
Informal sector employees	23.1	15.6	26.5	17.6	32.3
Domestic workers employed by households					
Total	100.0	100.0	100.0	100.0	100.0

* Members of producers' cooperatives

4. Informal non-agricultural self-employment as % of total non-agricultural self-employment by status in employment

Status in employment	Total	Women	Men	Urban	Rural
Employers & members of producers' co-operatives	6.3	6.3	8.3	4.8	9.1
Own-account workers	48.6	25.0	53.3	43.5	57.1
Enterprise owners	48.6	23.1	53.3	43.5	57.1
Total self-employment (incl. contributing family workers)	34.7	20.0	39.0	28.3	44.8

5. Informal wage employment as % of total wage employment by type of employees

Type of employees	Total	Women	Men	Urban	Rural
Agricultural employees	21.4	33.3	27.3	16.7	25.0
Non-agricultural employees	8.8	7.1	10.0	6.8	13.7
Formal sector employees	5.4	5.6	5.3	4.9	6.6
Informal sector employees	88.2	83.3	92.9	85.7	100.0
Domestic workers employed by households					
Total employees	9.2	7.0	10.7	6.9	14.5

6. Informal non-agricultural employment outside the informal sector by type (%)

Type of employment	Total	Women	Men	Urban	Rural
Producers of goods exclusively for own final use					
Contributing family workers: formal sector	14.8	9.1	18.8	11.8	23.8
Employees	85.2	90.9	81.3	88.2	76.2
Employees: formal sector	85.2	90.9	81.3	88.2	76.2
Employees: domestic work					
Total	100.0	100.0	100.0	100.0	100.0

7. Share of women in employment by type

Share of women in …	%
1. Total employment	38.6
2. Agricultural employment	39.3
2.1 Agricultural wage employment	21.4
2.1.1 Formal agricultural wage employment	18.2
2.1.2 Informal agricultural wage employment	33.3
2.2 Agricultural self-employment	42.1
3. Non-agricultural employment	38.2
3.1 Non-agricultural wage employment*	41.2
3.1.1 Formal non-agricultural wage employment	41.9
3.1.2 Informal non-agricultural wage employment	33.3
3.2 Non-agricultural self-employment	20.0
3.2.1 Formal non-agricultural self-employment	26.5
3.2.2 Informal non-agricultural self-employment	11.5

* = MDG Indicator No. 3.2: Share of women in wage employment in the non-agricultural sector

8. Share of women in informal non-agricultural employment by component

Share of women in …	%
1. Informal employment	24.6
1.1 Self-employment	11.5
1.2. Wage employment	33.3
2. Employment in the informal sector	12.8
2.1 Self-employment	9.1
2.2 Wage employment	17.6
3. Informal employment outside the informal sector	40.7
3.1 Self-employment	25.0
3.2 Wage employment	43.5
3.2.1 Formal sector	43.5
3.2.2 Domestic work	

Women and men in the informal economy: A statistical picture

9. Share of informal employment (%) by kind of non-agricultural activity

Share of informal employment in total employment in …	Total	Women	Men
All non-agricultural actitvities	12.4	8.1	15.2
Manufacturing	8.0	9.4	7.0
Construction	43.1	5.3	45.8
Trade	13.0	8.2	16.2
Transportation	16.5	7.3	18.0
Services other than trade or transportation	8.3	7.2	9.3

10. Non-agricultural employment by sex, formal/informal nature and kind of activity (%)

A. Both sexes

Kind of activity	Total	Formal	Informal
All non-agricultural actitvities	100.0	100.0	100.0
Manufacturing	27.9	29.4	17.9
Construction	7.9	5.2	27.4
Trade	18.6	18.5	19.5
Transportation	7.0	6.6	9.2
Services other than trade or transportation	38.5	40.3	25.8

B. Women

Kind of activity	Total	Formal	Informal
All non-agricultural actitvities	100.0	100.0	100.0
Manufacturing	29.8	29.4	34.9
Construction	1.4	1.4	0.9
Trade	19.3	19.3	19.8
Transportation	2.6	2.6	2.3
Services other than trade or transportation	46.8	47.3	42.0

C. Men

Kind of activity	Total	Formal	Informal
All non-agricultural actitvities	100.0	100.0	100.0
Manufacturing	26.8	29.3	12.4
Construction	12.0	7.6	36.2
Trade	18.2	18.0	19.5
Transportation	9.7	9.3	11.5
Services other than trade or transportation	33.4	35.7	20.5

Country: The Former Yugoslav Republic of Macedonia   **Year: 2010**

Non-agricultural employment

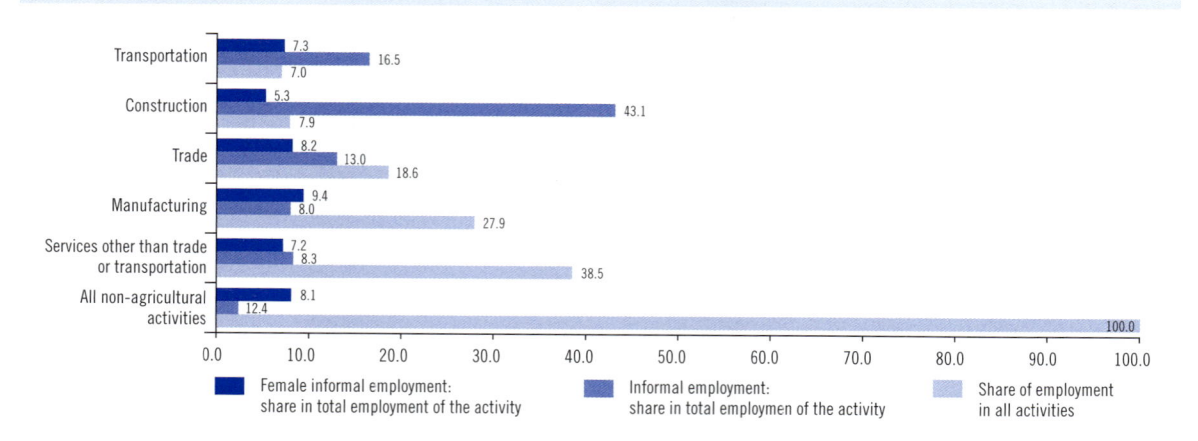

Annex II

Country: Madagascar
Source: Enquête Périodique auprès des Ménages

Year: 2005

1. Informal non-agricultural employment and its components

	Total	Women	Men	Urban	Rural
in 1,000					
Persons in informal employment	1'270.9	670.8	600.1		
Persons employed in the informal sector	893.4	528.2	365.2		
Persons in formal employment in the informal sector	0.4	0.0	0.4		
Persons in informal employment outside the informal sector	377.9	142.6	235.3		
as % of non-agricultural employment					
Persons in informal employment	73.6	81.0	66.8		
Persons employed in the informal sector	51.8	63.8	40.7		
Persons in formal employment in the informal sector	0.0	0.0	0.0		
Persons in informal employment outside the informal sector	21.9	17.2	26.2		

2. Employment in the informal sector by status in employment (%)

Status in employment	Total	Women	Men	Urban	Rural
Employers, own-account workers and MPCs*	51.7	48.1	57.0		
Contributing family workers	30.3	37.9	19.3		
Employees	18.0	14.0	23.7		
Total	100.0	100.0	100.0		

* Members of producers' cooperatives

3. Informal non-agricultural employment by status in employment (%)

Status in employment	Total	Women	Men	Urban	Rural
Employers, own-account workers and MPCs*	36.4	37.9	34.7		
Owners of informal sector enterprises	36.4	37.9	34.7		
Producers of goods exclusively for own final use					
Contributing family workers	21.3	29.8	11.8		
Employees	42.3	32.3	53.6		
Formal sector employees	29.7	21.3	39.2		
Informal sector employees	12.6	11.0	14.3		
Domestic workers employed by households					
Total	100.0	100.0	100.0		

* Members of producers' cooperatives

4. Informal non-agricultural self-employment as % of total non-agricultural self-employment by status in employment

Status in employment	Total	Women	Men	Urban	Rural
Employers and own-account workers	99.1	99.8	98.3		
Enterprise owners	99.1	99.8	98.3		
Total self-employment (incl. contributing family workers)	99.4	99.9	98.7		

Women and men in the informal economy: A statistical picture

5. Informal wage employment as % of total wage employment by type of employees

Type of employees	Total	Women	Men	Urban	Rural
Agricultural employees	91.1	94.5	88.1		
Non-agricultural employees	54.4	58.0	52.2		
Formal sector employees	45.6	47.6	44.5		
Informal sector employees	99.7	100.0	99.5		
Domestic workers employed by households					
Total employees	63.1	68.1	59.8		

6. Informal non-agricultural employment outside the informal sector by type (%)

Type of employment	Total	Women	Men	Urban	Rural
Producers of goods exclusively for own final use					
Contributing family workers: formal sector	0.0	0.0	0.0		
Employees	100.0	100.0	100.0		
Employees: formal sector	100.0	100.0	100.0		
Employees: domestic work					
Total	100.0	100.0	100.0		

7. Share of women in employment by type

Share of women in …	%
1. Total employment	49.4
2. Agricultural employment	49.7
2.1 Agricultural wage employment	46.2
2.1.1 Formal agricultural wage employment	28.6
2.1.2 Informal agricultural wage employment	47.9
2.2 Agricultural self-employment	49.9
3. Non-agricultural employment	48.0
3.1 Non-agricultural wage employment*	37.7
3.1.1 Formal non-agricultural wage employment	34.8
3.1.2 Informal non-agricultural wage employment	40.3
3.2 Non-agricultural self-employment	61.7
3.2.1 Formal non-agricultural self-employment	12.5
3.2.2 Informal non-agricultural self-employment	62.0

* = MDG Indicator No. 3.2: Share of women in wage employment in the non-agricultural sector

8. Share of women in informal non-agricultural employment by component

Share of women in …	%
1. Informal employment	52.8
1.1 Self-employment	62.0
1.2 Wage employment	40.3
2. Employment in the informal sector	59.1
2.1 Self-employment	62.0
2.2 Wage employment	46.1
3. Informal employment outside the informal sector	37.7
3.1 Self-employment	
3.2 Wage employment	37.7
3.2.1 Formal sector	37.7
3.2.2 Domestic work	

9. Share of informal employment (%) by kind of non-agricultural activity

Share of informal employment in total employment in …	Total	Women	Men
Data not available.			

10. Non-agricultural employment by sex, formal/informal nature and kind of activity (%)

Kind of activity	Total	Formal	Informal
Data not available.			

Women and men in the informal economy: A statistical picture

Country: Mali
Source: Enquête sur la main-d'oeuvre

Year: 2004

1. Informal non-agricultural employment and its components

	Total	Women	Men	Urban	Rural
in 1,000					
Persons in informal employment	1'180.1	652.2	527.9		
Persons employed in the informal sector	1'029.4	582.1	447.3		
Persons in formal employment in the informal sector	12.7	4.0	8.7		
Persons in informal employment outside the informal sector	163.4	74.0	89.4		
as % of non-agricultural employment					
Persons in informal employment	81.8	89.2	74.2		
Persons employed in the informal sector	71.4	79.6	62.9		
Persons in formal employment in the informal sector	0.9	0.5	1.2		
Persons in informal employment outside the informal sector	11.3	10.1	12.6		

2. Employment in the informal sector by status in employment (%)

Status in employment	Total	Women	Men	Urban	Rural
Employers, own-account workers and MPCs*	81.9	89.1	72.6		
Contributing family workers	5.9	4.9	7.1		
Employees	12.2	5.9	20.4		
Total	100.0	100.0	100.0		

* Members of producers' cooperatives

3. Informal non-agricultural employment by status in employment (%)

Status in employment	Total	Women	Men	Urban	Rural
Employers, own-account workers and MPCs*	71.5	79.6	61.5		
Owners of informal sector enterprises	71.5	79.6	61.5		
Producers of goods exclusively for own final use					
Contributing family workers	6.6	5.9	7.5		
Employees	21.9	14.5	31.0		
Formal sector employees	7.7	2.6	14.1		
Informal sector employees	9.6	4.7	15.6		
Domestic workers employed by households	4.6	7.3	1.4		
Total	100.0	100.0	100.0		

* Members of producers' cooperatives

4. Informal non-agricultural self-employment as % of total non-agricultural self-employment by status in employment

Status in employment	Total	Women	Men	Urban	Rural
Employers & members of producers' co-operatives)	87.0	95.8	75.9		
Own-account workers)					
Enterprise owners					
Total self-employment (incl. contributing family workers)	88.0	96.1	77.9		

5. Informal wage employment as % of total wage employment by type of employees

Type of employees	Total	Women	Men	Urban	Rural
Agricultural employees	63.7	32.0	66.0		
Non-agricultural employees	65.4	62.7	67.2		
Formal sector employees	50.3	44.5	51.7		
Informal sector employees	89.9	88.5	90.4		
Domestic workers employed by households	61.9	60.1	77.5		
Total employees	65.3	62.4	67.1		

6. Informal non-agricultural employment outside the informal sector by type (%)

Type of employment	Total	Women	Men	Urban	Rural
Producers of goods exclusively for own final use					
Contributing family workers: formal sector	10.8	13.2	8.8		
Employees	89.2	86.8	91.2		
Employees: formal sector	55.8	22.7	83.2		
Employees: domestic work	33.5	64.1	8.1		
Total	100.0	100.0	100.0		

7. Share of women in employment by type

Share of women in ...	%
1. Total employment	41.6
2. Agricultural employment	29.2
2.1 Agricultural wage employment	6.8
2.1.1 Formal agricultural wage employment	12.8
2.1.2 Informal agricultural wage employment	3.4
2.2 Agricultural self-employment	29.7
3. Non-agricultural employment	50.7
3.1 Non-agricultural wage employment*	38.2
3.1.1 Formal non-agricultural wage employment	41.3
3.1.2 Informal non-agricultural wage employment	36.6
3.2 Non-agricultural self-employment	55.4
3.2.1 Formal non-agricultural self-employment	18.1
3.2.2 Informal non-agricultural self-employment	60.5

* = MDG Indicator No. 3.2: Share of women in wage employment in the non-agricultural sector

8. Share of women in informal non-agricultural employment by component

Share of women in ...	%
1. Informal employment	55.3
1.1 Self-employment	60.5
1.2. Wage employment	36.6
2. Employment in the informal sector	56.5
2.1 Self-employment	60.6
2.2 Wage employment	27.5
3. Informal employment outside the informal sector	45.3
3.1 Self-employment	55.5
3.2 Wage employment	44.1
3.2.1 Formal sector	18.4
3.2.2 Domestic work	86.8

Women and men in the informal economy: A statistical picture

9. Share of informal employment (%) by kind of non-agricultural activity

Share of informal employment in total employment in ...	Total	Women	Men
Data not available.			

10. Non-agricultural employment by sex, formal/informal nature and kind of activity (%)

Kind of activity	Total	Formal	Informal
Data not available.			

Country: Mauritius
Source: Continuous Multipurpose Household Survey

Year: 2009

1. Informal non-agricultural employment and its components

	Total	Women	Men	Urban	Rural
in 1,000					
Persons in informal employment					
Persons employed in the informal sector	56.9	13.7	43.2		
Persons in formal employment in the informal sector					
Persons in informal employment outside the informal sector					
as % of non-agricultural employment					
Persons in informal employment					
Persons employed in the informal sector	11.9	8.2	13.9		
Persons in formal employment in the informal sector					
Persons in informal employment outside the informal sector					

2. Employment in the informal sector by status in employment (%)

Status in employment	Total	Women	Men	Urban	Rural
Employers, own-account workers and MPCs*	69.2	58.4	72.7		
Contributing family workers	8.6	24.1	3.7		
Employees	22.1	17.5	23.6		
Total	100.0	100.0	100.0		

* Members of producers' cooperatives

3. Informal non-agricultural employment by status in employment (%)

Status in employment	Total	Women	Men	Urban	Rural
Data not available.					

4. Informal non-agricultural self-employment as % of total non-agricultural self-employment by status in employment

Status in employment	Total	Women	Men	Urban	Rural
Employers & members of producers' co-operatives	29.0	14.8	31.4		
Own-account workers	58.2	57.1	58.5		
Enterprise owners	58.2	57.1	58.5		
Total self-employment (incl. contributing family workers)	56.1	64.9	52.9		

Women and men in the informal economy: A statistical picture

5. Informal wage employment as % of total wage employment by type of employees

Type of employees	Total	Women	Men	Urban	Rural
Data not available.					

6. Informal non-agricultural employment outside the informal sector by type (%)

Type of employment	Total	Women	Men	Urban	Rural
Data not available.					

7. Share of women in employment by type

Share of women in …	%
1. Total employment	34.8
2. Agricultural employment	31.5
2.1 Agricultural wage employment	30.1
2.1.1 Formal agricultural wage employment	
2.1.2 Informal agricultural wage employment	
2.2 Agricultural self-employment	33.5
3. Non-agricultural employment	35.1
3.1 Non-agricultural wage employment*	36.9
3.1.1 Formal non-agricultural wage employment	
3.1.2 Informal non-agricultural wage employment	
3.2 Non-agricultural self-employment	26.7
3.2.1 Formal non-agricultural self-employment	21.3
3.2.2 Informal non-agricultural self-employment	30.9

* = MDG Indicator No. 3.2: Share of women in wage employment in the non-agricultural sector

8. Share of women in informal non-agricultural employment by component

Share of women in …	%
1. Informal employment	
1.1 Self-employment	
1.2. Wage employment	
2. Employment in the informal sector	24.1
2.1 Self-employment	25.5
2.2 Wage employment	19.0
3. Informal employment outside the informal sector	
3.1 Self-employment	
3.2 Wage employment	
3.2.1 Formal sector	
3.2.2 Domestic work	

9. Share of informal employment (%) by kind of non-agricultural activity

Share of informal employment* in total employment in …	Total	Women	Men
All non-agricultural actitvities	16.0	18.1	14.9
Manufacturing	13.8	10.9	16.0
Construction	20.9	6.7	21.3
Trade	21.8	18.3	23.9
Transportation	18.6	1.8	21.3
Services other than trade or transportation	13.2	22.4	6.2

10. Non-agricultural employment by sex, formal/informal nature and kind of activity (%)

A. Both sexes

Kind of activity	Total	Formal**	Informal*
All non-agricultural actitvities	100.0	100.0	100.0
Manufacturing	20.1	20.7	17.4
Construction	11.6	10.9	15.1
Trade	15.5	14.4	21.1
Transportation	8.2	8.0	9.5
Services other than trade or transportation	44.5	46.0	36.8

B. Women

Kind of activity	Total	Formal**	Informal*
All non-agricultural actitvities	100.0	100.0	100.0
Manufacturing	24.5	26.7	14.8
Construction	0.9	1.0	0.3
Trade	16.3	16.2	16.4
Transportation	3.3	3.9	0.3
Services other than trade or transportation	55.0	52.1	68.1

C. Men

Kind of activity	Total	Formal**	Informal*
All non-agricultural actitvities	100.0	100.0	100.0
Manufacturing	17.7	17.5	19.0
Construction	17.4	16.1	24.9
Trade	15.1	13.5	24.2
Transportation	10.9	10.1	15.6
Services other than trade or transportation	38.9	42.8	16.2

* Informal sector employment and paid domestic work   ** Formal sector employment

Country: Mauritius   **Year: 2009**

Non-agricultural employment

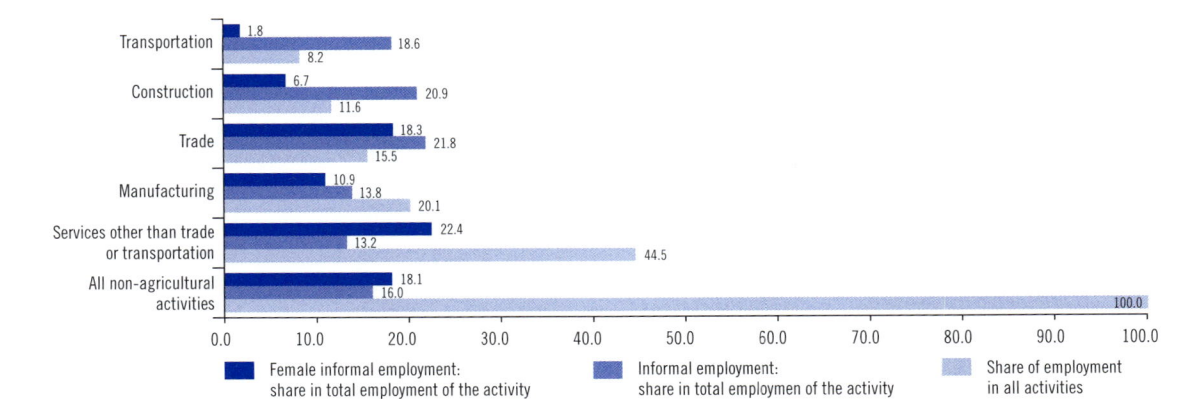

Women and men in the informal economy: A statistical picture

Country: Mexico
Source: Encuesta Nacional de Ocupación y Empleo

Year: 2009 (II)

1. Informal non-agricultural employment and its components

	Total	Women	Men	Urban	Rural
	in 1,000				
Persons in informal employment	20'257.5	9'065.9	11'191.6	10'462.6	9'794.9
Persons employed in the informal sector	12'860.8	4'993.2	7'867.6	6'162.0	6'698.8
Persons in formal employment in the informal sector	222.8	42.7	180.1	125.1	97.7
Persons in informal employment outside the informal sector	7'619.5	4'115.4	3'504.1	4'425.7	3'193.9
	as % of non-agricultural employment				
Persons in informal employment	53.7	57.8	50.8	45.8	65.9
Persons employed in the informal sector	34.1	31.8	35.7	27.0	45.1
Persons in formal employment in the informal sector	0.6	0.3	0.8	0.5	0.7
Persons in informal employment outside the informal sector	20.2	26.2	15.9	19.4	21.5

2. Employment in the informal sector by status in employment (%)

Status in employment	Total	Women	Men	Urban	Rural
Employers, own-account workers and MPCs*	56.0	66.5	49.3	60.6	51.8
Contributing family workers	8.8	15.7	4.4	7.3	10.2
Employees	35.2	17.8	46.3	32.1	38.1
Total	100.0	100.0	100.0	100.0	100.0

* Members of producers' cooperatives

3. Informal non-agricultural employment by status in employment (%)

Status in employment	Total	Women	Men	Urban	Rural
Employers, own-account workers and MPCs*	35.5	36.6	34.7	35.7	35.4
Owners of informal sector enterprises	35.5	36.6	34.7	35.7	35.4
Producers of goods exclusively for own final use					
Contributing family workers	8.8	13.6	5.0	7.9	9.8
Employees	55.6	49.8	60.3	56.4	54.7
Formal sector employees	25.5	22.3	28.1	30.1	20.6
Informal sector employees	21.2	9.3	30.9	17.7	25.0
Domestic workers employed by households	8.9	18.2	1.3	8.6	9.1
Total	100.0	100.0	100.0	100.0	100.0

* Members of producers' cooperatives

4. Informal non-agricultural self-employment as % of total non-agricultural self-employment by status in employment

Status in employment	Total	Women	Men	Urban	Rural
Employers & members of producers' co-operatives	43.8	39.0	45.0	35.7	56.5
Own-account workers	83.7	87.2	80.6	80.2	87.9
Enterprise owners	83.7	87.2	80.6	80.2	87.9
Total self-employment (incl. contributing family workers)	80.2	86.9	74.4	75.3	86.1

5. Informal wage employment as % of total wage employment by type of employees

Type of employees	Total	Women	Men	Urban	Rural
Agricultural employees	87.1	74.7	88.1	57.2	88.4
Non-agricultural employees	42.5	43.2	42.1	35.2	55.2
Formal sector employees	25.7	25.7	25.7	22.8	32.3
Informal sector employees	95.1	95.2	95.1	93.7	96.2
Domestic workers employed by households	95.2	96.0	86.4	93.0	97.6
Total employees	45.9	43.7	47.1	35.3	61.0

6. Informal non-agricultural employment outside the informal sector by type (%)

Type of employment	Total	Women	Men	Urban	Rural
Producers of goods exclusively for own final use					
Contributing family workers: formal sector	8.6	10.8	6.1	8.4	8.9
Employees	91.4	89.2	93.9	91.6	91.1
Employees: formal sector	67.9	49.1	89.9	71.1	63.3
Employees: domestic work	23.5	40.1	4.0	20.4	27.8
Total	100.0	100.0	100.0	100.0	100.0

7. Share of women in employment by type

Share of women in …	%
1. Total employment	37.5
2. Agricultural employment	9.8
2.1 Agricultural wage employment	7.9
2.1.1 Formal agricultural wage employment	15.4
2.1.2 Informal agricultural wage employment	6.7
2.2 Agricultural self-employment	11.0
3. Non-agricultural employment	41.6
3.1 Non-agricultural wage employment*	39.5
3.1.1 Formal non-agricultural wage employment	39.0
3.1.2 Informal non-agricultural wage employment	40.1
3.2 Non-agricultural self-employment	46.7
3.2.1 Formal non-agricultural self-employment	30.9
3.2.2 Informal non-agricultural self-employment	50.6

* = MDG Indicator No. 3.2: Share of women in wage employment in the non-agricultural sector

8. Share of women in informal non-agricultural employment by component

Share of women in …	%
1. Informal employment	44.8
1.1 Self-employment	50.6
1.2. Wage employment	40.1
2. Employment in the informal sector	38.8
2.1 Self-employment	49.3
2.2 Wage employment	19.6
3. Informal employment outside the informal sector	54.0
3.1 Self-employment	67.4
3.2 Wage employment	52.7
3.2.1 Formal sector	39.1
3.2.2 Domestic work	92.1

Women and men in the informal economy: A statistical picture

9. Share of informal employment (%) by kind of non-agricultural activity

Share of informal employment in total employment in …	Total	Women	Men
All non-agricultural actitvities	53.7	57.8	50.8
Manufacturing	42.9	53.7	36.8
Construction	77.8	22.4	79.6
Trade	65.8	73.7	58.5
Transportation	57.1	19.2	62.0
Services other than trade or transportation	39.9	46.6	32.0

10. Non-agricultural employment by sex, formal/informal nature and kind of activity (%)

A. Both sexes

Kind of activity	Total	Formal	Informal
All non-agricultural actitvities	100.0	100.0	100.0
Manufacturing	18.6	22.9	14.8
Construction	9.3	4.5	13.5
Trade	33.9	25.0	41.5
Transportation	5.5	5.1	5.9
Services other than trade or transportation	32.7	42.4	24.2

B. Women

Kind of activity	Total	Formal	Informal
All non-agricultural actitvities	100.0	100.0	100.0
Manufacturing	16.0	17.6	14.9
Construction	0.7	1.3	0.3
Trade	39.3	24.5	50.1
Transportation	1.5	2.9	0.5
Services other than trade or transportation	42.5	53.8	34.2

C. Men

Kind of activity	Total	Formal	Informal
All non-agricultural actitvities	100.0	100.0	100.0
Manufacturing	20.4	26.2	14.8
Construction	15.5	6.4	24.2
Trade	30.1	25.4	34.6
Transportation	8.4	6.5	10.3
Services other than trade or transportation	25.7	35.5	16.1

Country: Mexico Year: 2009 (II)
Non-agricultural employment

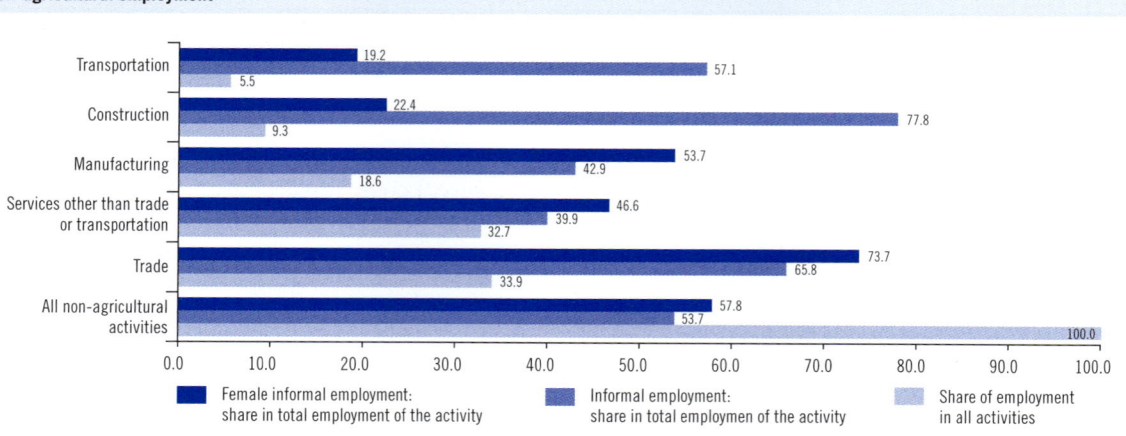

Annex II

Country: Republic of Moldova
Source: Labour Force Survey

Year: 2009

1. Informal non-agricultural employment and its components

	Total	Women	Men	Urban	Rural
in 1,000					
Persons in informal employment	135.5	50.1	85.3	74.7	60.7
Persons employed in the informal sector	62.3	11.5	50.8	30.5	31.8
Persons in formal employment in the informal sector	0.0	0.0	0.0	0.0	0.0
Persons in informal employment outside the informal sector	73.1	38.6	34.5	44.3	28.9
as % of non-agricultural employment					
Persons in informal employment	15.9	11.4	20.8	14.0	19.1
Persons employed in the informal sector	7.3	2.6	12.4	5.7	10.0
Persons in formal employment in the informal sector	0.0	0.0	0.0	0.0	0.0
Persons in informal employment outside the informal sector	8.6	8.8	8.4	8.3	9.1

2. Employment in the informal sector by status in employment (%)

Status in employment	Total	Women	Men	Urban	Rural
Employers, own-account workers and MPCs*	91.0	87.8	91.5	94.5	87.3
Contributing family workers	1.4	4.2	0.9	0.7	2.3
Employees	7.7	8.0	7.6	4.8	10.4
Total	100.0	100.0	100.0	100.0	100.0

* Members of producers' cooperatives

3. Informal non-agricultural employment by status in employment (%)

Status in employment	Total	Women	Men	Urban	Rural
Employers, own-account workers and MPCs*	41.8	20.1	54.5	38.6	45.7
Owners of informal sector enterprises	41.8	20.1	54.5	38.6	45.7
Producers of goods exclusively for own final use					
Contributing family workers	2.4	3.2	2.0	2.8	2.1
Employees	55.7	76.7	43.5	58.7	52.2
Formal sector employees	48.8	67.1	38.1	53.9	42.6
Informal sector employees	3.5	1.8	4.5	2.0	5.4
Domestic workers employed by households	3.4	7.7	0.9	2.8	4.1
Total	100.0	100.0	100.0	100.0	100.0

* Members of producers' cooperatives

4. Informal non-agricultural self-employment as % of total non-agricultural self-employment by status in employment

Status in employment	Total	Women	Men	Urban	Rural
Employers & members of producers' co-operatives	1.0	0.0	1.7	1.1	1.2
Own-account workers	70.3	40.8	83.2	61.0	83.2
Enterprise owners	70.2	40.8	83.2	61.0	83.2
Total self-employment (incl. contributing family workers)	63.9	39.5	75.1	55.1	76.9

Women and men in the informal economy: A statistical picture

5. Informal wage employment as % of total wage employment by type of employees

Type of employees	Total	Women	Men	Urban	Rural
Agricultural employees	35.3	38.4	33.6	23.5	37.0
Non-agricultural employees	10.0	9.3	10.7	9.2	11.3
Formal sector employees	8.8	8.3	9.5	8.5	9.4
Informal sector employees	100.0	100.0	100.0	100.0	100.0
Domestic workers employed by households	100.0	100.0	100.0	100.0	100.0
Total employees	12.4	11.1	13.8	9.5	16.4

6. Informal non-agricultural employment outside the informal sector by type (%)

Type of employment	Total	Women	Men	Urban	Rural
Producers of goods exclusively for own final use					
Contributing family workers: formal sector	3.3	2.9	3.7	4.3	1.8
Employees	96.7	97.1	96.3	95.7	98.2
Employees: formal sector	90.4	87.1	94.2	91.0	89.5
Employees: domestic work	6.3	10.0	2.1	4.7	8.7
Total	100.0	100.0	100.0	100.0	100.0

7. Share of women in employment by type

Share of women in …	%
1. Total employment	49.5
2. Agricultural employment	43.7
2.1 Agricultural wage employment	33.7
2.1.1 Formal agricultural wage employment	32.0
2.1.2 Informal agricultural wage employment	36.7
2.2 Agricultural self-employment	46.8
3. Non-agricultural employment	51.8
3.1 Non-agricultural wage employment*	54.3
3.1.1 Formal non-agricultural wage employment	54.7
3.1.2 Informal non-agricultural wage employment	50.9
3.2 Non-agricultural self-employment	31.5
3.2.1 Formal non-agricultural self-employment	52.8
3.2.2 Informal non-agricultural self-employment	19.5

* = MDG Indicator No. 3.2: Share of women in wage employment in the non-agricultural sector

8. Share of women in informal non-agricultural employment by component

Share of women in …	%
1. Informal employment	37.0
1.1 Self-employment	19.5
1.2. Wage employment	50.9
2. Employment in the informal sector	18.4
2.1 Self-employment	18.3
2.2 Wage employment	19.1
3. Informal employment outside the informal sector	52.8
3.1 Self-employment	47.5
3.2 Wage employment	53.0
3.2.1 Formal sector	50.9
3.2.2 Domestic work	83.9

Annex II

9. Share of informal employment (%) by kind of non-agricultural activity

Share of informal employment in total employment in …	Total	Women	Men
All non-agricultural actitvities	15.9	11.4	20.8
Manufacturing	9.8	7.3	11.8
Construction	58.1	41.1	60.4
Trade	24.9	27.1	22.2
Transportation	16.1	0.9	21.3
Services other than trade or transportation	5.4	5.5	5.3

10. Non-agricultural employment by sex, formal/informal nature and kind of activity (%)

A. Both sexes

Kind of activity	Total	Formal	Informal
All non-agricultural actitvities	100.0	100.0	100.0
Manufacturing	18.3	19.6	11.3
Construction	8.6	4.3	31.3
Trade	22.3	19.9	34.8
Transportation	8.0	8.0	8.1
Services other than trade or transportation	42.9	48.3	14.6

B. Women

Kind of activity	Total	Formal	Informal
All non-agricultural actitvities	100.0	100.0	100.0
Manufacturing	15.7	16.4	10.1
Construction	2.0	1.3	7.1
Trade	23.5	19.3	56.0
Transportation	4.0	4.4	0.3
Services other than trade or transportation	54.9	58.5	26.4

C. Men

Kind of activity	Total	Formal	Informal
All non-agricultural actitvities	100.0	100.0	100.0
Manufacturing	21.0	23.4	12.0
Construction	15.7	7.8	45.5
Trade	20.9	20.6	22.3
Transportation	12.3	12.3	12.6
Services other than trade or transportation	30.0	35.9	7.6

Country: Republic of Moldava Year: 2009

Non-agricultural employment

Activity	Female informal employment: share in total employment of the activity	Informal employment: share in total employmen of the activity	Share of employment in all activities
Transportation	0.9	16.1	8.0
Construction	41.1	58.1	8.6
Manufacturing	7.3	9.8	18.3
Trade	27.1	24.9	22.3
Services other than trade or transportation	5.5	5.4	42.9
All non-agricultural activities	11.4	15.9	100.0

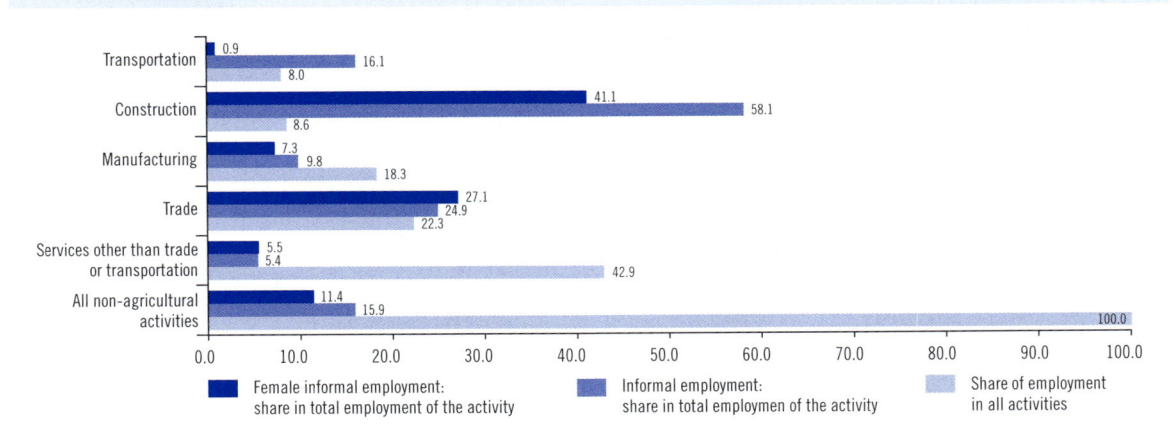

Women and men in the informal economy: A statistical picture

Country: Namibia
Source: Namibia Labour Force Survey

Year: 2008

1. Informal non-agricultural employment and its components

	Total	Women	Men	Urban	Rural
in 1,000					
Persons in informal employment	121.3	62.4	58.9	80.9	40.4
Persons employed in the informal sector					
Persons in formal employment in the informal sector					
Persons in informal employment outside the informal sector					
as % of non-agricultural employment					
Persons in informal employment	43.9	47.0	41.1	40.3	53.8
Persons employed in the informal sector					
Persons in formal employment in the informal sector					
Persons in informal employment outside the informal sector					

2. Employment in the informal sector by status in employment (%)

Status in employment	Total	Women	Men	Urban	Rural
Data not available.					

3. Informal non-agricultural employment by status in employment (%)

Status in employment	Total	Women	Men	Urban	Rural
Employers, own-account workers and MPCs*	23.9	27.4	20.0	20.1	31.4
Owners of informal sector enterprises	23.9	27.4	20.0	20.1	31.4
Producers of goods exclusively for own final use					
Contributing family workers	2.1	1.9	2.5	2.7	1.0
Employees	73.9	70.7	77.4	77.1	67.6
Formal sector employees					
Informal sector employees					
Domestic workers employed by households	25.3	34.9	15.1	24.1	28.0
Total	100.0	100.0	100.0	100.0	100.0

* Members of producers' cooperatives

4. Informal non-agricultural self-employment as % of total non-agricultural self-employment by status in employment

Status in employment	Total	Women	Men	Urban	Rural
Employers & members of producers' co-operatives)	69.4	81.8	56.5	61.7	82.5
Own-account workers)					
Enterprise owners					
Total self-employment (incl. contributing family workers)	71.2	82.8	59.4	64.7	82.9

5. Informal wage employment as % of total wage employment by type of employees

Type of employees	Total	Women	Men	Urban	Rural
Agricultural employees	61.9	57.6	62.6	48.8	63.5
Non-agricultural employees	38.7	39.8	37.7	36.2	46.0
Formal sector employees					
Informal sector employees					
Domestic workers employed by households	81.2	79.0	87.3	79.6	85.0
Total employees	42.0	40.7	43.0	36.5	52.5

6. Informal non-agricultural employment outside the informal sector by type (%)

Type of employment	Total	Women	Men	Urban	Rural
Data not available.					

7. Share of women in employment by type

Share of women in …	%
1. Total employment	43.8
2. Agricultural employment	21.9
2.1 Agricultural wage employment	15.5
2.1.1 Formal agricultural wage employment	17.2
2.1.2 Informal agricultural wage employment	14.4
2.2 Agricultural self-employment	37.3
3. Non-agricultural employment	48.1
3.1 Non-agricultural wage employment*	47.8
3.1.1 Formal non-agricultural wage employment	47.0
3.1.2 Informal non-agricultural wage employment	49.2
3.2 Non-agricultural self-employment	49.8
3.2.1 Formal non-agricultural self-employment	29.7
3.2.2 Informal non-agricultural self-employment	57.9

* = MDG Indicator No. 3.2: Share of women in wage employment in the non-agricultural sector

8. Share of women in informal non-agricultural employment by component

Share of women in …	%
1. Informal employment	51.4
1.1 Self-employment	57.9
1.2. Wage employment	49.2
2. Employment in the informal sector	
2.1 Self-employment	
2.2 Wage employment	
3. Informal employment outside the informal sector	
3.1 Self-employment	
3.2 Wage employment	
3.2.1 Formal sector	
3.2.2 Domestic work	71.0

Women and men in the informal economy: A statistical picture

9. Share of informal employment (%) by kind of non-agricultural activity

Share of informal employment in total employment in ...	Total	Women	Men
All non-agricultural actitvities	43.9	47.0	41.1
Manufacturing	30.7	35.7	28.3
Construction	69.5	61.9	70.3
Trade	58.1	66.0	48.8
Transportation	35.9	13.3	41.3
Services other than trade or transportation	37.7	41.7	31.9

10. Non-agricultural employment by sex, formal/informal nature and kind of activity (%)

A. Both sexes

Kind of activity	Total	Formal	Informal
All non-agricultural actitvities	100.0	100.0	100.0
Manufacturing	12.8	15.8	8.9
Construction	8.4	4.6	13.4
Trade	22.2	16.6	29.3
Transportation	5.7	6.5	4.6
Services other than trade or transportation	51.0	56.6	43.8

B. Women

Kind of activity	Total	Formal	Informal
All non-agricultural actitvities	100.0	100.0	100.0
Manufacturing	8.4	10.2	6.4
Construction	1.6	1.1	2.1
Trade	25.0	16.1	35.1
Transportation	2.3	3.7	0.6
Services other than trade or transportation	62.8	69.0	55.8

C. Men

Kind of activity	Total	Formal	Informal
All non-agricultural actitvities	100.0	100.0	100.0
Manufacturing	16.8	20.4	11.5
Construction	14.8	7.5	25.3
Trade	19.6	17.1	23.3
Transportation	8.8	8.8	8.8
Services other than trade or transportation	40.0	46.3	31.1

Country: Namibia **Year: 2008**

Non-agricultural employment

- Female informal employment: share in total employment of the activity
- Informal employment: share in total employmen of the activity
- Share of employment in all activities

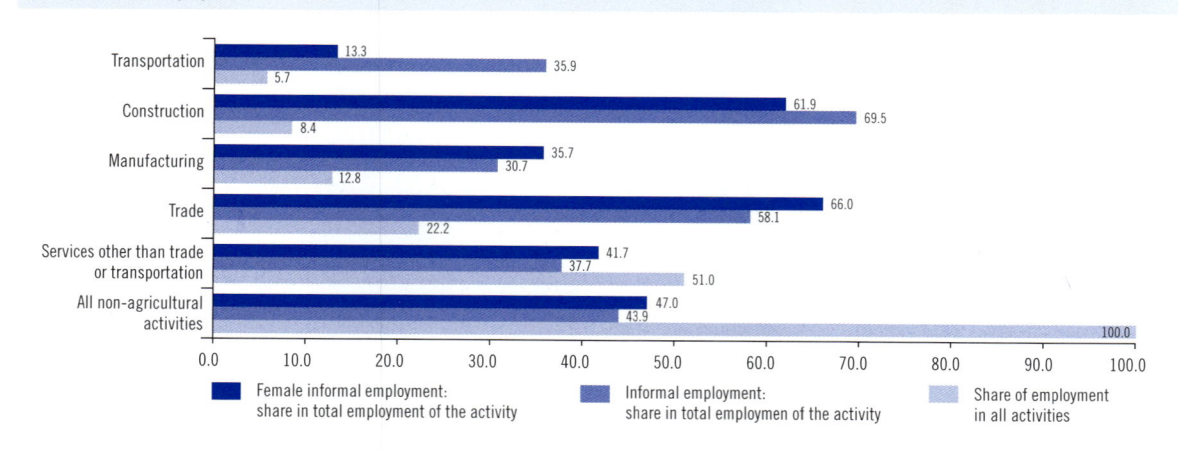

Annex II

Country: Nicaragua
Source: Encuesta de Hogares para la Medición del Empleo Urbano-Rural

Year: 2008

1. Informal non-agricultural employment and its components

	Total	Women	Men	Urban	Rural
in 1,000					
Persons in informal employment	1'024.1	505.1	519.0	741.1	283.0
Persons employed in the informal sector	846.8	399.8	446.9	627.9	218.8
Persons in formal employment in the informal sector	56.5	24.7	31.8	45.9	10.6
Persons in informal employment outside the informal sector	233.9	130.0	103.9	159.1	74.7
as % of non-agricultural employment					
Persons in informal employment	65.7	66.6	64.9	62.5	76.2
Persons employed in the informal sector	54.4	52.7	55.9	52.9	58.9
Persons in formal employment in the informal sector	3.6	3.3	4.0	3.9	2.9
Persons in informal employment outside the informal sector	15.0	17.2	13.0	13.4	20.1

2. Employment in the informal sector by status in employment (%)

Status in employment	Total	Women	Men	Urban	Rural
Employers, own-account workers and MPCs*	61.1	70.4	52.9	61.7	59.5
Contributing family workers	8.5	12.0	5.3	7.0	12.5
Employees	30.4	17.6	41.8	31.3	27.9
Total	100.0	100.0	100.0	100.0	100.0

* Members of producers' cooperatives

3. Informal non-agricultural employment by status in employment (%)

Status in employment	Total	Women	Men	Urban	Rural
Employers, own-account workers and MPCs*	50.6	55.7	45.5	52.3	46.0
Owners of informal sector enterprises	50.6	55.7	45.5	52.3	46.0
Producers of goods exclusively for own final use					
Contributing family workers	7.9	10.6	5.2	6.9	10.5
Employees	41.6	33.7	49.2	40.8	43.5
Formal sector employees	11.5	6.9	16.0	11.8	10.7
Informal sector employees	19.6	9.1	29.9	20.3	17.9
Domestic workers employed by households	10.4	17.8	3.3	8.7	14.9
Total	100.0	100.0	100.0	100.0	100.0

* Members of producers' cooperatives

4. Informal non-agricultural self-employment as % of total non-agricultural self-employment by status in employment

Status in employment	Total	Women	Men	Urban	Rural
Employers & members of producers' co-operatives	76.8	79.9	75.6	75.6	82.9
Own-account workers	95.0	95.8	93.9	94.5	96.4
Enterprise owners	95.0	95.8	93.9	94.5	96.4
Total self-employment (incl. contributing family workers)	94.2	95.8	92.2	93.4	96.4

Women and men in the informal economy: A statistical picture

5. Informal wage employment as % of total wage employment by type of employees

Type of employees	Total	Women	Men	Urban	Rural
Agricultural employees	86.5	67.9	88.0	70.8	90.1
Non-agricultural employees	46.1	41.7	49.7	42.2	59.9
Formal sector employees	21.4	14.3	27.0	19.4	30.6
Informal sector employees	78.0	65.0	83.0	76.6	82.7
Domestic workers employed by households	94.0	94.9	89.5	94.4	93.4
Total employees	52.7	42.5	59.1	43.5	72.5

6. Informal non-agricultural employment outside the informal sector by type (%)

Type of employment	Total	Women	Men	Urban	Rural
Producers of goods exclusively for own final use					
Contributing family workers: formal sector	3.8	4.3	3.2	4.3	2.9
Employees	96.2	95.7	96.8	95.7	97.1
Employees: formal sector	50.4	26.7	80.2	55.0	40.6
Employees: domestic work	45.7	69.0	16.6	40.7	56.4
Total	100.0	100.0	100.0	100.0	100.0

7. Share of women in employment by type

Share of women in ...	%
1. Total employment	37.3
2. Agricultural employment	8.3
2.1 Agricultural wage employment	7.3
2.1.1 Formal agricultural wage employment	17.4
2.1.2 Informal agricultural wage employment	5.7
2.2 Agricultural self-employment	8.7
3. Non-agricultural employment	48.7
3.1 Non-agricultural wage employment*	44.3
3.1.1 Formal non-agricultural wage employment	47.9
3.1.2 Informal non-agricultural wage employment	40.0
3.2 Non-agricultural self-employment	55.0
3.2.1 Formal non-agricultural self-employment	39.8
3.2.2 Informal non-agricultural self-employment	56.0

* = MDG Indicator No. 3.2: Share of women in wage employment in the non-agricultural sector

8. Share of women in informal non-agricultural employment by component

Share of women in ...	%
1. Informal employment	49.3
1.1 Self-employment	56.0
1.2 Wage employment	40.0
2. Employment in the informal sector	47.2
2.1 Self-employment	55.9
2.2 Wage employment	27.4
3. Informal employment outside the informal sector	55.6
3.1 Self-employment	62.7
3.2 Wage employment	55.3
3.2.1 Formal sector	29.4
3.2.2 Domestic work	83.9

9. Share of informal employment (%) by kind of non-agricultural activity

Share of informal employment in total employment in ...	Total	Women	Men
All non-agricultural actitvities	65.7	66.6	64.9
Manufacturing	57.9	62.6	53.6
Construction	85.4	50.0	86.2
Trade	81.4	84.0	78.1
Transportation	75.7	31.7	79.2
Services other than trade or transportation	49.8	54.0	43.7

10. Non-agricultural employment by sex, formal/informal nature and kind of activity (%)

A. Both sexes

Kind of activity	Total	Formal	Informal
All non-agricultural actitvities	100.0	100.0	100.0
Manufacturing	20.1	24.7	17.7
Construction	7.2	3.1	9.4
Trade	32.6	17.7	40.4
Transportation	5.6	4.0	6.5
Services other than trade or transportation	34.5	50.6	26.1

B. Women

Kind of activity	Total	Formal	Informal
All non-agricultural actitvities	100.0	100.0	100.0
Manufacturing	19.7	22.0	18.5
Construction	0.3	0.5	0.2
Trade	37.2	17.8	46.9
Transportation	0.9	1.8	0.4
Services other than trade or transportation	41.9	57.9	34.0

C. Men

Kind of activity	Total	Formal	Informal
All non-agricultural actitvities	100.0	100.0	100.0
Manufacturing	20.5	27.1	16.9
Construction	13.7	5.4	18.3
Trade	28.2	17.6	34.0
Transportation	10.1	6.0	12.4
Services other than trade or transportation	27.4	44.0	18.4

Country: Nicaragua   Year: 2008
Non-agricultural employment

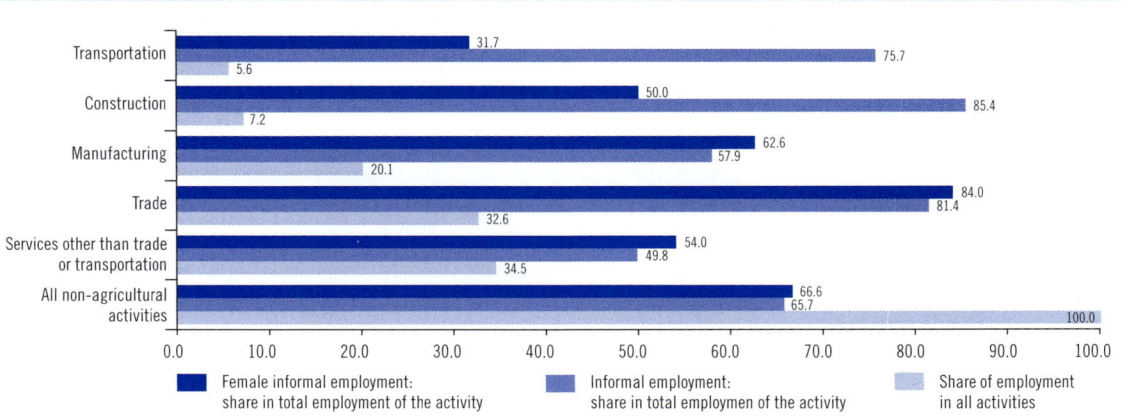

Women and men in the informal economy: A statistical picture

Country: Pakistan

Source: Labour Force Survey

Year: 2009–2010

1. Informal non-agricultural employment and its components

	Total	Women	Men	Urban	Rural
in 1,000					
Persons in informal employment	21'913	2'079	19'834	10'861	11'052
Persons employed in the informal sector	20'416	1'979	18'437	10'019	10'297
Persons in formal employment in the informal sector	722	119	603	441	281
Persons in informal employment outside the informal sector	2'319	219	2'100	1'283	1'036
as % of non-agricultural employment					
Persons in informal employment	78.4	75.7	78.7	75.8	81.1
Persons employed in the informal sector	73.0	72.1	73.1	69.9	75.6
Persons in formal employment in the informal sector	2.6	4.3	2.4	3.1	2.1
Persons in informal employment outside the informal sector	8.3	8.0	8.3	8.9	7.6

2. Employment in the informal sector by status in employment (%)

Status in employment	Total	Women	Men	Urban	Rural
Employers, own-account workers and MPCs*	45.0	32.8	46.3	46.4	44.0
Contributing family workers	10.5	18.6	9.6	12.5	8.5
Employees	44.1	48.6	43.6	41.0	47.5
Total	100.0	100.0	100.0	100.0	100.0

* Members of producers' cooperatives

3. Informal non-agricultural employment by status in employment (%)

Status in employment	Total	Women	Men	Urban	Rural
Employers, own-account workers and MPCs*	41.9	31.2	43.0	42.8	41.0
Owners of informal sector enterprises	41.9	31.2	43.0	42.8	41.0
Producers of goods exclusively for own final use					
Contributing family workers	10.2	19.9	9.2	12.0	8.5
Employees	47.9	48.9	47.8	45.2	50.5
Formal sector employees	10.0	8.2	10.2	11.4	8.7
Informal sector employees	37.8	40.5	37.5	33.8	41.7
Domestic workers employed by households	0.1	0.1	0.1	0.1	0.1
Total	100.0	100.0	100.0	100.0	100.0

* Members of producers' cooperatives

4. Informal non-agricultural self-employment as % of total non-agricultural self-employment by status in employment

Status in employment	Total	Women	Men	Urban	Rural
Employers & members of producers' co-operatives	85.1	100.0	84.7	83.8	89.7
Own-account workers	98.1	97.2	98.2	98.2	98.1
Enterprise owners	98.1	97.2	98.2	98.2	98.1
Total self-employment (incl. contributing family workers)	97.8	98.3	97.7	97.4	98.2

5. Informal wage employment as % of total wage employment by type of employees

Type of employees	Total	Women	Men	Urban	Rural
Agricultural employees	94.6	99.8	92.3	85.7	95.1
Non-agricultural employees	64.4	61.0	64.8	59.7	69.3
Formal sector employees	30.3	24.4	30.9	30.1	30.6
Informal sector employees	92.0	87.6	92.5	89.3	94.3
Domestic workers employed by households	70.8	100.0	66.7	60.0	78.6
Total employees	67.3	70.4	66.9	60.0	73.6

6. Informal non-agricultural employment outside the informal sector by type (%)

Type of employment	Total	Women	Men	Urban	Rural
Producers of goods exclusively for own final use					
Contributing family workers: formal sector	4.3	20.5	2.6	3.2	5.7
Employees	95.7	79.5	97.4	96.8	94.3
Employees: formal sector	95.0	78.1	96.7	96.3	93.2
Employees: domestic work	0.7	1.4	0.7	0.5	1.1
Total	100.0	100.0	100.0	100.0	100.0

7. Share of women in employment by type

Share of women in …	%
1. Total employment	21.2
2. Agricultural employment	36.1
2.1 Agricultural wage employment	30.7
2.1.1 Formal agricultural wage employment	1.1
2.1.2 Informal agricultural wage employment	32.4
2.2 Agricultural self-employment	36.6
3. Non-agricultural employment	9.8
3.1 Non-agricultural wage employment*	10.2
3.1.1 Formal non-agricultural wage employment	11.2
3.1.2 Informal non-agricultural wage employment	9.7
3.2 Non-agricultural self-employment	9.3
3.2.1 Formal non-agricultural self-employment	7.0
3.2.2 Informal non-agricultural self-employment	9.3

* = MDG Indicator No. 3.2: Share of women in wage employment in the non-agricultural sector

8. Share of women in informal non-agricultural employment by component

Share of women in …	%
1. Informal employment	9.5
1.1 Self-employment	9.3
1.2. Wage employment	9.7
2. Employment in the informal sector	9.7
2.1 Self-employment	9.0
2.2 Wage employment	10.7
3. Informal employment outside the informal sector	9.4
3.1 Self-employment	45.0
3.2 Wage employment	7.8
3.2.1 Formal sector	7.8
3.2.2 Domestic work	17.6

Women and men in the informal economy: A statistical picture

9. Share of informal employment (%) by kind of non-agricultural activity

Share of informal employment in total employment in …	Total	Women	Men
All non-agricultural actitvities	78.4	78.6	75.8
Manufacturing	80.0	76.7	96.9
Construction	96.7	96.7	96.2
Trade	96.1	96.0	99.1
Transportation	84.9	85.3	48.3
Services other than trade or transportation	41.5	38.9	51.9

10. Non-agricultural employment by sex, formal/informal nature and kind of activity (%)

A. Both sexes

Kind of activity	Total	Formal	Informal
All non-agricultural actitvities	100.0	100.0	100.0
Manufacturing	25.5	23.5	26.1
Construction	12.3	1.9	15.2
Trade	29.4	5.3	36.1
Transportation	9.6	6.7	10.4
Services other than trade or transportation	23.2	62.7	12.3

B. Women

Kind of activity	Total	Formal	Informal
All non-agricultural actitvities	100.0	100.0	100.0
Manufacturing	23.6	25.7	23.0
Construction	13.5	2.1	16.7
Trade	31.7	5.9	38.7
Transportation	10.5	7.2	11.4
Services other than trade or transportation	20.7	59.1	10.2

C. Men

Kind of activity	Total	Formal	Informal
All non-agricultural actitvities	100.0	100.0	100.0
Manufacturing	43.5	5.6	55.6
Construction	1.0	0.2	1.2
Trade	8.4	0.3	11.0
Transportation	1.1	2.3	0.7
Services other than trade or transportation	46.1	91.7	31.6

Country: Pakistan **Year: 2009–2010**
Non-agricultural employment

Activity	Female informal employment: share in total employment of the activity	Informal employment: share in total employmen of the activity	Share of employment in all activities
Transportation	85.3	84.9	9.6
Construction	96.7	96.7	12.3
Services other than trade or transportation	38.3	41.5	23.2
Manufacturing	76.7	80.0	25.5
Trade	96.0	96.1	29.4
All non-agricultural activities	78.6	78.4	100.0

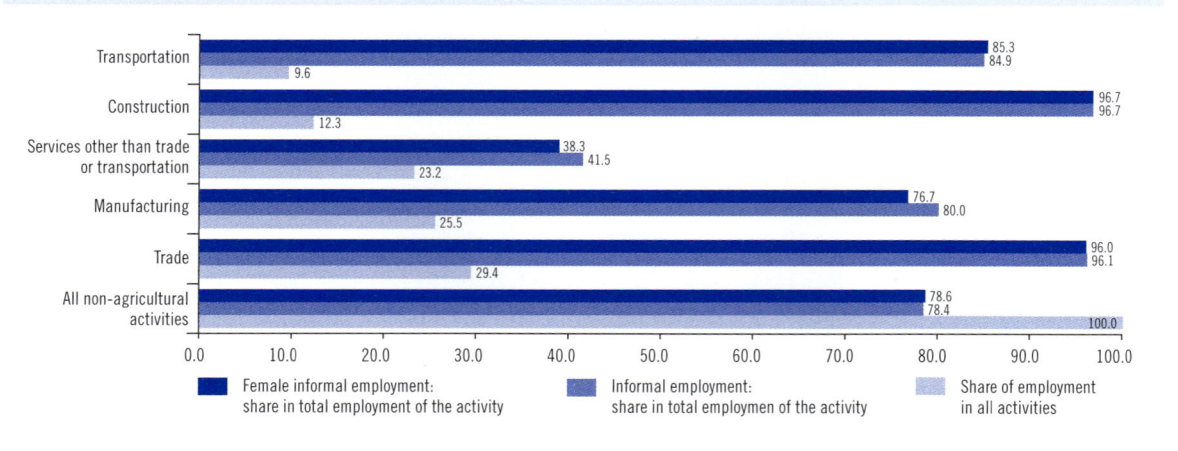

Annex II

Country: Panama
Source: Encuesta de Hogares de Propósitos Múltiples

Year: 2009 (August)

1. Informal non-agricultural employment and its components

	Total	Women	Men	Urban	Rural
in 1,000					
Persons in informal employment	517.5	232.3	285.2	365.0	152.5
Persons employed in the informal sector	327.0	129.9	197.0	224.5	102.6
Persons in formal employment in the informal sector	2.0	0.3	1.6	1.0	1.0
Persons in informal employment outside the informal sector	192.4	102.6	89.8	141.5	50.9
as % of non-agricultural employment					
Persons in informal employment	43.8	46.5	41.8	39.2	61.2
Persons employed in the informal sector	27.7	26.0	28.9	24.1	41.2
Persons in formal employment in the informal sector	0.2	0.1	0.2	0.1	0.4
Persons in informal employment outside the informal sector	16.3	20.6	13.2	15.2	20.4

2. Employment in the informal sector by status in employment (%)

Status in employment	Total	Women	Men	Urban	Rural
Employers, own-account workers and MPCs*	90.6	95.8	87.2	92.1	87.3
Contributing family workers	1.3	2.5	0.5	0.7	2.6
Employees	8.1	1.8	12.2	7.2	10.1
Total	100.0	100.0	100.0	100.0	100.0

* Members of producers' cooperatives

3. Informal non-agricultural employment by status in employment (%)

Status in employment	Total	Women	Men	Urban	Rural
Employers, own-account workers and MPCs*	57.3	53.6	60.3	56.6	58.8
Owners of informal sector enterprises	57.3	53.6	60.3	56.6	58.8
Producers of goods exclusively for own final use					
Contributing family workers	3.0	4.7	1.6	2.2	4.9
Employees	39.7	41.7	38.2	41.2	36.4
Formal sector employees	23.9	18.4	28.4	25.7	19.5
Informal sector employees	4.7	0.9	7.9	4.2	6.1
Domestic workers employed by households	11.1	22.5	1.9	11.3	10.7
Total	100.0	100.0	100.0	100.0	100.0

* Members of producers' cooperatives

4. Informal non-agricultural self-employment as % of total non-agricultural self-employment by status in employment

Status in employment	Total	Women	Men	Urban	Rural
Employers & members of producers' co-operatives	70.5	69.2	70.9	67.4	88.5
Own-account workers	98.9	99.3	98.5	98.7	99.2
Enterprise owners	98.9	99.3	98.5	98.7	99.2
Total self-employment (incl. contributing family workers)	95.5	97.3	94.2	94.2	98.6

Women and men in the informal economy: A statistical picture

5. Informal wage employment as % of total wage employment by type of employees

Type of employees	Total	Women	Men	Urban	Rural
Agricultural employees	60.5	41.0	61.4	33.1	64.8
Non-agricultural employees	24.1	26.9	22.0	21.3	36.8
Formal sector employees	16.3	14.5	17.5	14.8	24.5
Informal sector employees	92.6	87.4	93.4	94.0	90.3
Domestic workers employed by households	80.6	82.6	65.2	78.5	86.6
Total employees	27.1	27.0	27.1	21.5	45.4

6. Informal non-agricultural employment outside the informal sector by type (%)

Type of employment	Total	Women	Men	Urban	Rural
Producers of goods exclusively for own final use					
Contributing family workers: formal sector	5.9	7.6	3.9	4.5	9.5
Employees	94.1	92.4	96.1	95.5	90.5
Employees: formal sector	64.2	41.6	90.1	66.3	58.5
Employees: domestic work	29.9	50.8	6.0	29.2	32.0
Total	100.0	100.0	100.0	100.0	100.0

7. Share of women in employment by type

Share of women in …	%
1. Total employment	37.7
2. Agricultural employment	16.8
2.1 Agricultural wage employment	4.4
2.1.1 Formal agricultural wage employment	6.5
2.1.2 Informal agricultural wage employment	3.0
2.2 Agricultural self-employment	22.0
3. Non-agricultural employment	42.3
3.1 Non-agricultural wage employment*	42.1
3.1.1 Formal non-agricultural wage employment	40.6
3.1.2 Informal non-agricultural wage employment	47.1
3.2 Non-agricultural self-employment	42.7
3.2.1 Formal non-agricultural self-employment	26.1
3.2.2 Informal non-agricultural self-employment	43.4

* = MDG Indicator No. 3.2: Share of women in wage employment in the non-agricultural sector

8. Share of women in informal non-agricultural employment by component

Share of women in …	%
1. Informal employment	44.9
1.1 Self-employment	43.4
1.2 Wage employment	47.1
2. Employment in the informal sector	39.7
2.1 Self-employment	42.5
2.2 Wage employment	8.6
3. Informal employment outside the informal sector	53.3
3.1 Self-employment	69.1
3.2 Wage employment	52.4
3.2.1 Formal sector	34.5
3.2.2 Domestic work	90.6

9. Share of informal employment (%) by kind of non-agricultural activity

Share of informal employment in total employment in …	Total	Women	Men
All non-agricultural actitvities	43.8	46.5	41.8
Manufacturing	51.5	74.1	38.4
Construction	48.4	11.8	49.8
Trade	50.3	56.7	44.4
Transportation	53.5	17.9	59.5
Services other than trade or transportation	33.5	37.9	27.4

10. Non-agricultural employment by sex, formal/informal nature and kind of activity (%)

A. Both sexes

Kind of activity	Total	Formal	Informal
All non-agricultural actitvities	100.0	100.0	100.0
Manufacturing	11.6	10.0	13.6
Construction	11.8	10.8	13.0
Trade	27.7	24.5	31.8
Transportation	9.2	7.6	11.2
Services other than trade or transportation	39.7	47.0	30.3

B. Women

Kind of activity	Total	Formal	Informal
All non-agricultural actitvities	100.0	100.0	100.0
Manufacturing	10.1	4.9	16.0
Construction	1.0	1.7	0.3
Trade	31.4	25.4	38.2
Transportation	3.1	4.8	1.2
Services other than trade or transportation	54.4	63.2	44.3

C. Men

Kind of activity	Total	Formal	Informal
All non-agricultural actitvities	100.0	100.0	100.0
Manufacturing	12.7	13.5	11.7
Construction	19.7	17.0	23.4
Trade	25.0	23.9	26.5
Transportation	13.6	9.5	19.4
Services other than trade or transportation	29.0	36.2	19.0

Country: Panama **Year: 2009 (August)**

Non-agricultural employment

- Female informal employment: share in total employment of the activity
- Informal employment: share in total employmen of the activity
- Share of employment in all activities

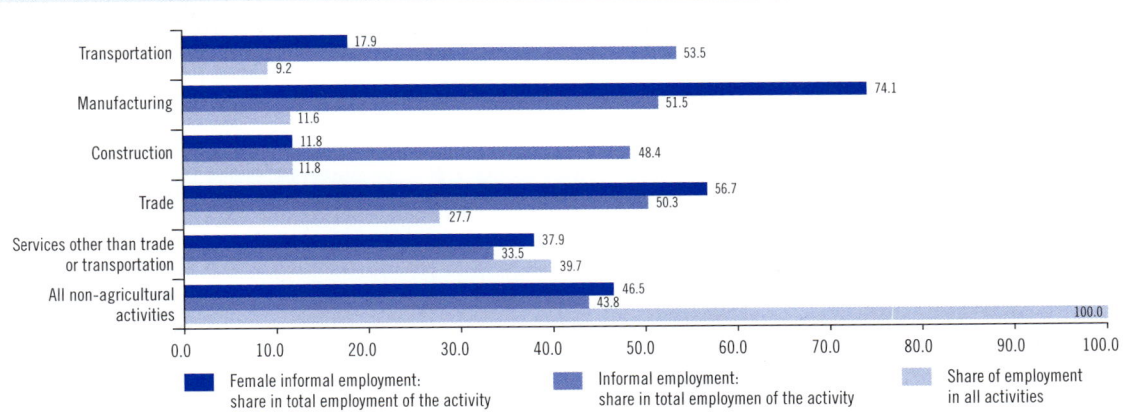

Women and men in the informal economy: A statistical picture

Country: Paraguay **Year: 2009**

Source: Encuesta Permanente de Hogares

1. Informal non-agricultural employment and its components

	Total	Women	Men	Urban	Rural
in 1,000					
Persons in informal employment	1'472.6	666.3	806.4	1'102.4	370.2
Persons employed in the informal sector	790.1	328.3	461.7	560.3	229.7
Persons in formal employment in the informal sector	0.7	-	0.7	0.7	-
Persons in informal employment outside the informal sector	683.2	337.9	345.3	542.8	140.5
as % of non-agricultural employment					
Persons in informal employment	70.7	74.4	67.9	67.7	81.3
Persons employed in the informal sector	37.9	36.7	38.9	34.4	50.4
Persons in formal employment in the informal sector	0.0	-	0.1	0.0	-
Persons in informal employment outside the informal sector	32.8	37.7	29.1	33.4	30.8

2. Employment in the informal sector by status in employment (%)

Status in employment	Total	Women	Men	Urban	Rural
Employers, own-account workers and MPCs*	62.8	75.5	53.8	62.6	63.3
Contributing family workers	11.2	14.3	9.0	11.5	10.3
Employees	26.0	10.2	37.3	25.9	26.4
Total	100.0	100.0	100.0	100.0	100.0

* Members of producers' cooperatives

3. Informal non-agricultural employment by status in employment (%)

Status in employment	Total	Women	Men	Urban	Rural
Employers, own-account workers and MPCs*	33.7	37.2	30.8	31.8	39.3
Owners of informal sector enterprises	33.7	37.2	30.8	31.8	39.3
Producers of goods exclusively for own final use					
Contributing family workers	6.5	7.8	5.4	6.4	6.9
Employees	59.8	55.0	63.8	61.8	53.8
Formal sector employees	32.4	23.1	40.1	35.5	23.3
Informal sector employees	13.9	5.0	21.3	13.1	16.4
Domestic workers employed by households	13.4	26.8	2.4	13.2	14.1
Total	100.0	100.0	100.0	100.0	100.0

* Members of producers' cooperatives

4. Informal non-agricultural self-employment as % of total non-agricultural self-employment by status in employment

Status in employment	Total	Women	Men	Urban	Rural
Employers & members of producers' co-operatives	45.4	41.5	46.5	40.5	65.9
Own-account workers	82.3	83.7	80.8	78.9	91.9
Enterprise owners	82.3	83.7	80.8	78.9	91.9
Total self-employment (incl. contributing family workers)	78.3	82.8	74.3	74.5	89.6

5. Informal wage employment as % of total wage employment by type of employees

Type of employees	Total	Women	Men	Urban	Rural
Agricultural employees	96.1	93.3	96.5	97.7	95.8
Non-agricultural employees	66.4	68.7	64.8	64.1	75.3
Formal sector employees	51.8	48.1	53.7	50.7	57.0
Informal sector employees	99.7	100.0	99.6	99.5	100.0
Domestic workers employed by households	99.8	99.8	100.0	100.0	99.3
Total employees	68.4	69.3	67.8	64.7	80.0

6. Informal non-agricultural employment outside the informal sector by type (%)

Type of employment	Total	Women	Men	Urban	Rural
Producers of goods exclusively for own final use					
Contributing family workers: formal sector	1.1	1.5	0.6	1.0	1.4
Employees	98.9	98.5	99.4	99.0	98.6
Employees: formal sector	69.9	45.6	93.7	72.1	61.5
Employees: domestic work	29.0	52.8	5.6	26.9	37.1
Total	100.0	100.0	100.0	100.0	100.0

7. Share of women in employment by type

Share of women in …	%
1. Total employment	38.7
2. Agricultural employment	28.4
2.1 Agricultural wage employment	13.1
2.1.1 Formal agricultural wage employment	22.6
2.1.2 Informal agricultural wage employment	12.8
2.2 Agricultural self-employment	30.3
3. Non-agricultural employment	43.0
3.1 Non-agricultural wage employment*	40.1
3.1.1 Formal non-agricultural wage employment	37.3
3.1.2 Informal non-agricultural wage employment	41.6
3.2 Non-agricultural self-employment	48.0
3.2.1 Formal non-agricultural self-employment	38.2
3.2.2 Informal non-agricultural self-employment	50.7

* = MDG Indicator No. 3.2: Share of women in wage employment in the non-agricultural sector

8. Share of women in informal non-agricultural employment by component

Share of women in …	%
1. Informal employment	45.2
1.1 Self-employment	50.7
1.2. Wage employment	41.6
2. Employment in the informal sector	41.6
2.1 Self-employment	50.4
2.2 Wage employment	16.3
3. Informal employment outside the informal sector	49.5
3.1 Self-employment	71.3
3.2 Wage employment	49.2
3.2.1 Formal sector	32.3
3.2.2 Domestic work	90.2

Women and men in the informal economy: A statistical picture

9. Share of informal employment (%) by kind of non-agricultural activity

Share of informal employment in total employment in …	Total	Women	Men
All non-agricultural actitvities	70.7	74.4	67.9
Manufacturing	72.0	82.8	66.5
Construction	92.6	100.0	92.5
Trade	78.6	82.2	75.5
Transportation	55.8	54.5	56.0
Services other than trade or transportation	59.4	66.6	49.0

10. Non-agricultural employment by sex, formal/informal nature and kind of activity (%)

A. Both sexes

Kind of activity	Total	Formal	Informal
All non-agricultural actitvities	100.0	100.0	100.0
Manufacturing	16.2	15.5	16.5
Construction	8.2	2.1	10.8
Trade	35.0	25.5	38.9
Transportation	6.2	9.3	4.9
Services other than trade or transportation	34.4	47.6	28.9

B. Women

Kind of activity	Total	Formal	Informal
All non-agricultural actitvities	100.0	100.0	100.0
Manufacturing	12.7	8.6	14.2
Construction	0.2	0.0	0.3
Trade	37.7	26.2	41.7
Transportation	1.9	3.3	1.4
Services other than trade or transportation	47.4	62.0	42.4

C. Men

Kind of activity	Total	Formal	Informal
All non-agricultural actitvities	100.0	100.0	100.0
Manufacturing	18.8	19.6	18.4
Construction	14.3	3.4	19.4
Trade	32.9	25.1	36.6
Transportation	9.4	12.9	7.8
Services other than trade or transportation	24.5	38.9	17.7

Country: Paraguay
Year: 2009
Non-agricultural employment

- Female informal employment: share in total employment of the activity
- Informal employment: share in total employmen of the activity
- Share of employment in all activities

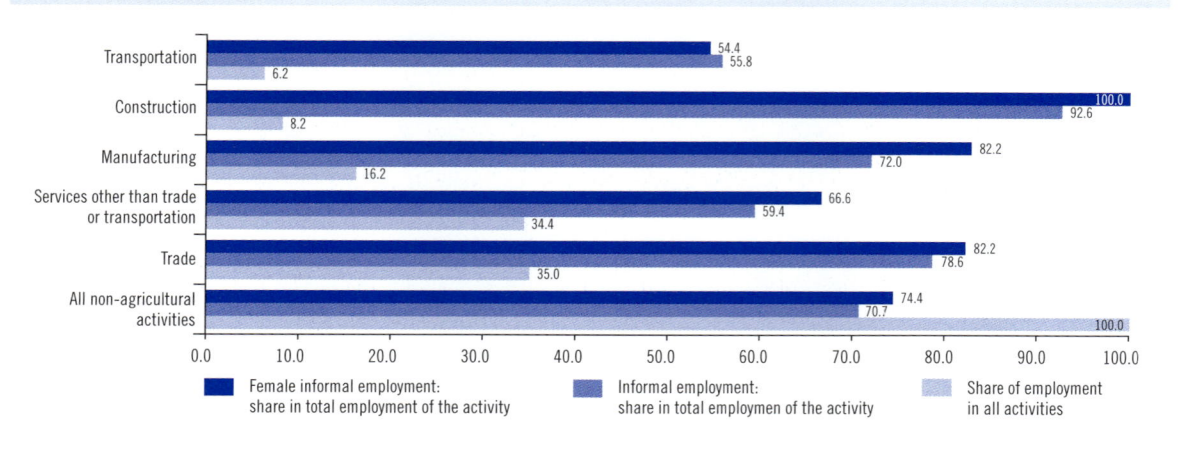

Annex II

Country: Peru
Source: Encuesta Nacional de Hogares

Year: 2009

1. Informal non-agricultural employment and its components

	Total	Women	Men	Urban	Rural
in 1,000					
Persons in informal employment	7'457.6	3'691.1	3'766.5	6'537.5	920.2
Persons employed in the informal sector	5'222.6	2'650.4	2'572.3	4'566.0	656.7
Persons in formal employment in the informal sector	77.7	40.4	37.3	74.8	3.0
Persons in informal employment outside the informal sector	2'312.7	1'081.2	1'231.6	2'046.3	266.5
as % of non-agricultural employment					
Persons in informal employment	69.9	75.7	65.1	68.0	87.8
Persons employed in the informal sector	49.0	54.3	44.4	47.5	62.6
Persons in formal employment in the informal sector	0.7	0.8	0.6	0.8	0.3
Persons in informal employment outside the informal sector	21.7	22.2	21.3	21.3	25.4

2. Employment in the informal sector by status in employment (%)

Status in employment	Total	Women	Men	Urban	Rural
Employers, own-account workers and MPCs*	71.0	74.8	67.0	70.9	71.4
Contributing family workers	11.0	13.8	8.1	11.2	9.4
Employees	18.0	11.4	24.8	17.9	19.1
Total	100.0	100.0	100.0	100.0	100.0

* Members of producers' cooperatives

3. Informal non-agricultural employment by status in employment (%)

Status in employment	Total	Women	Men	Urban	Rural
Employers, own-account workers and MPCs*	49.7	53.7	45.8	49.5	51.0
Owners of informal sector enterprises	49.7	53.7	45.8	49.5	51.0
Producers of goods exclusively for own final use					
Contributing family workers	8.4	10.8	6.0	8.5	7.3
Employees	41.9	35.5	48.2	41.9	41.8
Formal sector employees	24.8	17.7	31.8	24.9	23.9
Informal sector employees	11.6	7.1	16.0	11.3	13.3
Domestic workers employed by households	5.5	10.7	0.5	5.7	4.5
Total	100.0	100.0	100.0	100.0	100.0

* Members of producers' cooperatives

4. Informal non-agricultural self-employment as % of total non-agricultural self-employment by status in employment

Status in employment	Total	Women	Men	Urban	Rural
Employers & members of producers' co-operatives	63.2	69.2	60.9	62.2	79.9
Own-account workers	95.9	96.8	94.7	95.4	98.7
Enterprise owners	95.9	96.8	94.7	95.4	98.7
Total self-employment (incl. contributing family workers)	92.6	95.6	89.1	91.9	97.8

Women and men in the informal economy: A statistical picture

5. Informal wage employment as % of total wage employment by type of employees

Type of employees	Total	Women	Men	Urban	Rural
Agricultural employees	85.3	88.8	84.1	74.0	95.1
Non-agricultural employees	52.2	54.8	50.5	50.0	76.8
Formal sector employees	40.5	40.0	40.7	38.5	66.2
Informal sector employees	91.7	86.7	94.2	90.8	97.6
Domestic workers employed by households	86.6	87.0	78.5	85.6	97.2
Total employees	56.4	57.8	55.5	51.6	85.6

6. Informal non-agricultural employment outside the informal sector by type (%)

Type of employment	Total	Women	Men	Urban	Rural
Producers of goods exclusively for own final use					
Contributing family workers: formal sector	2.2	3.1	1.4	2.3	1.9
Employees	97.8	96.9	98.6	97.7	98.1
Employees: formal sector	80.0	60.5	97.1	79.7	82.4
Employees: domestic work	17.8	36.4	1.5	18.1	15.7
Total	100.0	100.0	100.0	100.0	100.0

7. Share of women in employment by type

Share of women in …	%
1. Total employment	44.0
2. Agricultural employment	39.4
2.1 Agricultural wage employment	26.3
2.1.1 Formal agricultural wage employment	20.0
2.1.2 Informal agricultural wage employment	27.3
2.2 Agricultural self-employment	42.8
3. Non-agricultural employment	45.7
3.1 Non-agricultural wage employment*	39.9
3.1.1 Formal non-agricultural wage employment	37.7
3.1.2 Informal non-agricultural wage employment	41.9
3.2 Non-agricultural self-employment	53.2
3.2.1 Formal non-agricultural self-employment	31.3
3.2.2 Informal non-agricultural self-employment	55.0

* = MDG Indicator No. 3.2: Share of women in wage employment in the non-agricultural sector

8. Share of women in informal non-agricultural employment by component

Share of women in …	%
1. Informal employment	49.5
1.1 Self-employment	55.0
1.2. Wage employment	41.9
2. Employment in the informal sector	50.7
2.1 Self-employment	54.8
2.2 Wage employment	32.2
3. Informal employment outside the informal sector	46.7
3.1 Self-employment	66.7
3.2 Wage employment	46.3
3.2.1 Formal sector	35.3
3.2.2 Domestic work	95.5

9. Share of informal employment (%) by kind of non-agricultural activity

Share of informal employment in total employment in ...	Total	Women	Men
All non-agricultural actitvities	69.9	75.7	65.1
Manufacturing	66.6	79.0	59.6
Construction	78.8	65.0	79.3
Trade	85.6	90.3	77.7
Transportation	83.4	67.1	86.0
Services other than trade or transportation	48.1	56.5	38.7

10. Non-agricultural employment by sex, formal/informal nature and kind of activity (%)

A. Both sexes

Kind of activity	Total	Formal	Informal
All non-agricultural actitvities	100.0	100.0	100.0
Manufacturing	16.5	18.3	15.7
Construction	6.9	4.9	7.8
Trade	34.3	16.4	41.9
Transportation	10.8	6.0	12.9
Services other than trade or transportation	31.6	54.5	21.7

B. Women

Kind of activity	Total	Formal	Informal
All non-agricultural actitvities	100.0	100.0	100.0
Manufacturing	12.9	11.2	13.5
Construction	0.5	0.8	0.5
Trade	46.9	18.7	56.0
Transportation	3.3	4.4	2.9
Services other than trade or transportation	36.4	64.9	27.2

C. Men

Kind of activity	Total	Formal	Informal
All non-agricultural acitvities	100.0	100.0	100.0
Manufacturing	19.5	22.5	17.9
Construction	12.3	7.3	15.0
Trade	23.6	15.1	28.2
Transportation	17.1	6.9	22.6
Services other than trade or transportation	27.5	48.3	16.4

Country: Peru **Year: 2009**

Non-agricultural employment

- Female informal employment: share in total employment of the activity
- Informal employment: share in total employmen of the activity
- Share of employment in all activities

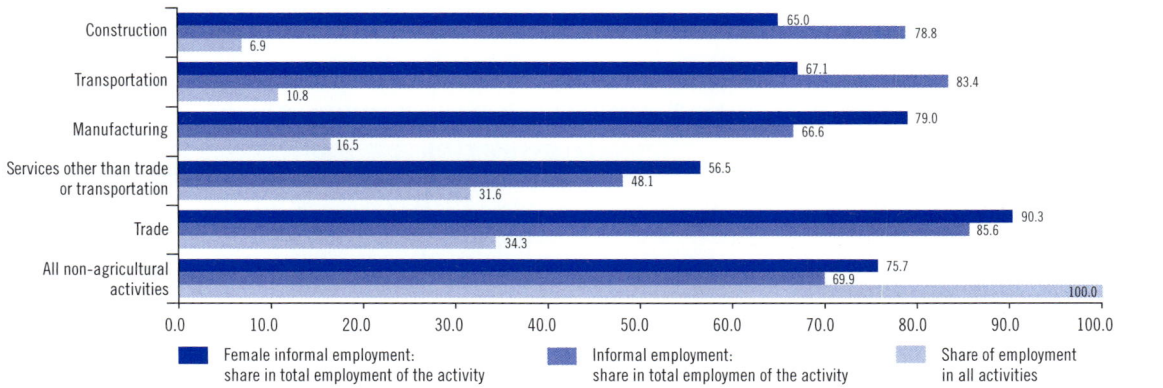

Women and men in the informal economy: A statistical picture

Country: Philippines
Source: Informal Sector Survey

Year: 2008

1. Informal non-agricultural employment and its components

	Total	Women	Men	Urban	Rural
	in 1,000				
Persons in informal employment	15'150.4	6'854.1	8'296.3		
Persons employed in the informal sector	15'680.0	6'617.6	9'062.4		
Persons in formal employment in the informal sector	3'019.4	1'410.0	1'609.5		
Persons in informal employment outside the informal sector	2'489.9	1'646.5	843.4		
	as % of non-agricultural employment				
Persons in informal employment	70.1	70.2	69.9		
Persons employed in the informal sector	72.5	67.8	76.4		
Persons in formal employment in the informal sector	14.0	14.4	13.6		
Persons in informal employment outside the informal sector	11.5	16.9	7.1		

2. Employment in the informal sector by status in employment (%)

Status in employment	Total	Women	Men	Urban	Rural
Employers, own-account workers and MPCs*	36.9	45.9	30.3		
Contributing family workers	7.6	11.6	4.7		
Employees	55.5	42.5	65.0		
Total	100.0	100.0	100.0		

* Members of producers' cooperatives

3. Informal non-agricultural employment by status in employment (%)

Status in employment	Total	Women	Men	Urban	Rural
Employers, own-account workers and MPCs*	39.3	45.2	34.4		
Owners of informal sector enterprises	38.2	44.3	33.1		
Producers of goods exclusively for own final use	1.1	0.8	1.4		
Contributing family workers	8.0	11.3	5.2		
Employees	52.8	43.5	60.4		
Formal sector employees	5.1	4.0	6.0		
Informal sector employees	37.5	20.4	51.6		
Domestic workers employed by households	10.1	19.1	2.8		
Total	100.0	100.0	100.0		

* Members of producers' cooperatives

4. Informal non-agricultural self-employment as % of total non-agricultural self-employment by status in employment

Status in employment	Total	Women	Men	Urban	Rural
Employers & members of producers' co-operatives	92.9	92.4	93.3		
Own-account workers	99.6	99.7	99.5		
Enterprise owners	99.6	99.7	99.5		
Total self-employment (incl. contributing family workers)	99.1	99.3	98.9		

5. Informal wage employment as % of total wage employment by type of employees

Type of employees	Total	Women	Men	Urban	Rural
Agricultural employees	93.8	93.9	93.8		
Non-agricultural employees	55.5	50.8	58.7		
Formal sector employees	18.8	16.0	20.7		
Informal sector employees	65.3	49.8	72.7		
Domestic workers employed by households	97.7	98.0	96.0		
Total employees	62.7	55.2	67.0		

6. Informal non-agricultural employment outside the informal sector by type (%)

Type of employment	Total	Women	Men	Urban	Rural
Producers of goods exclusively for own final use	6.8	3.4	13.4		
Contributing family workers: formal sector	0.4	0.5	0.3		
Employees	92.8	96.1	86.4		
Employees: formal sector	31.1	16.8	59.2		
Employees: domestic work	61.7	79.3	27.2		
Total	100.0	100.0	100.0		

7. Share of women in employment by type

Share of women in …	%
1. Total employment	38.1
2. Agricultural employment	25.1
2.1 Agricultural wage employment	19.8
2.1.1 Formal agricultural wage employment	19.5
2.1.2 Informal agricultural wage employment	19.9
2.2 Agricultural self-employment	27.2
3. Non-agricultural employment	45.2
3.1 Non-agricultural wage employment*	40.7
3.1.1 Formal non-agricultural wage employment	45.0
3.1.2 Informal non-agricultural wage employment	37.3
3.2 Non-agricultural self-employment	54.0
3.2.1 Formal non-agricultural self-employment	41.5
3.2.2 Informal non-agricultural self-employment	54.1

* = MDG Indicator No. 3.2: Share of women in wage employment in the non-agricultural sector

8. Share of women in informal non-agricultural employment by component

Share of women in …	%
1. Informal employment	45.2
1.1 Self-employment	54.1
1.2. Wage employment	37.3
2. Employment in the informal sector	42.2
2.1 Self-employment	54.5
2.2 Wage employment	32.3
3. Informal employment outside the informal sector	66.1
3.1 Self-employment	35.7
3.2 Wage employment	68.5
3.2.1 Formal sector	35.6
3.2.2 Domestic work	85.1

Women and men in the informal economy: A statistical picture

9. Share of informal employment (%) by kind of non-agricultural activity

Share of informal employment in total employment in …	Total	Women	Men
All non-agricultural actitvities	70.1	70.2	69.9
Manufacturing	61.8	62.4	61.3
Construction	87.2	49.0	88.0
Trade	86.7	89.7	82.1
Transportation	85.5	34.2	88.8
Services other than trade or transportation	50.6	57.3	41.5

10. Non-agricultural employment by sex, formal/informal nature and kind of activity (%)

A. Both sexes

Kind of activity	Total	Formal	Informal
All non-agricultural actitvities	100.0	100.0	100.0
Manufacturing	14.6	18.6	12.9
Construction	8.5	3.6	10.6
Trade	29.2	13.0	36.2
Transportation	11.9	5.8	14.5
Services other than trade or transportation	35.7	58.9	25.8

B. Women

Kind of activity	Total	Formal	Informal
All non-agricultural actitvities	100.0	100.0	100.0
Manufacturing	13.4	16.9	12.0
Construction	0.4	0.7	0.3
Trade	38.8	13.4	49.6
Transportation	1.6	3.5	0.8
Services other than trade or transportation	45.7	65.4	37.4

C. Men

Kind of activity	Total	Formal	Informal
All non-agricultural actitvities	100.0	100.0	100.0
Manufacturing	15.5	20.0	13.6
Construction	15.2	6.1	19.2
Trade	21.3	12.7	25.0
Transportation	20.4	7.6	25.9
Services other than trade or transportation	27.5	53.6	16.3

Country: Philippines **Year: 2008**
Non-agricultural employment

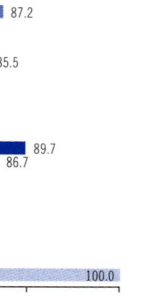

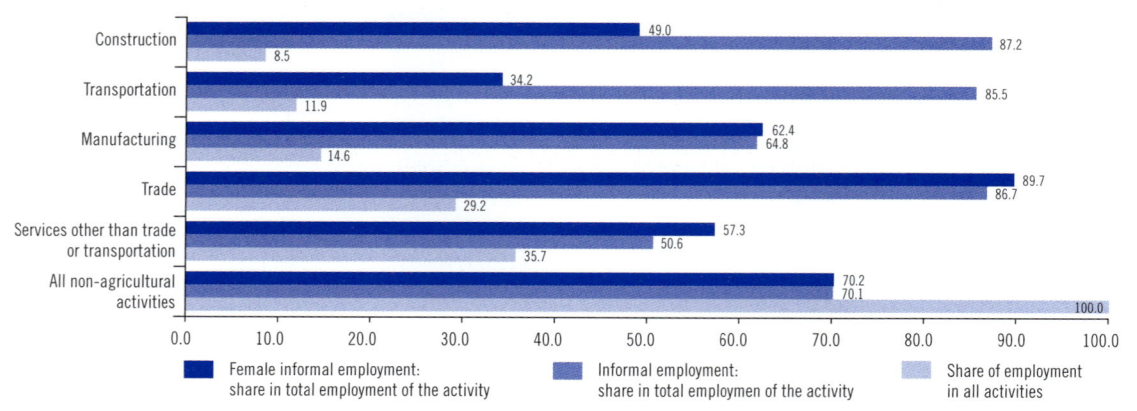

Country: Russian Federation
Source: Labour Force Survey

Year: 2010

1. Informal non-agricultural employment and its components

	Total	Women	Men	Urban	Rural
in 1,000					
Persons in informal employment					
Persons employed in the informal sector	7'784.6	3'535.6	4'249.0	5'868.9	1'915.7
Persons in formal employment in the informal sector					
Persons in informal employment outside the informal sector					
as % of non-agricultural employment					
Persons in informal employment					
Persons employed in the informal sector	12.1	10.9	13.3	11.3	15.3
Persons in formal employment in the informal sector					
Persons in informal employment outside the informal sector					

2. Employment in the informal sector by status in employment (%)

Status in employment	Total	Women	Men	Urban	Rural
Employers, own-account workers and MPCs*	30.7	27.6	33.3	31.1	29.7
Contributing family workers	2.2	2.1	2.3	2.0	2.8
Employees	67.1	70.3	64.4	66.9	67.6
Total	100.0	100.0	100.0	100.0	100.0

* Members of producers' cooperatives

3. Informal non-agricultural employment by status in employment (%)

Status in employment	Total	Women	Men	Urban	Rural
Data not available.					

4. Informal non-agricultural self-employment as % of total non-agricultural self-employment by status in employment

Status in employment	Total	Women	Men	Urban	Rural
Employers & members of producers' co-operatives	78.3	82.4	75.8	77.8	80.5
Own-account workers	95.7	95.8	95.7	95.3	96.9
Enterprise owners	95.7	95.8	95.7	95.3	96.9
Total self-employment (incl. contributing family workers)	90.9	92.5	89.8	90.0	93.8

5. Informal wage employment as % of total wage employment by type of employees

Type of employees	Total	Women	Men	Urban	Rural
Data not available.					

Women and men in the informal economy: A statistical picture

6. Informal non-agricultural employment outside the informal sector by type (%)

Type of employment	Total	Women	Men	Urban	Rural
Data not available.					

7. Share of women in employment by type

Share of women in ...	%
1. Total employment	49.1
2. Agricultural employment	35.6
2.1 Agricultural wage employment	29.4
2.1.1 Formal agricultural wage employment	
2.1.2 Informal agricultural wage employment	
2.2 Agricultural self-employment	47.1
3. Non-agricultural employment	50.3
3.1 Non-agricultural wage employment*	50.8
3.1.1 Formal non-agricultural wage employment	
3.1.2 Informal non-agricultural wage employment	
3.2 Non-agricultural self-employment	40.5
3.2.1 Formal non-agricultural self-employment	33.2
3.2.2 Informal non-agricultural self-employment	41.3

* = MDG Indicator No. 3.2: Share of women in wage employment in the non-agricultural sector

8. Share of women in informal non-agricultural employment by component

Share of women in ...	%
1. Informal employment	
1.1 Self-employment	
1.2. Wage employment	
2. Employment in the informal sector	45.4
2.1 Self-employment	41.0
2.2 Wage employment	47.6
3. Informal employment outside the informal sector	
3.1 Self-employment	
3.2 Wage employment	
3.2.1 Formal sector	
3.2.2 Domestic work	

9. Share of informal employment (%) by kind of non-agricultural activity

Share of informal employment in total employment in ...	Total	Women	Men
Data not available.			

10. Non-agricultural employment by sex, formal/informal nature and kind of activity (%)

A. Both sexes

Kind of activity	Total	Formal	Informal
All non-agricultural actitvities	100.0		
Manufacturing	22.2		
Construction	7.8		
Trade	16.9		
Transportation	10.1		
Services other than trade or transportation	42.9		

B. Women

Kind of activity	Total	Formal	Informal
All non-agricultural actitvities	100.0		
Manufacturing	16.4		
Construction	2.5		
Trade	20.9		
Transportation	5.6		
Services other than trade or transportation	54.6		

C. Men

Kind of activity	Total	Formal	Informal
All non-agricultural actitvities	100.0		
Manufacturing	28.2		
Construction	13.2		
Trade	12.9		
Transportation	14.7		
Services other than trade or transportation	31.1		

Women and men in the informal economy: A statistical picture

Country: Serbia
Source: Labour Force survey

Year: 2010

1. Informal non-agricultural employment and its components

	Total	Women	Men	Urban	Rural
in 1,000					
Persons in informal employment	113.4	34.7	78.7	57.8	55.6
Persons employed in the informal sector	65.8	17.3	48.5	34.4	31.4
Persons in formal employment in the informal sector	8.9	4.0	4.9	6.4	2.5
Persons in informal employment outside the informal sector	56.5	21.4	35.1	29.9	26.7
as % of non-agricultural employment					
Persons in informal employment	6.1	4.3	7.5	4.6	9.2
Persons employed in the informal sector	3.5	2.1	4.6	2.7	5.2
Persons in formal employment in the informal sector	0.5	0.5	0.5	0.5	0.4
Persons in informal employment outside the informal sector	3.0	2.6	3.3	2.4	4.4

2. Employment in the informal sector by status in employment (%)

Status in employment	Total	Women	Men	Urban	Rural
Employers, own-account workers and MPCs*	65.0	64.4	65.2	66.6	63.2
Contributing family workers	2.4	4.5	1.7	0.4	4.7
Employees	32.6	31.1	33.1	33.0	32.2
Total	100.0	100.0	100.0	100.0	100.0

* Members of producers' cooperatives

3. Informal non-agricultural employment by status in employment (%)

Status in employment	Total	Women	Men	Urban	Rural
Employers, own-account workers and MPCs*	37.7	32.0	40.2	39.6	35.7
Owners of informal sector enterprises	37.7	32.0	40.2	39.6	35.7
Producers of goods exclusively for own final use					
Contributing family workers	9.0	11.7	7.8	7.3	10.7
Employees	53.4	56.3	52.1	53.2	53.6
Formal sector employees	42.3	52.3	37.9	44.6	39.9
Informal sector employees	11.1	4.0	14.2	8.6	13.7
Domestic workers employed by households					
Total	100.0	100.0	100.0	100.0	100.0

* Members of producers' cooperatives

4. Informal non-agricultural self-employment as % of total non-agricultural self-employment by status in employment

Status in employment	Total	Women	Men	Urban	Rural
Employers & members of producers' co-operatives	2.0	1.6	2.1	1.7	2.6
Own-account workers	21.2	16.8	23.3	17.0	29.2
Enterprise owners	21.2	16.8	23.3	17.0	29.2
Total self-employment (incl. contributing family workers)	18.4	16.5	19.2	14.1	26.9

5. Informal wage employment as % of total wage employment by type of employees

Type of employees	Total	Women	Men	Urban	Rural
Agricultural employees	26.6	34.5	24.9	17.9	31.6
Non-agricultural employees	3.8	2.7	4.8	2.9	5.9
Formal sector employees	3.1	2.6	3.5	2.4	4.5
Informal sector employees	58.5	25.9	69.4	43.8	75.1
Domestic workers employed by households					
Total employees	4.5	3.2	5.6	3.1	7.4

6. Informal non-agricultural employment outside the informal sector by type (%)

Type of employment	Total	Women	Men	Urban	Rural
Producers of goods exclusively for own final use					
Contributing family workers: formal sector	15.1	15.2	15.1	13.6	16.8
Employees	84.9	84.8	84.9	86.4	83.2
Employees: formal sector	84.9	84.8	84.9	86.4	83.2
Employees: domestic work					
Total	100.0	100.0	100.0	100.0	100.0

7. Share of women in employment by type

Share of women in ...	%
1. Total employment	42.7
2. Agricultural employment	40.1
2.1 Agricultural wage employment	23.3
2.1.1 Formal agricultural wage employment	20.9
2.1.2 Informal agricultural wage employment	30.1
2.2 Agricultural self-employment	41.7
3. Non-agricultural employment	43.5
3.1 Non-agricultural wage employment*	45.6
3.1.1 Formal non-agricultural wage employment	46.1
3.1.2 Informal non-agricultural wage employment	32.3
3.2 Non-agricultural self-employment	31.9
3.2.1 Formal non-agricultural self-employment	32.6
3.2.2 Informal non-agricultural self-employment	28.7

* = MDG Indicator No. 3.2: Share of women in wage employment in the non-agricultural sector

8. Share of women in informal non-agricultural employment by component

Share of women in ...	%
1. Informal employment	30.6
1.1 Self-employment	28.7
1.2. Wage employment	32.3
2. Employment in the informal sector	26.2
2.1 Self-employment	26.8
2.2 Wage employment	25.0
3. Informal employment outside the informal sector	37.9
3.1 Self-employment	38.1
3.2 Wage employment	37.9
3.2.1 Formal sector	37.9
3.2.2 Domestic work	

Women and men in the informal economy: A statistical picture

9. Share of informal employment (%) by kind of non-agricultural activity

Share of informal employment in total employment in …	Total	Women	Men
All non-agricultural actitvities	6.1	4.3	7.5
Manufacturing	3.9	3.8	4.0
Construction	26.1	0.0	30.2
Trade	7.2	6.6	7.9
Transportation	3.1	1.4	3.6
Services other than trade or transportation	4.4	3.9	5.0

10. Non-agricultural employment by sex, formal/informal nature and kind of activity (%)

A. Both sexes

Kind of activity	Total	Formal	Informal
All non-agricultural actitvities	100.0	100.0	100.0
Manufacturing	27.0	27.6	17.3
Construction	6.5	5.1	27.8
Trade	17.5	17.3	20.8
Transportation	6.7	7.0	3.5
Services other than trade or transportation	42.3	43.1	30.6

B. Women

Kind of activity	Total	Formal	Informal
All non-agricultural actitvities	100.0	100.0	100.0
Manufacturing	18.4	18.5	16.2
Construction	2.0	2.1	0.0
Trade	20.9	20.4	32.1
Transportation	3.4	3.5	1.1
Services other than trade or transportation	55.3	55.5	50.7

C. Men

Kind of activity	Total	Formal	Informal
All non-agricultural actitvities	100.0	100.0	100.0
Manufacturing	33.6	34.8	17.8
Construction	9.9	7.5	40.1
Trade	14.9	14.8	15.8
Transportation	9.3	9.7	4.5
Services other than trade or transportation	32.3	33.2	21.8

Country: Serbia **Year: 2010**

Non-agricultural employment

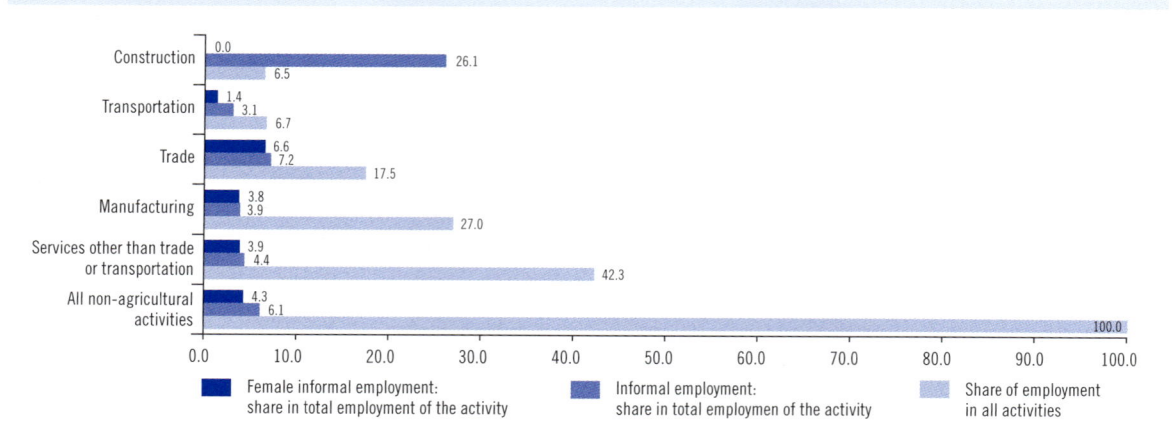

Country: South Africa
Source: Quarterly Labour Force Survey

Year: 2010 (IV)

1. Informal non-agricultural employment and its components

	Total	Women	Men	Urban	Rural
in 1,000					
Persons in informal employment	4'089.1	2'018.4	2'070.8	2'827.4	1'261.8
Persons employed in the informal sector	2'225.3	922.1	1'303.2	1'438.7	786.6
Persons in formal employment in the informal sector	0.0	0.0	0.0	0.0	0.0
Persons in informal employment outside the informal sector	1'863.9	1'096.3	767.6	1'388.7	475.2
as % of non-agricultural employment					
Persons in informal employment	32.7	36.8	29.5	28.2	51.7
Persons employed in the informal sector	17.8	16.8	18.6	14.3	32.2
Persons in formal employment in the informal sector	0.0	0.0	0.0	0.0	0.0
Persons in informal employment outside the informal sector	14.9	20.0	10.9	13.8	19.5

2. Employment in the informal sector by status in employment (%)

Status in employment	Total	Women	Men	Urban	Rural
Employers, own-account workers and MPCs*	61.0	66.0	57.5	59.9	63.0
Contributing family workers	2.7	3.4	2.2	2.3	3.5
Employees	36.3	30.6	40.3	37.8	33.5
Total	100.0	100.0	100.0	100.0	100.0

* Members of producers' cooperatives

3. Informal non-agricultural employment by status in employment (%)

Status in employment	Total	Women	Men	Urban	Rural
Employers, own-account workers and MPCs*	33.2	30.1	36.2	30.5	39.3
Owners of informal sector enterprises	33.2	30.1	36.2	30.5	39.3
Producers of goods exclusively for own final use					
Contributing family workers	2.3	2.7	2.0	2.3	2.4
Employees	64.5	67.2	61.8	67.2	58.4
Formal sector employees	17.8	11.1	24.3	19.8	13.3
Informal sector employees	19.7	14.0	25.4	19.2	20.9
Domestic workers employed by households	27.0	42.1	12.1	28.2	24.2
Total	100.0	100.0	100.0	100.0	100.0

* Members of producers' cooperatives

4. Informal non-agricultural self-employment as % of total non-agricultural self-employment by status in employment

Status in employment	Total	Women	Men	Urban	Rural
Employers & members of producers' co-operatives	36.8	26.5	39.8	30.6	65.8
Own-account workers	91.5	94.2	88.8	87.1	99.9
Enterprise owners	91.5	94.2	88.8	87.1	99.9
Total self-employment (incl. contributing family workers)	72.5	81.2	66.5	64.6	92.5

Women and men in the informal economy: A statistical picture

5. Informal wage employment as % of total wage employment by type of employees

Type of employees	Total	Women	Men	Urban	Rural
Agricultural employees	39.5	34.4	42.1	36.4	40.7
Non-agricultural employees	25.1	29.1	22.0	22.1	39.3
Formal sector employees	8.5	6.3	10.0	7.7	12.9
Informal sector employees	100.0	100.0	100.0	100.0	100.0
Domestic workers employed by households	98.7	99.4	96.3	99.0	97.7
Total employees	25.8	29.3	23.2	22.4	39.6

6. Informal non-agricultural employment outside the informal sector by type (%)

Type of employment	Total	Women	Men	Urban	Rural
Producers of goods exclusively for own final use					
Contributing family workers: formal sector	1.9	2.0	1.6	2.3	0.5
Employees	98.1	98.0	98.4	97.7	99.5
Employees: formal sector	39.0	20.4	65.6	40.2	35.3
Employees: domestic work	59.1	77.6	32.8	57.4	64.1
Total	100.0	100.0	100.0	100.0	100.0

7. Share of women in employment by type

Share of women in ...	%
1. Total employment	43.3
2. Agricultural employment	33.3
2.1 Agricultural wage employment	34.2
2.1.1 Formal agricultural wage employment	37.0
2.1.2 Informal agricultural wage employment	29.8
2.2 Agricultural self-employment	24.8
3. Non-agricultural employment	43.9
3.1 Non-agricultural wage employment*	44.5
3.1.1 Formal non-agricultural wage employment	42.2
3.1.2 Informal non-agricultural wage employment	51.5
3.2 Non-agricultural self-employment	40.7
3.2.1 Formal non-agricultural self-employment	27.7
3.2.2 Informal non-agricultural self-employment	45.6

* = MDG Indicator No. 3.2: Share of women in wage employment in the non-agricultural sector

8. Share of women in informal non-agricultural employment by component

Share of women in ...	%
1. Informal employment	49.4
1.1 Self-employment	45.6
1.2 Wage employment	51.5
2. Employment in the informal sector	41.4
2.1 Self-employment	45.1
2.2 Wage employment	35.0
3. Informal employment outside the informal sector	58.8
3.1 Self-employment	63.9
3.2 Wage employment	58.7
3.2.1 Formal sector	30.7
3.2.2 Domestic work	77.2

Annex II

9. Share of informal employment (%) by kind of non-agricultural activity

Share of informal employment in total employment in ...	Total	Women	Men
All non-agricultural actitvities	32.7	36.8	29.5
Manufacturing	19.4	27.9	14.9
Construction	47.8	15.1	51.6
Trade	42.7	44.5	41.1
Transportation	34.6	19.5	38.4
Services other than trade or transportation	28.7	36.6	19.4

10. Non-agricultural employment by sex, formal/informal nature and kind of activity (%)

A. Both sexes

Kind of activity	Total	Formal	Informal
All non-agricultural actitvities	100.0	100.0	100.0
Manufacturing	14.3	17.1	8.5
Construction	8.4	6.5	12.3
Trade	23.8	20.2	31.1
Transportation	6.1	5.9	6.4
Services other than trade or transportation	47.4	50.2	41.7

B. Women

Kind of activity	Total	Formal	Informal
All non-agricultural actitvities	100.0	100.0	100.0
Manufacturing	11.2	12.7	8.5
Construction	2.0	2.7	0.8
Trade	25.6	22.5	31.0
Transportation	2.8	3.5	1.5
Services other than trade or transportation	58.5	58.6	58.3

C. Men

Kind of activity	Total	Formal	Informal
All non-agricultural actitvities	100.0	100.0	100.0
Manufacturing	16.7	20.1	8.5
Construction	13.5	9.3	23.6
Trade	22.4	18.7	31.2
Transportation	8.7	7.6	11.3
Services other than trade or transportation	38.8	44.3	25.5

Country: South Africa   Year: 2010 (IV)

Non-agricultural employment

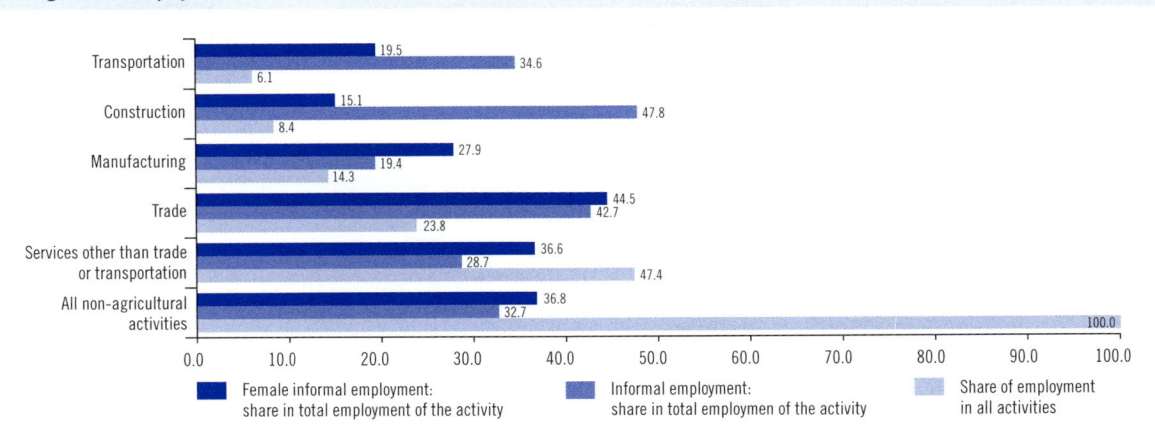

Women and men in the informal economy: A statistical picture

Country: Sri Lanka (excl. Northern Province)
Source: Sri Lanka Labour Force Survey

Year: 2009

1. Informal non-agricultural employment and its components

	Total	Women	Men	Urban	Rural
in 1,000					
Persons in informal employment	3'184.4	932.6	2'251.8	446.5	2'737.9
Persons employed in the informal sector (a)	2'587.8	700.3	1'887.5	348.2	2'239.7
Persons in formal employment in the informal sector (a)	0.0	0.0	0.0	0.0	0.0
Persons in informal employment outside the informal sector (b)	596.6	232.3	364.3	98.3	498.3
as % of non-agricultural employment					
Persons in informal employment	62.1	55.7	65.2	58.1	62.8
Persons employed in the informal sector (a)	50.5	41.8	54.7	45.3	51.4
Persons in formal employment in the informal sector (a)	0.0	0.0	0.0	0.0	0.0
Persons in informal employment outside the informal sector (b)	11.6	13.9	10.6	12.8	11.4

2. Employment in the informal sector (a) by status in employment (%)

Status in employment	Total	Women	Men	Urban	Rural
Employers, own-account workers and MPCs*	40.8	46.0	38.9	46.0	40.0
Contributing family workers	7.2	18.5	3.0	5.2	7.5
Employees	52.0	35.5	58.1	48.8	52.5
Total	100.0	100.0	100.0	100.0	100.0

* Members of producers' cooperatives

3. Informal non-agricultural employment by status in employment (%)

Status in employment	Total	Women	Men	Urban	Rural
Employers, own-account workers and MPCs*	33.2	34.5	32.6	35.9	32.7
Owners of informal sector enterprises (c)	33.2	34.5	32.6	35.9	32.7
Producers of goods exclusively for own final use					
Contributing family workers	7.7	17.7	3.5	6.2	7.9
Employees	59.2	47.8	63.9	57.9	59.4
Formal sector employees	16.9	21.1	15.2	19.9	16.4
Informal sector employees (d)	42.2	26.7	48.7	38.1	42.9
Domestic workers employed by households					
Total	100.0	100.0	100.0	100.0	100.0

* Members of producers' cooperatives

4. Informal non-agricultural self-employment as % of total non-agricultural self-employment by status in employment

Status in employment	Total	Women	Men	Urban	Rural
Employers & members of producers' co-operatives	48.7	48.1	48.7	41.4	51.4
Own-account workers	90.8	94.0	89.3	93.6	90.3
Enterprise owners (c)	90.8	94.0	89.3	93.6	90.3
Total self-employment (incl. contributing family workers)	87.6	94.5	84.0	84.0	88.3

5. Informal wage employment as % of total wage employment by type of employees

Type of employees	Total	Women	Men	Urban	Rural
Agricultural employees	62.2	49.4	70.6	94.0	61.6
Non-agricultural employees	51.7	38.5	57.9	47.5	52.5
Formal sector employees	23.4	21.6	24.6	23.7	23.4
Informal sector employees (d)	100.0	100.0	100.0	100.0	100.0
Domestic workers employed by households					
Total employees	53.5	40.6	59.8	48.7	54.2

6. Informal non-agricultural employment outside the informal sector by type (%)

Type of employment	Total	Women	Men	Urban	Rural
Producers of goods exclusively for own final use					
Contributing family workers: formal sector	9.7	15.3	6.1	9.7	9.7
Employees	90.3	84.7	93.9	90.3	90.3
Employees: formal sector	90.3	84.7	93.9	90.3	90.3
Employees: domestic work					
Total	100.0	100.0	100.0	100.0	100.0

7. Share of women in employment by type

Share of women in …	%
1. Total employment	34.7
2. Agricultural employment	39.0
2.1 Agricultural wage employment	39.3
2.1.1 Formal agricultural wage employment	52.7
2.1.2 Informal agricultural wage employment	31.2
2.2 Agricultural self-employment	38.8
3. Non-agricultural employment	32.7
3.1 Non-agricultural wage employment*	31.8
3.1.1 Formal non-agricultural wage employment	40.5
3.1.2 Informal non-agricultural wage employment	23.7
3.2 Non-agricultural self-employment	34.7
3.2.1 Formal non-agricultural self-employment	15.5
3.2.2 Informal non-agricultural self-employment	37.4

* = MDG Indicator No. 3.2: Share of women in wage employment in the non-agricultural sector

8. Share of women in informal non-agricultural employment by component

Share of women in …	%
1. Informal employment	29.3
1.1 Self-employment	37.4
1.2. Wage employment	23.7
2. Employment in the informal sector	27.1
2.1 Self-employment	36.3
2.2 Wage employment	18.5
3. Informal employment outside the informal sector	38.9
3.1 Self-employment	61.4
3.2 Wage employment	36.5
3.2.1 Formal sector	36.5
3.2.2 Domestic work	

Women and men in the informal economy: A statistical picture

9. Share of informal employment (%) by kind of non-agricultural activity

Share of informal employment in total employment in ...	Total	Women	Men
All non-agricultural actitvities	62.1	55.7	65.2
Manufacturing	62.6	63.3	61.9
Construction	92.7	74.7	93.2
Trade	78.2	84.5	76.0
Transportation	74.9	41.4	77.4
Services other than trade or transportation	42.7	38.8	45.1

10. Non-agricultural employment by sex, formal/informal nature and kind of activity (%)

A. Both sexes

Kind of activity	Total	Formal	Informal
All non-agricultural actitvities	100.0	100.0	100.0
Manufacturing	26.3	26.0	26.5
Construction	9.3	1.8	13.8
Trade	19.1	10.9	24.0
Transportation	8.7	5.7	10.5
Services other than trade or transportation	36.7	55.5	25.2

B. Women

Kind of activity	Total	Formal	Informal
All non-agricultural actitvities	100.0	100.0	100.0
Manufacturing	38.6	32.1	43.9
Construction	0.8	0.4	1.0
Trade	15.6	5.5	23.7
Transportation	1.8	2.4	1.3
Services other than trade or transportation	43.2	59.7	30.1

C. Men

Kind of activity	Total	Formal	Informal
All non-agricultural actitvities	100.0	100.0	100.0
Manufacturing	20.3	22.2	19.3
Construction	13.4	2.6	19.1
Trade	20.7	14.3	24.1
Transportation	12.0	7.8	14.3
Services other than trade or transportation	33.6	53.0	23.2

(a) Including domestic employees and producers of goods exclusively for own final use by the household. (b) Excluding domestic employees and producers of goods exclusively for own final use by the household. (c) Including producers of goods exclusively for own final use by the household. (d) Including domestic employees.

Country: Sri Lanka (excl. Northern Province)   Year: 2009

Non-agricultural employment

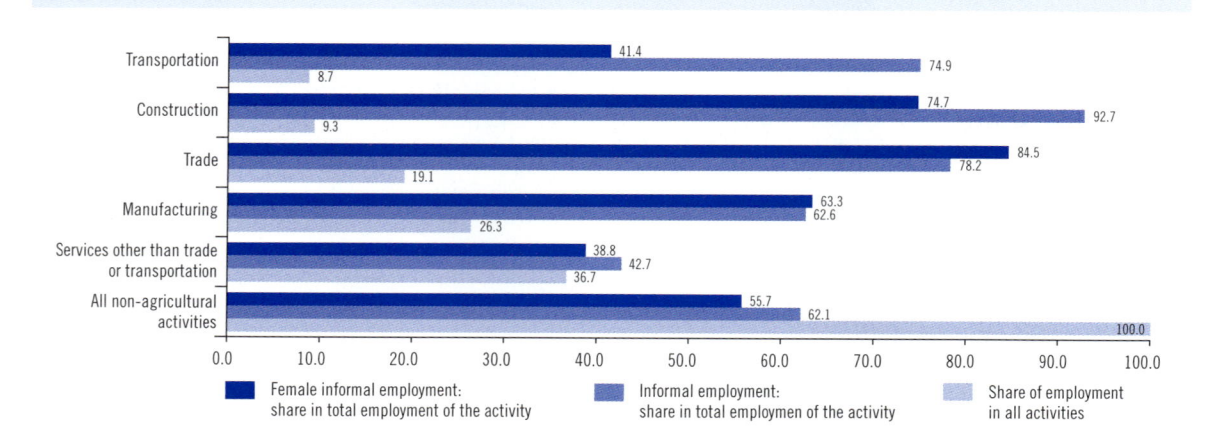

Annex II

Country: Tanzania, United Republic of
Source: Integrated Labour Force Survey

Year: 2005–2006

1. Informal non-agricultural employment and its components

	Total	Women	Men	Urban	Rural
in 1,000					
Persons in informal employment	3466.9	1672.2	1794.7	2316.8	1150.1
Persons employed in the informal sector	2352.7	1006.1	1346.6	1605.2	747.5
Persons in formal employment in the informal sector	22.5	6.0	16.5	19.5	3.0
Persons in informal employment outside the informal sector	1136.7	672.1	464.6	731.1	405.6
as % of non-agricultural employment					
Persons in informal employment	76.2	82.8	70.9	75.6	77.5
Persons employed in the informal sector	51.7	49.8	53.2	52.4	50.3
Persons in formal employment in the informal sector	0.5	0.3	0.7	0.6	0.2
Persons in informal employment outside the informal sector	25.0	33.3	18.4	23.9	27.3

2. Employment in the informal sector by status in employment (%)

Status in employment	Total	Women	Men	Urban	Rural
Employers, own-account workers and MPCs*	80.3	87.0	75.4	79.1	83.1
Contributing family workers	3.7	5.0	2.7	3.3	4.6
Employees	16.0	7.9	21.9	17.7	12.3
Total	100.0	100.0	100.0	100.0	100.0

* Members of producers' cooperatives

3. Informal non-agricultural employment by status in employment (%)

Status in employment	Total	Women	Men	Urban	Rural
Employers, own-account workers and MPCs*	70.3	79.2	62.0	68.7	73.6
Owners of informal sector enterprises	54.5	52.3	56.6	54.8	54.0
Producers of goods exclusively for own final use	15.8	26.8	5.5	13.9	19.6
Contributing family workers	2.9	3.6	2.3	2.7	3.3
Employees	26.8	17.2	35.7	28.6	23.1
Formal sector employees	12.9	6.6	18.8	12.7	13.4
Informal sector employees	10.2	4.4	15.5	11.4	7.7
Domestic workers employed by households	3.7	6.1	1.4	4.5	2.0
Total	100.0	100.0	100.0	100.0	100.0

* Members of producers' cooperatives

4. Informal non-agricultural self-employment as % of total non-agricultural self-employment by status in employment

Status in employment	Total	Women	Men	Urban	Rural
Employers & members of producers' co-operatives	60.8	68.6	57.5	61.5	59.2
Own-account workers	86.8	90.4	82.6	87.8	85.2
Enterprise owners	83.3	85.9	81.1	84.8	80.4
Total self-employment (incl. contributing family workers)	84.7	89.6	79.5	85.4	83.4

Women and men in the informal economy: A statistical picture

5. Informal wage employment as % of total wage employment by type of employees

Type of employees	Total	Women	Men	Urban	Rural
Agricultural employees	89.2	91.2	88.6	84.3	90.8
Non-agricultural employees	59.8	60.7	59.4	58.8	62.6
Formal sector employees	42.8	38.4	44.5	39.9	49.9
Informal sector employees	94.0	92.5	94.4	93.1	96.8
Domestic workers employed by households	96.8	98.1	91.8	97.3	94.5
Total employees	63.2	63.3	63.1	59.9	70.0

6. Informal non-agricultural employment outside the informal sector by type (%)

Type of employment	Total	Women	Men	Urban	Rural
Producers of goods exclusively for own final use	48.2	66.8	21.2	44.0	55.6
Contributing family workers: formal sector	1.2	1.5	0.9	1.4	0.9
Employees	50.6	31.8	77.9	54.6	43.5
Employees: formal sector	39.4	16.5	72.5	40.2	37.9
Employees: domestic work	11.2	15.3	5.4	14.4	5.6
Total	100.0	100.0	100.0	100.0	100.0

7. Share of women in employment by type

Share of women in …	%
1. Total employment	51.1
2. Agricultural employment	53.3
2.1 Agricultural wage employment	22.1
2.1.1 Formal agricultural wage employment	17.9
2.1.2 Informal agricultural wage employment	22.6
2.2 Agricultural self-employment	53.8
3. Non-agricultural employment	44.4
3.1 Non-agricultural wage employment*	30.5
3.1.1 Formal non-agricultural wage employment	29.8
3.1.2 Informal non-agricultural wage employment	31.0
3.2 Non-agricultural self-employment	51.6
3.2.1 Formal non-agricultural self-employment	35.1
3.2.2 Informal non-agricultural self-employment	54.5

* = MDG Indicator No. 3.2: Share of women in wage employment in the non-agricultural sector

8. Share of women in informal non-agricultural employment by component

Share of women in …	%
1. Informal employment	48.2
1.1 Self-employment	54.5
1.2. Wage employment	31.0
2. Employment in the informal sector	42.8
2.1 Self-employment	46.8
2.2 Wage employment	21.3
3. Informal employment outside the informal sector	59.1
3.1 Self-employment	81.7
3.2 Wage employment	37.1
3.2.1 Formal sector	24.7
3.2.2 Domestic work	80.5

9. Share of informal employment (%) by kind of non-agricultural activity

Share of informal employment in total employment in ...	Total	Women	Men
All non-agricultural actitvities	77.0	82.7	72.8
Manufacturing	79.7	83.1	77.7
Construction	83.2	64.5	83.8
Trade	79.3	84.5	75.4
Transportation	74.4	63.7	75.0
Services other than trade or transportation	74.1	81.8	65.1

10. Non-agricultural employment by sex, formal/informal nature and kind of activity (%)

A. Both sexes

Kind of activity	Total	Formal	Informal
All non-agricultural actitvities	100.0	100.0	100.0
Manufacturing	14.1	12.5	14.6
Construction	4.5	3.3	4.8
Trade	33.2	30.0	34.1
Transportation	5.4	6.1	5.3
Services other than trade or transportation	42.8	48.2	41.2

B. Women

Kind of activity	Total	Formal	Informal
All non-agricultural actitvities	100.0	100.0	100.0
Manufacturing	12.1	11.9	12.2
Construction	0.3	0.7	0.3
Trade	32.8	29.3	33.5
Transportation	0.6	1.4	0.5
Services other than trade or transportation	54.1	56.8	53.5

C. Men

Kind of activity	Total	Formal	Informal
All non-agricultural actitvities	100.0	100.0	100.0
Manufacturing	15.6	12.8	16.7
Construction	7.5	4.5	8.7
Trade	33.4	30.3	34.6
Transportation	9.0	8.3	9.3
Services other than trade or transportation	34.4	44.1	30.7

Country: Tanzania, United Republic of   Year: 2005–2006

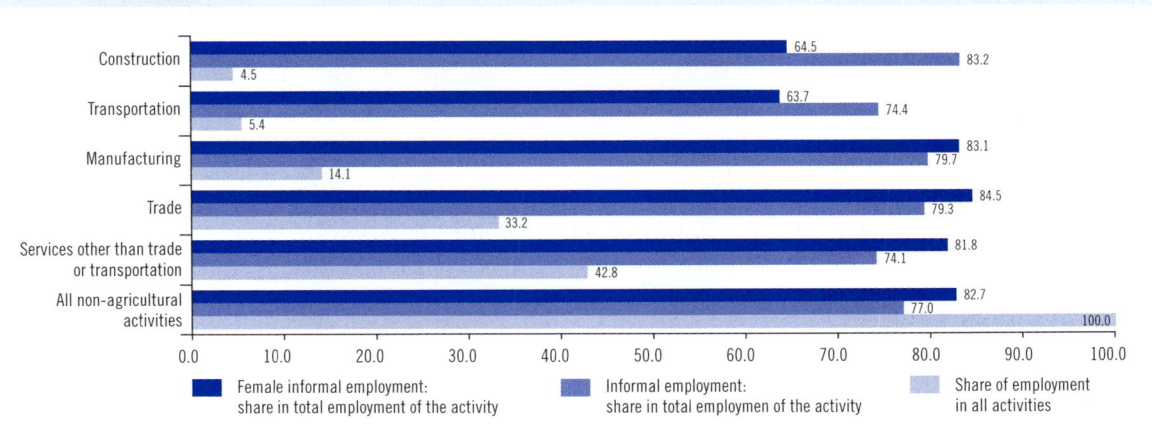

Non-agricultural employment

Women and men in the informal economy: A statistical picture

Country: Thailand
Source: Informal Employment Survey

Year: 2010

1. Informal non-agricultural employment and its components

	Total	Women	Men	Urban	Rural
in 1,000					
Persons in informal employment	9'642.0	4'729.8	4'912.2		
Persons employed in the informal sector					
Persons in formal employment in the informal sector					
Persons in informal employment outside the informal sector					
as % of non-agricultural employment					
Persons in informal employment	42.3	43.5	41.2		
Persons employed in the informal sector					
Persons in formal employment in the informal sector					
Persons in informal employment outside the informal sector					

2. Employment in the informal sector by status in employment (%)

Status in employment	Total	Women	Men	Urban	Rural
Data not available.					

3. Informal non-agricultural employment by status in employment (%)

Status in employment	Total	Women	Men	Urban	Rural
Data not available.					

4. Informal non-agricultural self-employment as % of total non-agricultural self-employment by status in employment

Status in employment	Total	Women	Men	Urban	Rural
Data not available.					

5. Informal wage employment as % of total wage employment by type of employees

Type of employees	Total	Women	Men	Urban	Rural
Data not available.					

6. Informal non-agricultural employment outside the informal sector by type (%)

Type of employment	Total	Women	Men	Urban	Rural
Data not available.					

7. Share of women in employment by type

Share of women in …	%
1. Total employment	46.0
2. Agricultural employment	43.7
2.1 Agricultural wage employment	42.8
2.1.1 Formal agricultural wage employment	
2.1.2 Informal agricultural wage employment	
2.2 Agricultural self-employment	43.9
3. Non-agricultural employment	47.5
3.1 Non-agricultural wage employment*	45.0
3.1.1 Formal non-agricultural wage employment	
3.1.2 Informal non-agricultural wage employment	
3.2 Non-agricultural self-employment	51.6
3.2.1 Formal non-agricultural self-employment	
3.2.2 Informal non-agricultural self-employment	

* = MDG Indicator No. 3.2: Share of women in wage employment in the non-agricultural sector

8. Share of women in informal non-agricultural employment by component

Share of women in …	%
1. Informal employment	49.1
1.1 Self-employment	
1.2. Wage employment	
2. Employment in the informal sector	
2.1 Self-employment	
2.2 Wage employment	
3. Informal employment outside the informal sector	
3.1 Self-employment	
3.2 Wage employment	
3.2.1 Formal sector	
3.2.2 Domestic work	

9. Share of informal employment (%) by kind of non-agricultural activity

Share of informal employment in total employment in …	Total	Women	Men
All non-agricultural actitvities	42.3	43.5	41.2
Manufacturing	21.2	22.2	20.2
Construction	46.6	45.7	46.7
Trade	66.1	71.2	61.1
Transportation	49.8	22.0	55.3
Services other than trade or transportation	36.0	38.8	32.3

Women and men in the informal economy: A statistical picture

10. Non-agricultural employment by sex, formal/informal nature and kind of activity (%)

A. Both sexes

Kind of activity	Total	Formal	Informal
All non-agricultural actitvities	100.0	100.0	100.0
Manufacturing	22.8	31.1	11.4
Construction	9.1	8.5	10.1
Trade	26.8	15.8	41.9
Transportation	4.6	4.0	5.4
Services other than trade or transportation	36.7	40.7	31.2

B. Women

Kind of activity	Total	Formal	Informal
All non-agricultural actitvities	100.0	100.0	100.0
Manufacturing	24.7	34.0	12.6
Construction	2.8	2.7	3.0
Trade	27.4	14.0	44.9
Transportation	1.6	2.2	0.8
Services other than trade or transportation	43.5	47.1	38.8

C. Men

Kind of activity	Total	Formal	Informal
All non-agricultural actitvities	100.0	100.0	100.0
Manufacturing	21.0	28.5	10.3
Construction	14.9	13.5	16.9
Trade	26.2	17.3	39.0
Transportation	7.3	5.6	9.9
Services other than trade or transportation	30.5	35.1	24.0

Country: Thailand **Year: 2010**

Non-agricultural employment

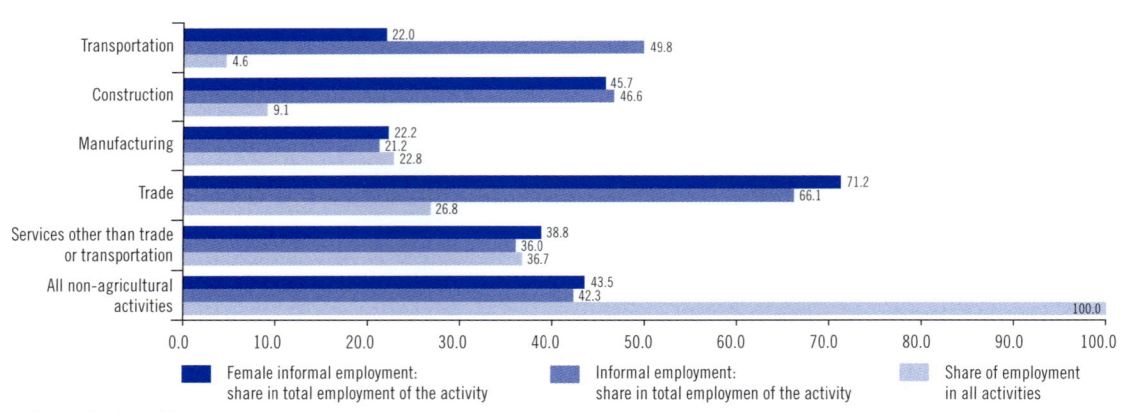

Activity	Female informal employment: share in total employment of the activity	Informal employment: share in total employmen of the activity	Share of employment in all activities
Transportation	22.0	49.8	4.6
Construction	45.7	46.6	9.1
Manufacturing	22.2	21.2	22.8
Trade	71.2	66.1	26.8
Services other than trade or transportation	38.8	36.0	36.7
All non-agricultural activities	43.5	42.3	100.0

Source: Informal Employment Survey

Country: Turkey
Source: Household Labour Force Survey

Year: **2009**

1. Informal non-agricultural employment and its components

	Total	Women	Men	Urban	Rural
in 1,000					
Persons in informal employment	4'903	1'116	3'788	3'780	1'126
Persons employed in the informal sector					
Persons in formal employment in the informal sector					
Persons in informal employment outside the informal sector					
as % of non-agricultural employment					
Persons in informal employment	30.6	32.6	30.1	28.5	40.5
Persons employed in the informal sector					
Persons in formal employment in the informal sector					
Persons in informal employment outside the informal sector					

2. Employment in the informal sector by status in employment (%)

Status in employment	Total	Women	Men	Urban	Rural
Data not available.					

3. Informal non-agricultural employment by status in employment (%)

Status in employment	Total	Women	Men	Urban	Rural
Employers, own-account workers and MPCs*	30.7	26.7	31.9	29.4	35.4
Owners of informal sector enterprises	30.7	26.7	31.9	29.4	35.4
Producers of goods exclusively for own final use					
Contributing family workers	9.2	16.8	7.0	8.7	11.2
Employees	60.0	56.5	61.0	62.0	53.4
Formal sector employees					
Informal sector employees					
Domestic workers employed by households					
Total	100.0	100.0	100.0	100.0	100.0

* Members of producers' cooperatives

4. Informal non-agricultural self-employment as % of total non-agricultural self-employment by status in employment

Status in employment	Total	Women	Men	Urban	Rural
Employers & members of producers' co-operatives	14.6	18.6	14.4	13.6	22.2
Own-account workers	62.7	83.3	58.8	61.0	68.0
Enterprise owners	62.7	83.3	58.8	61.0	68.0
Total self-employment (incl. contributing family workers)	52.7	81.0	47.3	49.4	64.8

Women and men in the informal economy: A statistical picture

5. Informal wage employment as % of total wage employment by type of employees

Type of employees	Total	Women	Men	Urban	Rural
Agricultural employees	87.1	96.5	81.8	83.8	89.2
Non-agricultural employees	23.9	22.3	24.4	22.7	30.5
Formal sector employees					
Informal sector employees					
Domestic workers employed by households					
Total employees	26.2	26.6	26.1	23.6	38.3

6. Informal non-agricultural employment outside the informal sector by type (%)

Type of employment	Total	Women	Men	Urban	Rural
Data not available.					

7. Share of women in employment by type

Share of women in ...	%
1. Total employment	27.6
2. Agricultural employment	46.5
2.1 Agricultural wage employment	37.1
2.1.1 Formal agricultural wage employment	10.0
2.1.2 Informal agricultural wage employment	41.1
2.2 Agricultural self-employment	47.5
3. Non-agricultural employment	21.4
3.1 Non-agricultural wage employment*	23.0
3.1.1 Formal non-agricultural wage employment	23.4
3.1.2 Informal non-agricultural wage employment	21.4
3.2 Non-agricultural self-employment	16.1
3.2.1 Formal non-agricultural self-employment	6.5
3.2.2 Informal non-agricultural self-employment	24.7

* = MDG Indicator No. 3.2: Share of women in wage employment in the non-agricultural sector

8. Share of women in informal non-agricultural employment by component

Share of women in ...	%
1. Informal employment	22.8
1.1 Self-employment	24.7
1.2. Wage employment	21.4
2. Employment in the informal sector	
2.1 Self-employment	
2.2 Wage employment	
3. Informal employment outside the informal sector	
3.1 Self-employment	
3.2 Wage employment	
3.2.1 Formal sector	
3.2.2 Domestic work	

9. Share of informal employment (%) by kind of non-agricultural activity

Share of informal employment in total employment in ...	Total	Women	Men
All non-agricultural actitvities	30.1	31.3	29.7
Manufacturing	26.5	43.3	22.1
Construction	55.2	23.1	56.3
Trade	39.6	40.9	39.3
Transportation	35.0	13.5	36.9
Services other than trade or transportation	17.1	21.8	14.8

10. Non-agricultural employment by sex, formal/informal nature and kind of activity (%)

A. Both sexes

Kind of activity	Total	Formal	Informal
All non-agricultural actitvities	100.0	100.0	100.0
Manufacturing	25.8	27.1	22.7
Construction	7.8	5.0	14.3
Trade	28.4	24.5	37.3
Transportation	6.7	6.3	7.8
Services other than trade or transportation	31.3	37.1	17.9

B. Women

Kind of activity	Total	Formal	Informal
All non-agricultural actitvities	100.0	100.0	100.0
Manufacturing	25.2	20.8	34.8
Construction	1.1	1.3	0.8
Trade	22.5	19.4	29.5
Transportation	2.6	3.3	1.1
Services other than trade or transportation	48.6	55.3	33.8

C. Men

Kind of activity	Total	Formal	Informal
All non-agricultural actitvities	100.0	100.0	100.0
Manufacturing	25.9	28.8	19.2
Construction	9.6	6.0	18.2
Trade	29.9	25.9	39.5
Transportation	7.9	7.1	9.8
Services other than trade or transportation	26.6	32.3	13.3

Country: Turkey **Year: 2009**

Non-agricultural employment

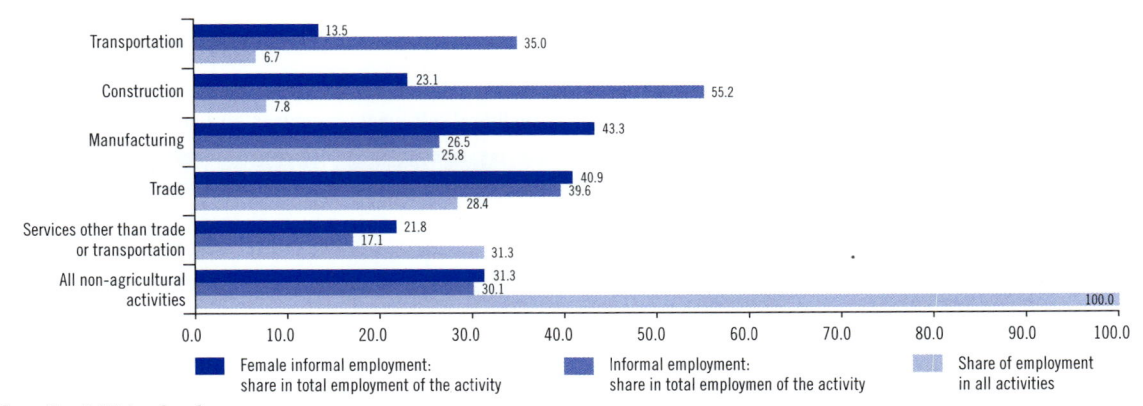

Source: Household Labour Force Survey

Women and men in the informal economy: A statistical picture

Country: Uganda
Source: Uganda National Household Survey

Year: 2010

1. Informal non-agricultural employment and its components

	Total	Women	Men	Urban	Rural
		in 1,000			
Persons in informal employment	2'720.3	1'232.4	1'488.0	1'169.7	1'550.5
Persons employed in the informal sector	2'343.7	1'066.3	1'277.4	982.8	1'360.9
Persons in formal employment in the informal sector	160.1	42.9	117.1	96.2	63.9
Persons in informal employment outside the informal sector	536.6	208.9	327.7	283.0	253.4
	as % of non-agricultural employment				
Persons in informal employment	69.4	71.9	67.5	66.1	72.1
Persons employed in the informal sector	59.8	62.2	57.9	55.5	63.3
Persons in formal employment in the informal sector	4.1	2.5	5.3	5.4	3.0
Persons in informal employment outside the informal sector	13.7	12.2	14.9	16.0	11.8

2. Employment in the informal sector by status in employment (%)

Status in employment	Total	Women	Men	Urban	Rural
Employers, own-account workers and MPCs*	61.7	68.0	56.5	53.0	68.0
Contributing family workers	9.8	14.2	6.1	13.6	7.1
Employees	28.5	17.8	37.4	33.4	24.9
Total	100.0	100.0	100.0	100.0	100.0

* Members of producers' cooperatives

3. Informal non-agricultural employment by status in employment (%)

Status in employment	Total	Women	Men	Urban	Rural
Employers, own-account workers and MPCs*	53.2	58.8	48.5	44.5	59.7
Owners of informal sector enterprises	53.2	58.8	48.5	44.5	59.7
Producers of goods exclusively for own final use					
Contributing family workers	12.1	16.3	8.6	16.0	9.1
Employees	34.8	24.9	42.9	39.5	31.2
Formal sector employees	13.3	8.2	17.5	16.6	10.8
Informal sector employees	18.7	12.0	24.2	19.9	17.8
Domestic workers employed by households	2.8	4.7	1.2	3.0	2.6
Total	100.0	100.0	100.0	100.0	100.0

* Members of producers' cooperatives

4. Informal non-agricultural self-employment as % of total non-agricultural self-employment by status in employment

Status in employment	Total	Women	Men	Urban	Rural
Employers & members of producers' co-operatives	73.2	61.6	75.2	80.6	63.6
Own-account workers	86.4	88.0	84.7	84.2	87.6
Enterprise owners	86.4	88.0	84.7	84.2	87.6
Total self-employment (incl. contributing family workers)	87.9	89.9	85.8	87.6	88.1

5. Informal wage employment as % of total wage employment by type of employees

Type of employees	Total	Women	Men	Urban	Rural
Agricultural employees	83.7	87.4	82.0	64.2	84.7
Non-agricultural employees	49.8	44.8	52.5	48.0	51.5
Formal sector employees	33.1	26.7	36.6	34.7	31.5
Informal sector employees	76.0	77.5	75.5	70.7	81.2
Domestic workers employed by households	54.3	50.8	70.0	48.0	61.0
Total employees	59.3	55.7	61.2	48.6	65.8

6. Informal non-agricultural employment outside the informal sector by type (%)

Type of employment	Total	Women	Men	Urban	Rural
Producers of goods exclusively for own final use					
Contributing family workers: formal sector	18.3	23.6	15.0	18.8	17.8
Employees	81.7	76.4	85.0	81.2	82.2
Employees: formal sector	67.5	48.6	79.5	68.7	66.1
Employees: domestic work	14.2	27.8	5.5	12.5	16.1
Total	100.0	100.0	100.0	100.0	100.0

7. Share of women in employment by type

Share of women in …	%
1. Total employment	51.9
2. Agricultural employment	55.5
2.1 Agricultural wage employment	31.8
2.1.1 Formal agricultural wage employment	24.6
2.1.2 Informal agricultural wage employment	33.2
2.2 Agricultural self-employment	57.7
3. Non-agricultural employment	43.7
3.1 Non-agricultural wage employment*	36.1
3.1.1 Formal non-agricultural wage employment	39.6
3.1.2 Informal non-agricultural wage employment	32.5
3.2 Non-agricultural self-employment	51.0
3.2.1 Formal non-agricultural self-employment	42.5
3.2.2 Informal non-agricultural self-employment	52.1

* = MDG Indicator No. 3.2: Share of women in wage employment in the non-agricultural sector

8. Share of women in informal non-agricultural employment by component

Share of women in …	%
1. Informal employment	45.3
1.1 Self-employment	52.1
1.2. Wage employment	32.5
2. Employment in the informal sector	45.5
2.1 Self-employment	52.3
2.2 Wage employment	28.5
3. Informal employment outside the informal sector	38.9
3.1 Self-employment	50.1
3.2 Wage employment	36.4
3.2.1 Formal sector	28.0
3.2.2 Domestic work	76.3

Women and men in the informal economy: A statistical picture

9. Share of informal employment (%) by kind of non-agricultural activity

Share of informal employment in total employment in …	Total	Women	Men
All non-agricultural actitvities	70.1	73.2	67.7
Manufacturing	87.5	95.3	81.7
Construction	76.3	100.0	75.5
Trade	86.0	89.4	82.2
Transportation	67.9	39.6	68.3
Services other than trade or transportation	37.9	41.3	34.1

10. Non-agricultural employment by sex, formal/informal nature and kind of activity (%)

A. Both sexes

Kind of activity	Total	Formal	Informal
All non-agricultural actitvities	100.0	100.0	100.0
Manufacturing	20.0	8.4	24.9
Construction	6.8	5.4	7.4
Trade	36.2	16.9	44.4
Transportation	7.7	8.3	7.4
Services other than trade or transportation	29.3	61.0	15.9

B. Women

Kind of activity	Total	Formal	Informal
All non-agricultural actitvities	100.0	100.0	100.0
Manufacturing	19.3	3.4	25.1
Construction	0.5	0.0	0.6
Trade	44.2	17.5	53.9
Transportation	0.2	0.5	0.1
Services other than trade or transportation	35.8	78.6	20.2

C. Men

Kind of activity	Total	Formal	Informal
All non-agricultural actitvities	100.0	100.0	100.0
Manufacturing	20.5	11.6	24.7
Construction	11.8	8.9	13.1
Trade	30.0	16.6	36.4
Transportation	13.5	13.3	13.6
Services other than trade or transportation	24.3	49.7	12.2

Country: Uganda **Year: 2010**
Non-agricultural employment

Activity	Female informal employment: share in total employment of the activity	Informal employment: share in total employmen of the activity	Share of employment in all activities
Construction	100.0	48.2	6.7
Transportation	30.4	77.6	8.9
Manufacturing	57.6	42.9	14.6
Services other than trade or transportation	65.8	64.4	23.4
Trade	43.7	39.4	46.4
All non-agricultural activities	49.6	49.7	100.0

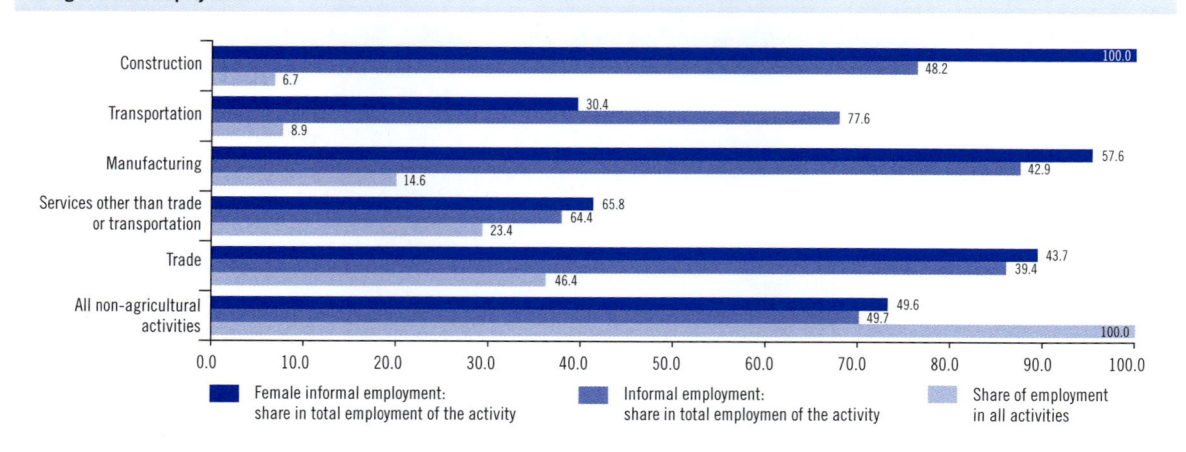

Country: Ukraine

Source: Population Sample Survey on Economic Activity

Year: 2009

1. Informal non-agricultural employment and its components

	Total	Women	Men	Urban	Rural
in 1,000					
Persons in informal employment					
Persons employed in the informal sector	1'524.5	518.2	1'006.3	1'105.9	418.6
Persons in formal employment in the informal sector					
Persons in informal employment outside the informal sector					
as % of non-agricultural employment					
Persons in informal employment					
Persons employed in the informal sector	9.4	6.4	12.4	8.4	13.7
Persons in formal employment in the informal sector					
Persons in informal employment outside the informal sector					

2. Employment in the informal sector by status in employment (%)

Status in employment	Total	Women	Men	Urban	Rural
Employers, own-account workers and MPCs*	9.9	8.0	10.8	11.7	5.0
Contributing family workers	1.9	2.4	1.6	2.0	1.5
Employees	88.2	89.6	87.5	86.3	93.4
Total	100.0	100.0	100.0	100.0	100.0

* Members of producers' cooperatives

3. Informal non-agricultural employment by status in employment (%)

Status in employment	Total	Women	Men	Urban	Rural
Data not available.					

4. Informal non-agricultural self-employment as % of total non-agricultural self-employment by status in employment

Status in employment	Total	Women	Men	Urban	Rural
Employers & members of producers' co-operatives	2.0	0.9	2.6	2.1	1.8
Own-account workers	21.1	14.9	25.2	20.7	24.6
Enterprise owners	21.1	14.9	25.2	20.7	24.6
Total self-employment (incl. contributing family workers)	19.6	15.3	22.3	19.2	22.2

5. Informal wage employment as % of total wage employment by type of employees

Status in employment	Total	Women	Men	Urban	Rural
Data not available.					

Women and men in the informal economy: A statistical picture

6. Informal non-agricultural employment outside the informal sector by type (%)

Status in employment	Total	Women	Men	Urban	Rural
Data not available.					

7. Share of women in employment by type

Share of women in …	%
1. Total employment	49.4
2. Agricultural employment	47.3
2.1 Agricultural wage employment	29.2
2.1.1 Formal agricultural wage employment	
2.1.2 Informal agricultural wage employment	
2.2 Agricultural self-employment	55.2
3. Non-agricultural employment	49.9
3.1 Non-agricultural wage employment*	50.6
3.1.1 Formal non-agricultural wage employment	
3.1.2 Informal non-agricultural wage employment	
3.2 Non-agricultural self-employment	38.6
3.2.1 Formal non-agricultural self-employment	40.6
3.2.2 Informal non-agricultural self-employment	30.1

* = MDG Indicator No. 3.2: Share of women in wage employment in the non-agricultural sector

8. Share of women in informal non-agricultural employment by component

Share of women in …	%
1. Informal employment	
1.1 Self-employment	
1.2. Wage employment	
2. Employment in the informal sector	34.0
2.1 Self-employment	30.1
2.2 Wage employment	34.5
3. Informal employment outside the informal sector	
3.1 Self-employment	
3.2 Wage employment	
3.2.1 Formal sector	
3.2.2 Domestic work	

9. Share of informal employment (%) by kind of non-agricultural activity

Share of informal employment* in total employment in …	Total	Women	Men
All non-agricultural actitvities	9.4	6.4	12.4
Manufacturing	4.1	3.5	4.4
Construction	40.9	15.4	44.1
Trade	16.3	17.1	15.2
Transportation	5.5	0.9	7.6
Services other than trade or transportation	3.7	3.1	5.0

10. Non-agricultural employment by sex, formal/informal nature and kind of activity (%)

A. Both sexes

Kind of activity	Total	Formal**	Informal*
All non-agricultural actitvities	100.0	100.0	100.0
Manufacturing	24.1	25.5	10.4
Construction	8.1	5.3	34.9
Trade	19.8	18.3	34.1
Transportation	9.2	9.6	5.3
Services other than trade or transportation	38.9	41.4	15.2

B. Women

Kind of activity	Total	Formal**	Informal*
All non-agricultural actitvities	100.0	100.0	100.0
Manufacturing	17.2	17.7	9.2
Construction	1.8	1.6	4.2
Trade	22.8	20.2	60.7
Transportation	5.8	6.1	0.8
Services other than trade or transportation	52.4	54.3	25.0

C. Men

Kind of activity	Total	Formal**	Informal*
All non-agricultural actitvities	100.0	100.0	100.0
Manufacturing	30.9	33.8	11.0
Construction	14.3	9.1	50.7
Trade	16.7	16.2	20.4
Transportation	12.6	13.3	7.7
Services other than trade or transportation	25.4	27.6	10.2

* Informal sector employment   ** Formal sector employment

Country: Ukraine   Year: 2009

Non-agricultural employment

Activity	Female informal SECTOR employment: share in total employment of the activity	Informal SECTOR employment: share in total employment of the activity	Share of employment in all activities
Construction	15.4	40.9	8.1
Transportation	0.9	5.5	9.2
Trade	17.1	16.3	19.8
Manufacturing	3.5	4.1	24.1
Services other than trade or transportation	3.1	3.7	38.9
All non-agricultural activities	6.4	9.4	100.0

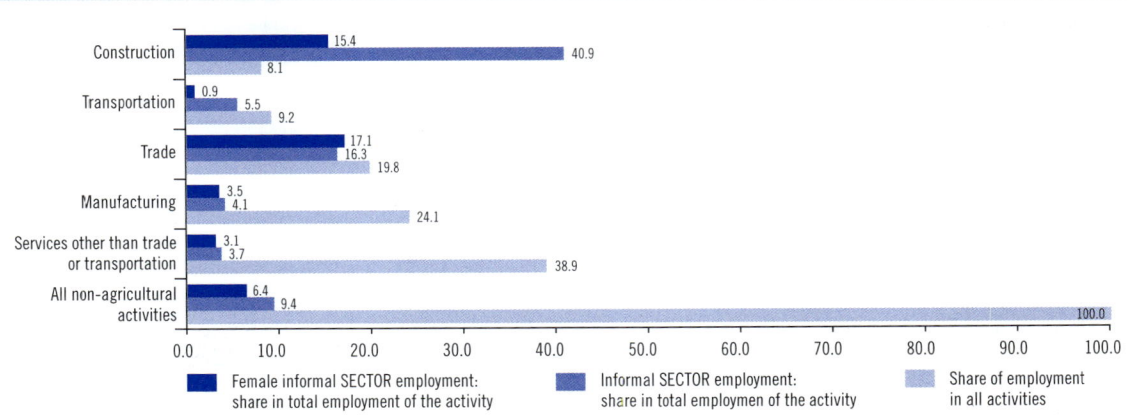

Source: Population Sample Survey on Economic Activity

Women and men in the informal economy: A statistical picture

Country: Uruguay

Source: Encuesta Continua de Hogares

Year: 2009

1. Informal non-agricultural employment and its components

	Total	Women	Men	Urban	Rural
in 1,000					
Persons in informal employment	571.8	269.8	302.0	571.8	
Persons employed in the informal sector	487.3	193.5	293.7	487.3	
Persons in formal employment in the informal sector	56.9	24.4	32.6	56.9	
Persons in informal employment outside the informal sector	141.4	100.7	40.8	141.4	
as % of non-agricultural employment					
Persons in informal employment	39.8	40.3	39.4	39.8	
Persons employed in the informal sector	33.9	28.9	38.3	33.9	
Persons in formal employment in the informal sector	4.0	3.6	4.2	4.0	
Persons in informal employment outside the informal sector	9.8	15.0	5.3	9.8	

2. Employment in the informal sector by status in employment (%)

Status in employment	Total	Women	Men	Urban	Rural
Employers, own-account workers and MPCs*	70.5	70.8	70.3	70.5	
Contributing family workers	3.5	6.1	1.8	3.5	
Employees	26.0	23.1	27.9	26.0	
Total	100.0	100.0	100.0	100.0	

* Members of producers' cooperatives

3. Informal non-agricultural employment by status in employment (%)

Status in employment	Total	Women	Men	Urban	Rural
Employers, own-account workers and MPCs*	62.5	55.8	68.6	62.5	
Owners of informal sector enterprises	60.1	50.8	68.4	60.1	
Producers of goods exclusively for own final use	2.5	5.0	0.2	2.5	
Contributing family workers	3.2	4.7	1.9	3.2	
Employees	34.3	39.5	29.6	34.3	
Formal sector employees	10.1	7.3	12.5	10.1	
Informal sector employees	12.2	7.6	16.3	12.2	
Domestic workers employed by households	12.0	24.6	0.7	12.0	
Total	100.0	100.0	100.0	100.0	

* Members of producers' cooperatives

4. Informal non-agricultural self-employment as % of total non-agricultural self-employment by status in employment

Status in employment	Total	Women	Men	Urban	Rural
Employers & members of producers' co-operatives	66.3	69.9	64.8	66.3	
Own-account workers	100.0	100.0	100.0	100.0	
Enterprise owners	100.0	100.0	100.0	100.0	
Total self-employment (incl. contributing family workers)	94.8	96.8	93.2	94.8	

5. Informal wage employment as % of total wage employment by type of employees

Type of employees	Total	Women	Men	Urban	Rural
Agricultural employees	31.5	20.5	33.2	31.5	
Non-agricultural employees	18.9	21.3	16.6	18.9	
Formal sector employees	7.3	5.7	8.4	7.3	
Informal sector employees	55.0	45.6	60.2	55.0	
Domestic workers employed by households	57.1	59.6	25.2	57.1	
Total employees	19.6	21.3	18.2	19.6	

6. Informal non-agricultural employment outside the informal sector by type (%)

Type of employment	Total	Women	Men	Urban	Rural
Producers of goods exclusively for own final use	9.9	13.4	1.3	9.9	
Contributing family workers: formal sector	0.8	0.9	0.6	0.8	
Employees	89.3	85.7	98.1	89.3	
Employees: formal sector	40.7	19.7	92.6	40.7	
Employees: domestic work	48.6	66.1	5.5	48.6	
Total	100.0	100.0	100.0	100.0	

7. Share of women in employment by type

Share of women in …	%
1. Total employment	44.5
2. Agricultural employment	15.9
2.1 Agricultural wage employment	13.6
2.1.1 Formal agricultural wage employment	15.8
2.1.2 Informal agricultural wage employment	8.8
2.2 Agricultural self-employment	20.3
3. Non-agricultural employment	46.6
3.1 Non-agricultural wage employment*	48.2
3.1.1 Formal non-agricultural wage employment	46.7
3.1.2 Informal non-agricultural wage employment	54.4
3.2 Non-agricultural self-employment	42.5
3.2.1 Formal non-agricultural self-employment	25.6
3.2.2 Informal non-agricultural self-employment	43.4

* = MDG Indicator No. 3.2: Share of women in wage employment in the non-agricultural sector

8. Share of women in informal non-agricultural employment by component

Share of women in …	%
1. Informal employment	47.2
1.1 Self-employment	43.4
1.2. Wage employment	54.4
2. Employment in the informal sector	39.7
2.1 Self-employment	41.3
2.2 Wage employment	35.4
3. Informal employment outside the informal sector	71.2
3.1 Self-employment	95.0
3.2 Wage employment	68.3
3.2.1 Formal sector	34.4
3.2.2 Domestic work	96.7

Women and men in the informal economy: A statistical picture

9. Share of informal employment (%) by kind of non-agricultural activity

Share of informal employment in total employment in …	Total	Women	Men
All non-agricultural actitvities*	38.8	38.3	39.3
Manufacturing	36.9	46.7	31.8
Construction	53.9	23.4	54.9
Trade	51.8	52.4	51.2
Transportation	29.2	19.8	31.5
Services other than trade or transportation	31.1	32.7	28.2

10. Non-agricultural employment by sex, formal/informal nature and kind of activity (%)

A. Both sexes

Kind of activity	Total	Formal	Informal
All non-agricultural actitvities*	100.0	100.0	100.0
Manufacturing	15.8	16.3	15.0
Construction	7.9	5.9	10.9
Trade	21.2	16.7	28.2
Transportation	6.2	7.2	4.7
Services other than trade or transportation	45.7	51.5	36.6

B. Women

Kind of activity	Total	Formal	Informal
All non-agricultural actitvities*	100.0	100.0	100.0
Manufacturing	11.7	10.1	14.2
Construction	0.5	0.7	0.3
Trade	22.2	17.1	30.4
Transportation	2.6	3.4	1.4
Services other than trade or transportation	62.0	67.7	53.0

C. Men

Kind of activity	Total	Formal	Informal
All non-agricultural actitvities*	100.0	100.0	100.0
Manufacturing	19.4	21.8	15.7
Construction	14.3	10.6	19.9
Trade	20.2	16.3	26.4
Transportation	9.4	10.6	7.5
Services other than trade or transportation	31.5	37.2	22.6

* Including persons with unknown kind of activity.

Country: Uruguay Year: 2009
Non-agricultural employment

* Including persons with unknown kind of activity.

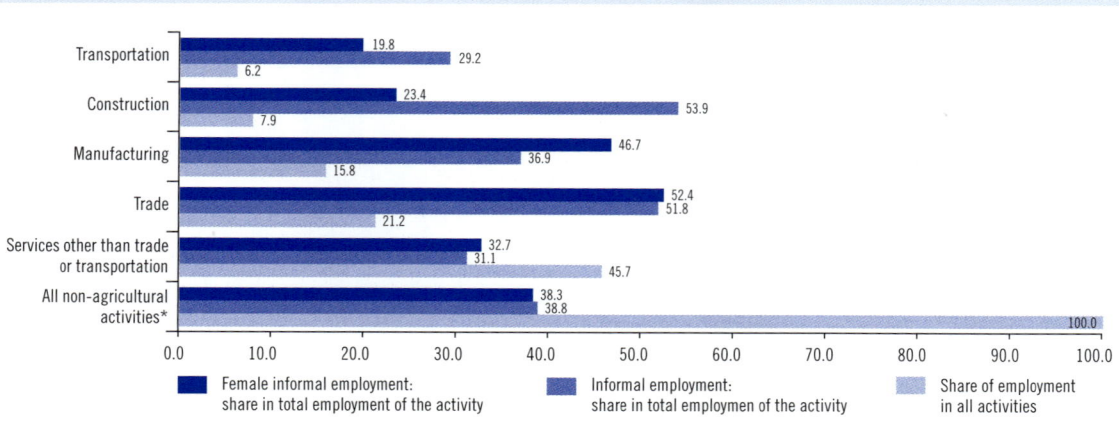

Annex II

Country: Venezuela
Source: Encuesta de Hogares por Muestreo

Year: 2009 (I)

1. Informal non-agricultural employment and its components

	Total	Women	Men	Urban	Rural
in 1,000					
Persons in informal employment	5'131.2	2'159.1	2'972.1		
Persons employed in the informal sector	3'919.8	1'552.4	2'367.4		
Persons in formal employment in the informal sector	63.2	16.4	46.8		
Persons in informal employment outside the informal sector	1'274.6	623.1	651.6		
as % of non-agricultural employment					
Persons in informal employment	47.5	47.4	47.5		
Persons employed in the informal sector	36.3	34.1	37.8		
Persons in formal employment in the informal sector	0.6	0.4	0.7		
Persons in informal employment outside the informal sector	11.8	13.7	10.4		

2. Employment in the informal sector by status in employment (%)

Status in employment	Total	Women	Men	Urban	Rural
Employers, own-account workers and MPCs*	84.2	91.7	79.3		
Contributing family workers	1.2	2.2	0.6		
Employees	14.6	6.1	20.1		
Total	100.0	100.0	100.0		

* Members of producers' cooperatives

3. Informal non-agricultural employment by status in employment (%)

Status in employment	Total	Women	Men	Urban	Rural
Employers, own-account workers and MPCs*	64.3	65.9	63.2		
Owners of informal sector enterprises	64.3	65.9	63.2		
Producers of goods exclusively for own final use					
Contributing family workers	1.3	2.2	0.7		
Employees	34.3	31.9	36.1		
Formal sector employees	22.2	23.0	21.7		
Informal sector employees	9.9	3.7	14.4		
Domestic workers employed by households	2.2	5.3	0.0		
Total	100.0	100.0	100.0		

* Members of producers' cooperatives

4. Informal non-agricultural self-employment as % of total non-agricultural self-employment by status in employment

Status in employment	Total	Women	Men	Urban	Rural
Employers & members of producers' co-operatives	27.4	26.3	27.6		
Own-account workers	87.3	89.2	85.9		
Enterprise owners	87.3	89.2	85.9		
Total self-employment (incl. contributing family workers)	79.6	85.3	75.6		

Women and men in the informal economy: A statistical picture

5. Informal wage employment as % of total wage employment by type of employees

Type of employees	Total	Women	Men	Urban	Rural
Agricultural employees	64.2	61.6	64.4		
Non-agricultural employees	26.8	24.3	28.7		
Formal sector employees	19.5	19.3	19.7		
Informal sector employees	88.9	82.8	90.1		
Domestic workers employed by households	66.2	66.6	44.5		
Total employees	28.9	24.7	31.8		

6. Informal non-agricultural employment outside the informal sector by type (%)

Type of employment	Total	Women	Men	Urban	Rural
Producers of goods exclusively for own final use					
Contributing family workers: formal sector	1.6	2.1	1.0		
Employees	98.4	97.9	99.0		
Employees: formal sector	89.4	79.6	98.8		
Employees: domestic work	9.0	18.2	0.2		
Total	100.0	100.0	100.0		

7. Share of women in employment by type

Share of women in …	%
1. Total employment	39.3
2. Agricultural employment	8.3
2.1 Agricultural wage employment	8.0
2.1.1 Formal agricultural wage employment	8.6
2.1.2 Informal agricultural wage employment	7.7
2.2 Agricultural self-employment	8.5
3. Non-agricultural employment	42.1
3.1 Non-agricultural wage employment*	43.1
3.1.1 Formal non-agricultural wage employment	44.5
3.1.2 Informal non-agricultural wage employment	39.1
3.2 Non-agricultural self-employment	40.7
3.2.1 Formal non-agricultural self-employment	29.2
3.2.2 Informal non-agricultural self-employment	43.6

* = MDG Indicator No. 3.2: Share of women in wage employment in the non-agricultural sector

8. Share of women in informal non-agricultural employment by component

Share of women in …	%
1. Informal employment	42.1
1.1 Self-employment	43.6
1.2 Wage employment	39.1
2. Employment in the informal sector	39.6
2.1 Self-employment	43.5
2.2 Wage employment	16.7
3. Informal employment outside the informal sector	48.9
3.1 Self-employment	67.0
3.2 Wage employment	48.6
3.2.1 Formal sector	43.5
3.2.2 Domestic work	98.7

9. Share of informal employment (%) by kind of non-agricultural activity

Share of informal employment in total employment in …	Total	Women	Men
All non-agricultural actitvities	47.5	47.4	47.5
Manufacturing	39.9	50.1	35.7
Construction	66.0	19.3	68.6
Trade	60.7	67.8	53.0
Transportation	58.9	29.0	62.2
Services other than trade or transportation	34.5	36.5	31.9

10. Non-agricultural employment by sex, formal/informal nature and kind of activity (%)

A. Both sexes

Kind of activity	Total	Formal	Informal
All non-agricultural actitvities	100.0	100.0	100.0
Manufacturing	14.7	16.9	12.4
Construction	9.8	6.4	13.7
Trade	25.7	19.2	32.8
Transportation	9.6	7.5	11.9
Services other than trade or transportation	40.2	50.0	29.2

B. Women

Kind of activity	Total	Formal	Informal
All non-agricultural actitvities	100.0	100.0	100.0
Manufacturing	10.2	9.7	10.8
Construction	1.2	1.9	0.5
Trade	31.6	19.3	45.2
Transportation	2.3	3.1	1.4
Services other than trade or transportation	54.7	66.1	42.1

C. Men

Kind of activity	Total	Formal	Informal
All non-agricultural actitvities	100.0	100.0	100.0
Manufacturing	18.0	22.1	13.5
Construction	16.1	9.6	23.2
Trade	21.3	19.1	23.8
Transportation	15.0	10.8	19.6
Services other than trade or transportation	29.6	38.4	19.8

Country: Venezuela   **Year: 2009 (I)**

Non-agricultural employment

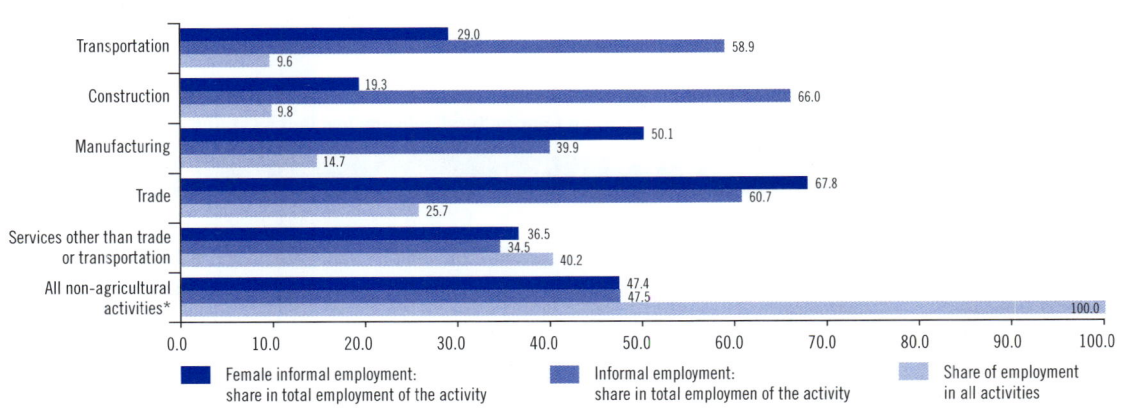

* Including persons with unknown kind of activity.

Women and men in the informal economy: A statistical picture

Country: Viet Nam
Year: 2009
Source: The Viet Nam 2009 Labour Force Survey

1. Informal non-agricultural employment and its components

	Total	Women	Men	Urban	Rural
in 1,000					
Persons in informal employment	17'172.3	7'800.5	9'371.8	6'956.7	10'215.6
Persons employed in the informal sector	10'947.7	5'105.6	5'842.1	4'030.2	6'917.5
Persons in formal employment in the informal sector	78.3	43.2	35.1		
Persons in informal employment outside the informal sector	6'303.1	2'738.2	3'564.9	1'294.4	1'261.4
as % of non-agricultural employment					
Persons in informal employment	68.2	66.8	69.4	60.4	74.7
Persons employed in the informal sector	43.5	43.7	43.3	35.0	50.6
Persons in formal employment in the informal sector	0.3	0.4	0.3		
Persons in informal employment outside the informal sector	25.0	23.4	26.4	11.2	9.2

2. Employment in the informal sector by status in employment (%)

Status in employment	Total	Women	Men	Urban	Rural
Employers, own-account workers and MPCs*	60.7	74.0	49.1	66.9	57.1
Contributing family workers	9.7	11.9	7.8	10.0	9.5
Employees	29.6	14.2	43.1	23.1	33.4
Total	100.0	100.0	100.0	100.0	100.0

* Members of producers' cooperatives

3. Informal non-agricultural employment by status in employment (%)

Status in employment	Total	Women	Men	Urban	Rural
Employers, own-account workers and MPCs*	49.9	61.6	40.1	52.3	48.3
Owners of informal sector enterprises	38.7	48.4	30.6	38.7	38.7
Producers of goods exclusively for own final use	11.2	13.2	9.5	13.5	9.6
Contributing family workers	9.9	12.3	7.9	10.9	9.2
Employees	40.2	26.1	52.0	36.8	42.6
Formal sector employees	21.8	17.4	25.5		
Informal sector employees	18.4	8.7	26.5		
Domestic workers employed by households					
Total	100.0	100.0	100.0	100.0	100.0

* Members of producers' cooperatives

4. Informal non-agricultural self-employment as % of total non-agricultural self-employment by status in employment

Status in employment	Total	Women	Men	Urban	Rural
Employers & members of producers' co-operatives	43.9	41.0	45.4	33.8	55.2
Own-account workers	100.0	100.0	100.0	100.0	100.0
Enterprise owners	100.0	100.0	100.0	100.0	100.0
Total self-employment (incl. contributing family workers)	92.1	94.9	88.8	88.9	94.7

5. Informal wage employment as % of total wage employment by type of employees

Type of employees	Total	Women	Men	Urban	Rural
Agricultural employees	89.2	92.6	86.9	83.3	90.3
Non-agricultural employees	49.2	36.4	57.7	39.0	58.2
Formal sector employees	34.7	27.8	40.4		
Informal sector employees	97.6	94.0	98.6		
Domestic workers employed by households					
Total employees	54.2	43.5	61.3	40.9	64.1

6. Informal non-agricultural employment outside the informal sector by type (%)

Type of employment	Total	Women	Men	Urban	Rural
Producers of goods exclusively for own final use	30.5	37.6	25.0	72.6	77.7
Contributing family workers: formal sector	10.1	12.8	8.0	27.4	22.3
Employees	59.5	49.6	67.0		
Employees: formal sector	59.5	49.6	67.0		
Employees: domestic work					
Total	100.0	100.0	100.0	100.0	100.0

7. Share of women in employment by type

Share of women in ...	%
1. Total employment	48.7
2. Agricultural employment	51.2
2.1 Agricultural wage employment	41.1
2.1.1 Formal agricultural wage employment	28.4
2.1.2 Informal agricultural wage employment	42.7
2.2 Agricultural self-employment	52.2
3. Non-agricultural employment	46.4
3.1 Non-agricultural wage employment*	39.9
3.1.1 Formal non-agricultural wage employment	50.0
3.1.2 Informal non-agricultural wage employment	29.5
3.2 Non-agricultural self-employment	54.5
3.2.1 Formal non-agricultural self-employment	35.2
3.2.2 Informal non-agricultural self-employment	56.2

* = MDG Indicator No. 3.2: Share of women in wage employment in the non-agricultural sector

8. Share of women in informal non-agricultural employment by component

Share of women in ...	%
1. Informal employment	45.4
1.1 Self-employment	56.2
1.2. Wage employment	29.5
2. Employment in the informal sector	46.6
2.1 Self-employment	56.9
2.2 Wage employment	22.3
3. Informal employment outside the informal sector	43.4
3.1 Self-employment	54.0
3.2 Wage employment	36.2
3.2.1 Formal sector	36.2
3.2.2 Domestic work	

Women and men in the informal economy: A statistical picture

9. Share of informal employment (%) by kind of non-agricultural activity

Share of informal employment in total employment in …	Total	Women	Men
All non-agricultural actitvities	63.7	61.6	65.4
Manufacturing	58.7	57.2	60.1
Construction	89.9	81.8	91.0
Trade	75.8	79.0	71.2
Transportation	72.7	47.6	75.2
Services other than trade or transportation	47.0	50.3	42.8

10. Non-agricultural employment by sex, formal/informal nature and kind of activity (%)

A. Both sexes

Kind of activity	Total	Formal	Informal
All non-agricultural actitvities	100.0	100.0	100.0
Manufacturing	29.6	33.7	27.3
Construction	12.1	3.3	17.0
Trade	22.7	15.1	27.0
Transportation	5.8	4.4	6.7
Services other than trade or transportation	29.8	43.5	22.0

B. Women

Kind of activity	Total	Formal	Informal
All non-agricultural actitvities	100.0	100.0	100.0
Manufacturing	31.1	34.7	28.9
Construction	2.9	1.4	3.8
Trade	28.8	15.8	37.0
Transportation	1.2	1.6	0.9
Services other than trade or transportation	36.0	46.6	29.4

C. Men

Kind of activity	Total	Formal	Informal
All non-agricultural actitvities	100.0	100.0	100.0
Manufacturing	28.3	32.7	26.0
Construction	20.0	5.2	27.8
Trade	17.4	14.5	18.9
Transportation	9.9	7.1	11.3
Services other than trade or transportation	24.5	40.6	16.0

Country: Viet Nam **Year: 2009**
Non-agricultural employment

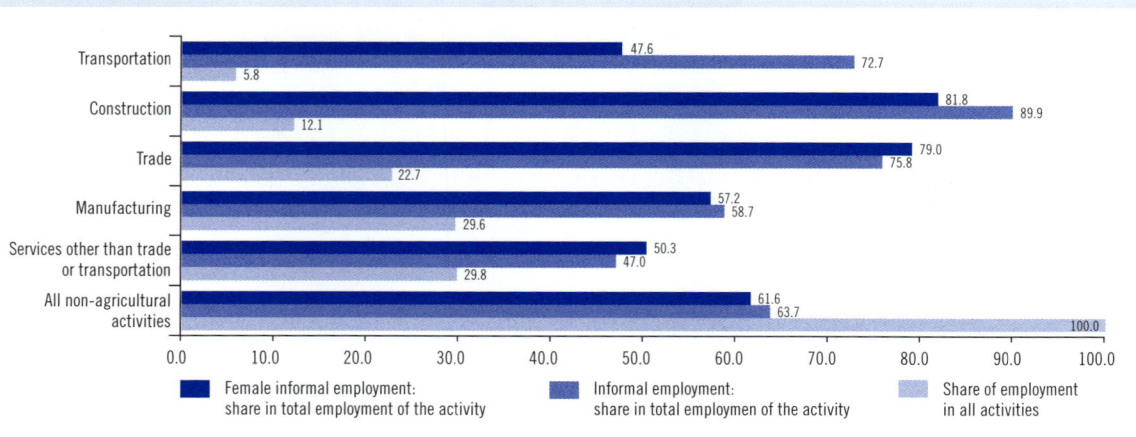

Annex II

Territory: West Bank and Gaza Strip **Year: 2010**
Source: Labour Force Survey

1. Informal non-agricultural employment and its components

	Total	Women	Men	Urban	Rural
in 1,000					
Persons in informal employment	375	42	333	272	76
Persons employed in the informal sector	140	14	126	97	33
Persons in formal employment in the informal sector	0	0	0	0	0
Persons in informal employment outside the informal sector	235	28	207	175	43
as % of non-agricultural employment					
Persons in informal employment	57.2	42.0	59.9	57.0	62.3
Persons employed in the informal sector	21.3	14.0	22.7	20.3	27.0
Persons in formal employment in the informal sector	0.0	0.0	0.0	0.0	0.0
Persons in informal employment outside the informal sector	35.8	28.0	37.2	36.7	35.2

2. Employment in the informal sector by status in employment (%)

Status in employment	Total	Women	Men	Urban	Rural
Employers, own-account workers and MPCs*	47.9	57.1	46.8	49.5	39.4
Contributing family workers	14.3	28.6	12.7	15.5	12.1
Employees	37.9	14.3	40.5	35.1	48.5
Total	100.0	100.0	100.0	100.0	100.0

* Members of producers' cooperatives

3. Informal non-agricultural employment by status in employment (%)

Status in employment	Total	Women	Men	Urban	Rural
Employers, own-account workers and MPCs*	18.1	19.0	18.0	18.0	17.1
Owners of informal sector enterprises	17.9	19.0	17.7	17.6	17.1
Producers of goods exclusively for own final use	0.3	0.0	0.3	0.4	0.0
Contributing family workers	5.3	9.5	4.8	5.5	5.3
Employees	76.5	71.4	77.2	76.5	77.6
Formal sector employees	50.9	61.9	49.5	51.5	47.4
Informal sector employees	14.1	4.8	15.3	12.5	21.1
Domestic workers employed by households	11.5	4.8	12.3	12.5	9.2
Total	100.0	100.0	100.0	100.0	100.0

* Members of producers' cooperatives

4. Informal non-agricultural self-employment as % of total non-agricultural self-employment by status in employment

Status in employment	Total	Women	Men	Urban	Rural
Employers & members of producers' co-operatives	-	-	-	-	-
Own-account workers	60.7	80.0	58.8	59.8	59.1
Enterprise owners	60.4	80.0	58.4	59.3	59.1
Total self-employment (incl. contributing family workers)	66.7	85.7	64.4	66.0	65.4

Women and men in the informal economy: A statistical picture

5. Informal wage employment as % of total wage employment by type of employees

Type of employees	Total	Women	Men	Urban	Rural
Agricultural employees	100.0	-	100.0	100.0	100.0
Non-agricultural employees	54.8	34.9	58.7	54.7	61.5
Formal sector employees	44.6	31.7	47.7	44.9	49.3
Informal sector employees	100.0	100.0	100.0	100.0	100.0
Domestic workers employed by households	100.0	100.0	100.0	100.0	100.0
Total employees	56.5	34.9	60.6	56.5	63.4

6. Informal non-agricultural employment outside the informal sector by type (%)

Type of employment	Total	Women	Men	Urban	Rural
Producers of goods exclusively for own final use	0.4	0.0	0.5	0.6	0.0
Contributing family workers: formal sector	0.0	0.0	0.0	0.0	0.0
Employees	99.6	100.0	99.5	99.4	100.0
Employees: formal sector	81.3	92.9	79.7	80.0	83.7
Employees: domestic work	18.3	7.1	19.8	19.4	16.3
Total	100.0	100.0	100.0	100.0	100.0

7. Share of women in employment by type

Share of women in …	%
1. Total employment	16.9
2. Agricultural employment	29.5
2.1 Agricultural wage employment	0.0
2.1.1 Formal agricultural wage employment	-
2.1.2 Informal agricultural wage employment	0.0
2.2 Agricultural self-employment	38.8
3. Non-agricultural employment	15.2
3.1 Non-agricultural wage employment*	16.4
3.1.1 Formal non-agricultural wage employment	23.6
3.1.2 Informal non-agricultural wage employment	10.5
3.2 Non-agricultural self-employment	10.6
3.2.1 Formal non-agricultural self-employment	4.5
3.2.2 Informal non-agricultural self-employment	13.6

* = MDG Indicator No. 3.2: Share of women in wage employment in the non-agricultural sector

8. Share of women in informal non-agricultural employment by component

Share of women in …	%
1. Informal employment	11.2
1.1 Self-employment	13.6
1.2. Wage employment	10.5
2. Employment in the informal sector	10.0
2.1 Self-employment	13.8
2.2 Wage employment	3.8
3. Informal employment outside the informal sector	11.9
3.1 Self-employment	0.0
3.2 Wage employment	12.0
3.2.1 Formal sector	13.6
3.2.2 Domestic work	4.7

9. Share of informal employment (%) by kind of non-agricultural activity

Share of informal employment in total employment in …	Total	Women	Men
All non-agricultural actitvities	52.3	40.0	54.5
Manufacturing	77.6	90.0	76.0
Construction	96.9	-	96.9
Trade	72.0	80.0	71.4
Transportation	48.9	50.0	51.2
Services other than trade or transportation	20.0	28.2	16.9

10. Non-agricultural employment by sex, formal/informal nature and kind of activity (%)

A. Both sexes

Kind of activity	Total	Formal	Informal
All non-agricultural actitvities	100.0	100.0	100.0
Manufacturing	13.0	6.1	19.2
Construction	14.8	1.0	27.4
Trade	21.8	12.8	30.0
Transportation	6.9	7.0	6.4
Services other than trade or transportation	43.4	72.8	16.6

B. Women

Kind of activity	Total	Formal	Informal
All non-agricultural actitvities	100.0	100.0	100.0
Manufacturing	10.0	1.7	22.5
Construction	-	-	-
Trade	10.0	3.3	20.0
Transportation	2.0	1.7	2.5
Services other than trade or transportation	78.0	93.3	55.0

C. Men

Kind of activity	Total	Formal	Informal
All non-agricultural actitvities	100.0	100.0	100.0
Manufacturing	13.5	7.1	18.8
Construction	17.4	1.2	31.0
Trade	23.9	15.0	31.4
Transportation	7.7	8.3	7.3
Services other than trade or transportation	37.2	68.0	11.6

Country: West Bank and Gaza Strip   Year: 2010

Non-agricultural employment

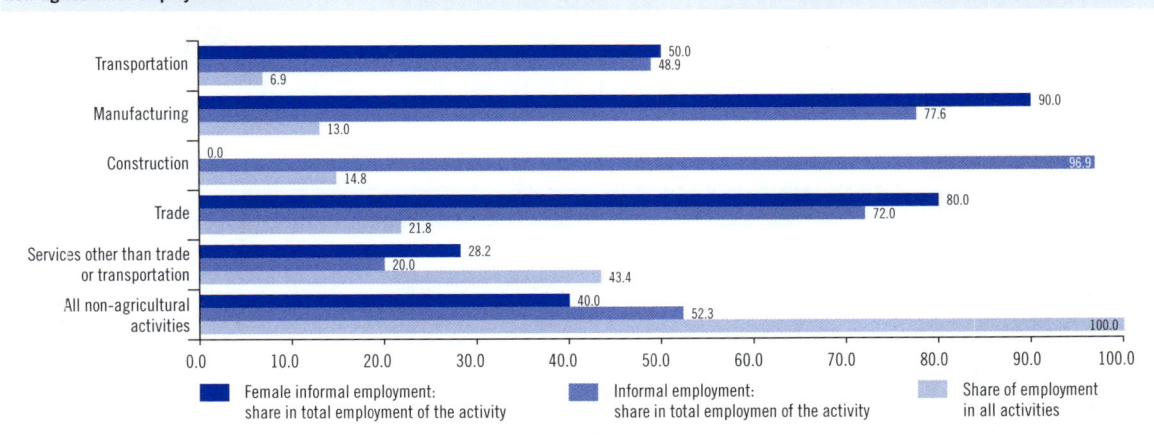

Women and men in the informal economy: A statistical picture

Country: Zambia
Source: Labour Force Survey

Year: 2008

1. Informal non-agricultural employment and its components

	Total	Women	Men	Urban	Rural
in 1,000					
Persons in informal employment	920	407	513	605	315
Persons employed in the informal sector	854	357	497	579	275
Persons in formal employment in the informal sector	89	13	76	86	3
Persons in informal employment outside the informal sector	155	63	92	112	43
as % of non-agricultural employment					
Persons in informal employment	69.5	80.1	62.9	61.6	92.6
Persons employed in the informal sector	64.6	70.3	60.9	59.0	80.9
Persons in formal employment in the informal sector	6.7	2.6	9.3	8.8	0.9
Persons in informal employment outside the informal sector	11.7	12.4	11.3	11.4	12.6

2. Employment in the informal sector by status in employment (%)

Status in employment	Total	Women	Men	Urban	Rural
Employers, own-account workers and MPCs*	53.6	57.4	50.9	61.3	37.5
Contributing family workers	14.5	24.1	7.6	3.5	37.8
Employees	31.9	18.5	41.4	35.2	24.7
Total	100.0	100.0	100.0	100.0	100.0

* Members of producers' cooperatives

3. Informal non-agricultural employment by status in employment (%)

Status in employment	Total	Women	Men	Urban	Rural
Employers, own-account workers and MPCs*	49.8	50.4	49.3	58.7	32.7
Owners of informal sector enterprises	49.8	50.4	49.3	58.7	32.7
Producers of goods exclusively for own final use					
Contributing family workers	14.9	23.6	8.0	3.5	36.8
Employees	35.3	26.0	42.7	37.9	30.5
Formal sector employees	10.9	6.9	14.0	12.1	8.6
Informal sector employees	19.9	13.0	25.3	19.5	20.6
Domestic workers employed by households	4.6	6.1	3.3	6.3	1.3
Total	100.0	100.0	100.0	100.0	100.0

* Members of producers' cooperatives

4. Informal non-agricultural self-employment as % of total non-agricultural self-employment by status in employment

Status in employment	Total	Women	Men	Urban	Rural
Employers & members of producers' co-operatives	53.1	53.3	52.9	52.0	57.1
Own-account workers	88.2	90.8	86.2	87.5	90.8
Enterprise owners	88.2	90.8	86.2	87.5	90.8
Total self-employment (incl. contributing family workers)	88.9	91.8	86.2	86.0	94.4

Annex II

5. Informal wage employment as % of total wage employment by type of employees

Type of employees	Total	Women	Men	Urban	Rural
Agricultural employees	66.7	36.7	79.0	55.9	69.4
Non-agricultural employees	49.7	58.8	46.1	41.9	88.9
Formal sector employees	29.9	32.9	28.8	24.5	73.0
Informal sector employees	67.3	80.3	63.1	57.8	95.6
Domestic workers employed by households	89.4	86.2	89.5	88.4	100.0
Total employees	53.2	54.1	52.8	42.8	78.1

6. Informal non-agricultural employment outside the informal sector by type (%)

Type of employment	Total	Women	Men	Urban	Rural
Producers of goods exclusively for own final use					
Contributing family workers: formal sector	8.4	15.9	3.3	0.9	27.9
Employees	91.6	84.1	96.7	99.1	72.1
Employees: formal sector	64.5	44.4	78.3	65.2	62.8
Employees: domestic work	27.1	39.7	18.5	33.9	9.3
Total	100.0	100.0	100.0	100.0	100.0

7. Share of women in employment by type

Share of women in ...	%
1. Total employment	48.0
2. Agricultural employment	51.9
2.1 Agricultural wage employment	29.2
2.1.1 Formal agricultural wage employment	55.4
2.1.2 Informal agricultural wage employment	16.1
2.2 Agricultural self-employment	53.1
3. Non-agricultural employment	38.4
3.1 Non-agricultural wage employment*	27.5
3.1.1 Formal non-agricultural wage employment	22.6
3.1.2 Informal non-agricultural wage employment	32.6
3.2 Non-agricultural self-employment	49.0
3.2.1 Formal non-agricultural self-employment	36.5
3.2.2 Informal non-agricultural self-employment	50.6

* = MDG Indicator No. 3.2: Share of women in wage employment in the non-agricultural sector

8. Share of women in informal non-agricultural employment by component

Share of women in ...	%
1. Informal employment	44.2
1.1 Self-employment	50.6
1.2. Wage employment	32.6
2. Employment in the informal sector	41.8
2.1 Self-employment	50.0
2.2 Wage employment	24.3
3. Informal employment outside the informal sector	40.6
3.1 Self-employment	76.9
3.2 Wage employment	37.3
3.2.1 Formal sector	28.0
3.2.2 Domestic work	59.5

Women and men in the informal economy: A statistical picture

9. Share of informal employment (%) by kind of non-agricultural activity

Share of informal employment in total employment in ...	Total	Women	Men
All non-agricultural actitvities	66.7	76.1	60.9
Manufacturing	76.7	84.9	71.7
Construction	82.5	66.7	83.1
Trade	93.4	96.4	90.0
Transportation	68.4	64.3	69.1
Services other than trade or transportation	41.4	53.0	34.2

10. Non-agricultural employment by sex, formal/informal nature and kind of activity (%)

A. Both sexes

Kind of activity	Total	Formal	Informal
All non-agricultural actitvities	100.0	100.0	100.0
Manufacturing	12.0	8.4	13.8
Construction	6.0	3.2	7.5
Trade	32.1	6.6	45.0
Transportation	7.2	6.6	7.4
Services other than trade or transportation	42.6	75.2	26.4

B. Women

Kind of activity	Total	Formal	Informal
All non-agricultural actitvities	100.0	100.0	100.0
Manufacturing	4.5	5.7	11.9
Construction	0.6	0.8	0.5
Trade	44.1	6.6	55.9
Transportation	2.7	4.1	2.3
Services other than trade or transportation	42.2	82.8	29.4

C. Men

Kind of activity	Total	Formal	Informal
All non-agricultural actitvities	100.0	100.0	100.0
Manufacturing	13.0	9.5	15.4
Construction	9.5	4.1	12.9
Trade	24.6	6.6	36.4
Transportation	10.0	7.6	11.3
Services other than trade or transportation	42.8	72.2	24.0

Country: Zambia Year: 2008
Non-agricultural employment

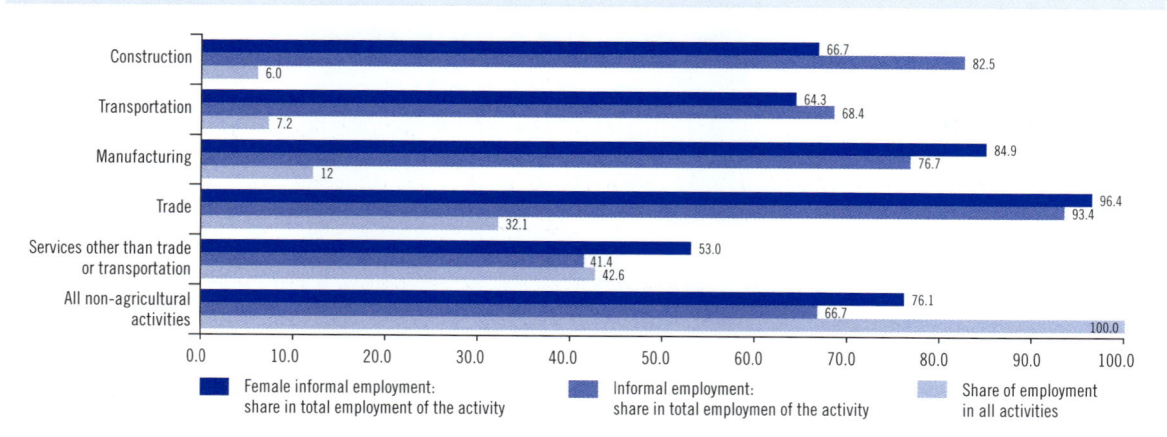

Annex II

Country: Zimbabwe

Year: 2004

Source: Labour Force Survey

1. Informal non-agricultural employment and its components

	Total	Women	Men	Urban	Rural
in 1,000					
Persons in informal employment	908.8	446.9	462.0		
Persons employed in the informal sector	697.7	360.2	337.5		
Persons in formal employment in the informal sector					
Persons in informal employment outside the informal sector					
as % of non-agricultural employment					
Persons in informal employment	51.6	65.9	42.7		
Persons employed in the informal sector	39.6	53.1	31.2		
Persons in formal employment in the informal sector					
Persons in informal employment outside the informal sector					

2. Employment in the informal sector by status in employment (%)

	Total	Women	Men	Urban	Rural
Data not available.					

3. Informal non-agricultural employment by status in employment (%)

	Total	Women	Men	Urban	Rural
Data not available.					

4. Informal non-agricultural self-employment as % of total non-agricultural self-employment by status in employment

	Total	Women	Men	Urban	Rural
Data not available.					

5. Informal wage employment as % of total wage employment by type of employees

	Total	Women	Men	Urban	Rural
Data not available.					

6. Informal non-agricultural employment outside the informal sector by type (%)

	Total	Women	Men	Urban	Rural
Data not available.					

Women and men in the informal economy: A statistical picture

7. Share of women in employment by type

Share of women in ...	%
1. Total employment	48.2
2. Agricultural employment	53.4
2.1 Agricultural wage employment	
2.1.1 Formal agricultural wage employment	
2.1.2 Informal agricultural wage employment	
2.2 Agricultural self-employment	
3. Non-agricultural employment	38.5
3.1 Non-agricultural wage employment*	
3.1.1 Formal non-agricultural wage employment	
3.1.2 Informal non-agricultural wage employment	
3.2 Non-agricultural self-employment	
3.2.1 Formal non-agricultural self-employment	
3.2.2 Informal non-agricultural self-employment	

* = MDG Indicator No. 3.2: Share of women in wage employment in the non-agricultural sector

8. Share of women in informal non-agricultural employment by component

Share of women in ...	%
1. Informal employment	49.2
1.1 Self-employment	
1.2. Wage employment	
2. Employment in the informal sector	51.6
2.1 Self-employment	
2.2 Wage employment	
3. Informal employment outside the informal sector	
3.1 Self-employment	
3.2 Wage employment	
3.2.1 Formal sector	
3.2.2 Domestic work	

9. Share of informal employment (%) by kind of non-agricultural activity

Share of informal employment in total employment in ...	Total	Women	Men
All non-agricultural actitvities	51.7	66.1	42.7
Manufacturing	48.2	72.6	39.9
Construction	67.1	68.2	67.1
Trade	42.5	55.6	32.4
Transportation	23.7	24.2	23.7
Services other than trade or transportation	56.8	67.5	46.7

10. Non-agricultural employment by sex, formal/informal nature and kind of activity (%)

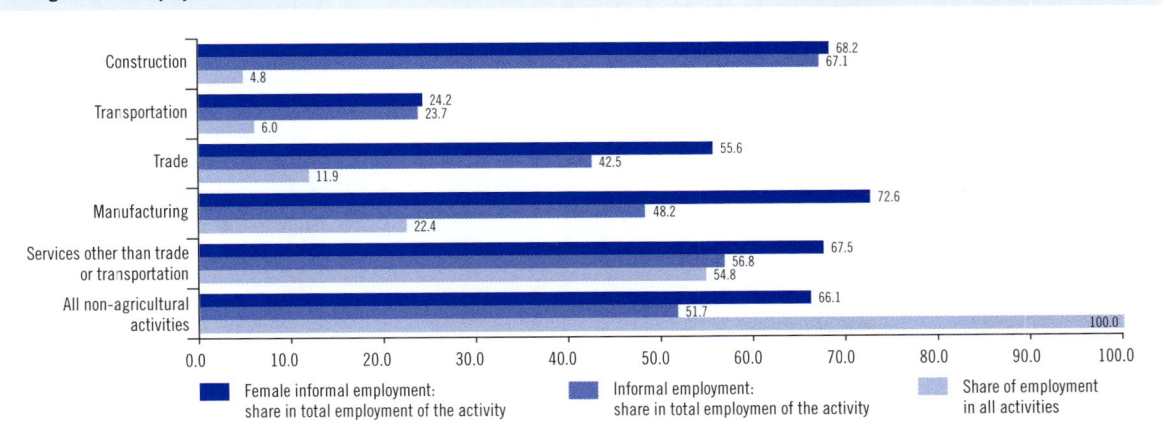

A. Both sexes

Kind of activity	Total	Formal	Informal
All non-agricultural actitvities	100.0	100.0	100.0
Manufacturing	22.4	24.0	20.9
Construction	4.8	3.3	6.3
Trade	11.9	14.1	9.8
Transportation	6.0	9.5	2.8
Services other than trade or transportation	54.8	49.0	60.3

B. Women

Kind of activity	Total	Formal	Informal
All non-agricultural actitvities	100.0	100.0	100.0
Manufacturing	14.8	11.9	16.2
Construction	1.3	1.2	1.3
Trade	13.5	17.7	11.4
Transportation	1.3	3.1	0.5
Services other than trade or transportation	69.1	66.1	70.6

C. Men

Kind of activity	Total	Formal	Informal
All non-agricultural actitvities	100.0	100.0	100.0
Manufacturing	27.2	28.5	25.5
Construction	7.0	4.0	11.0
Trade	10.8	12.8	8.2
Transportation	9.0	12.0	5.0
Services other than trade or transportation	45.9	42.7	50.3

Country: Zimbabwe **Year: 2004**
Non-agricultural employment

Activity	Female informal employment: share in total employment of the activity	Informal employment: share in total employment of the activity	Share of employment in all activities
Construction	68.2	67.1	4.8
Transportation	24.2	23.7	6.0
Trade	55.6	42.5	11.9
Manufacturing	72.6	48.2	22.4
Services other than trade or transportation	67.5	56.8	54.8
All non-agricultural activities	66.1	51.7	100.0